Scale

Scale is a word which underlies much of architectural and urban design practice, its history and theory, and its technology. Its connotations have traditionally been linked with the humanities, in the sense of relating to human societies and to human form. 'To build in scale' is an aspiration that is usually taken for granted by most of those involved in architectural production, as well as by members of the public; yet in a world where value systems of all kinds are being questioned, the term has come under renewed scrutiny. The older, more particular, meanings in the humanities, pertaining to classical Western culture, are where the sense of scale often resides in cultural production.

Scale may be traced back, ultimately, to the discovery of musical harmonies, and in the arithmetic proportional relationship of the building to its parts. One might question the continued relevance of this understanding of scale in the global world of today. What, in other words, is culturally specific about scale? And what does scale mean in a world where an intuitive, visual understanding is often undermined or superseded by other senses, or by hyper-reality? Structured thematically in three parts, this book addresses various issues of scale. The book includes an introduction which sets the scene in terms of current architectural discourse and also contains a visual essay in each section. It is of interest to undergraduate and postgraduate students, academics and practitioners in architecture and architectural theory as well as to students in a range of other disciplines including art history and theory, geography, anthropology and landscape architecture.

Gerald Adler runs the BA (Hons) Architecture programme at the Kent School of Architecture, University of Kent, UK, where he is Deputy Head of School.

Timothy Brittain-Catlin is Senior Lecturer at the Kent School of Architecture.

Gordana Fontana-Giusti is an architect specialising in architectural theory who has been involved in establishing postgraduate studies and research at the Kent School of Architecture.

The editors are members of CREAte, the Centre for Research in European Architecture at the Kent School of Architecture.

CRITIQUES: Critical Studies in Architectural Humanities
A project of the Architectural Humanities Research Association

Series Editor: Jonathan Hale (University of Nottingham)
Editorial Board:
Sarah Chaplin
Mark Dorrian (Newcastle University)
Murray Fraser (University College London)
Hilde Heynen (Catholic University of Leuven)
Andrew Leach (Griffith University)
Thomas Mical (Rensselaer Polytechnic Institute)
Jane Rendell (University College London)
Adam Sharr (Newcastle University)
Igea Troiani (Oxford Brookes University)

This original series of edited books contains selected papers from the AHRA Annual International Conferences. Each year the event has its own thematic focus while sharing an interest in new and emerging critical research in the areas of architectural history, theory, culture, design and urbanism.

1. **Critical Architecture**
   Edited by: Jane Rendell, Jonathan Hill, Murray Fraser and Mark Dorrian
2. **From Models to Drawings: Imagination and Representation in Architecture**
   Edited by: Marco Frascari, Jonathan Hale and Bradley Starkey
3. **The Politics of Making**
   Edited by: Mark Swenarton, Igea Troiani and Helena Webster
4. **Curating Architecture and the City**
   Edited by: Sarah Chaplin and Alexandra Stara
5. **Agency: Working with Uncertain Architectures**
   Edited by: Florrian Kossak, Doina Petrescu, Tatjana Schneider, Renata Tyszczuk and Stephen Walker
6. **Architecture and Field/Work**
   Edited by: Suzanne Ewing, Jérémie Michael McGowan, Chris Speed and Victoria Clare Bernie
7. **Scale: Imagination, Perception and Practice in Architecture**
   Edited by: Gerald Adler, Timothy Brittain-Catlin and Gordana Fontana-Giusti

AHRA provides an inclusive and comprehensive support network for humanities researchers in architecture across the UK and beyond. It promotes, supports, develops and disseminates high-quality research in all areas of architectural humanities.

www.ahra-architecture.org.uk

Scale

Imagination, Perception and Practice in Architecture

Edited by Gerald Adler,
Timothy Brittain-Catlin and
Gordana Fontana-Giusti

LONDON AND NEW YORK

First published 2012
by Routledge
2 Park Square, Milton Park, Abingdon, Oxon OX14 4RN

Simultaneously published in the USA and Canada
by Routledge
711 Third Avenue, New York, NY 10017

Routledge is an imprint of the Taylor & Francis Group, an informa business

© 2012 selection and editorial material, Gerald Adler, Timothy Brittain-Catlin and Gordana Fontana-Giusti: individual chapters, the contributors

The right of the editors to be identified as the authors of the editorial material, and of the authors for their individual chapters, has been asserted in accordance with sections 77 and 78 of the Copyright, Designs and Patents Act 1988.

All rights reserved. No part of this book may be reprinted or reproduced or utilised in any form or by any electronic, mechanical, or other means, now known or hereafter invented, including photocopying and recording, or in any information storage or retrieval system, without permission in writing from the publishers. Every effort has been made to contact and acknowledge copyright owners. If any material has been included without permission, the publishers offer their apologies. The publishers would be pleased to have any errors or omissions brought to their attention so that corrections may be published at later printing.

Trademark notice: Product or corporate names may be trademarks or registered trademarks, and are used only for identification and explanation without intent to infringe.

British Library Cataloguing in Publication Data
A catalogue record for this book is available from the British Library

Library of Congress Cataloging in Publication Data
  Scale: imagination, perception, and practice in architecture/edited by Gerald Adler, Timothy Brittain-Catlin, and Gordana Fontana-Giusti.
  p. cm. – (Critiques : critical studies in architectural humanities)
  Selected papers from the AHRA Annual International Conferences.
  'A project of the Architectural Humanities Research Association'.
  Includes bibliographical references and index.
  I. Adler, Gerald, 1955– II. Brittain-Catlin, Timothy. III. Fontana-Giusti, Gordana.
  IV. Architectural Humanities Research Association. V. Title: Imagination, perception, and practice in architecture.
  NA2760.S32 2012
  720–dc23
  2011019716

ISBN: 978–0-415–68711–9 (hbk)
ISBN: 978–0-415–68712–6 (pbk)

Typeset in Univers by
Florence Production Ltd, Stoodleigh, Devon

Printed and bound in Great Britain by
TJ International Ltd, Padstow, Cornwall

Contents

Illustration credits — *viii*
Contributors — *xi*
Acknowledgements — *xiv*

Introduction — 1
Gerald Adler

Excursus 1: The scale of the detail — 11
Michel da Costa Gonçalves and Nathalie Rozencwajg

Scale before the twentieth century — 19

The role of small-scale images by Wenceslaus Hollar: the rebuilding of London in the late seventeenth century — 21
Gordana Fontana-Giusti

Mildendo and Masdar: a tale of two cities — 34
Adam Sharr

'Examining the knots . . . counting the bricks': John Ruskin's innocent eye — 43
Stephen Kite

The worm's eye as a measure of man: Choisy's development of axonometry in architectural representation — 54
Hilary Bryon

Excursus 2: Scale in recent projects by MVRDV — 65
Nathalie de Vries

Contents

Scale in art and perception — 77

Colour scales — 79
Fay Zika

Scales of interaction: aligning the qualitative with the quantitative in music and architecture — 88
Fiona Smyth

Architectural scale: psychoanalysis and Adrian Stokes — 99
Janet Sayers

Sublime indifference — 107
Helen Mallinson

Measuring up: measurement pieces and the redefinition of scale in conceptual art — 117
Elise Noyez

Scaling haptics – haptic scaling: studying scale and scaling in the haptic design process of two architects who lost their sight — 127
Peter-Willem Vermeersch and Ann Heylighen

Scale adjustment in architecture and music — 136
Richard Coyne

Excursus 3: Complex ordinariness in Oxford: 'House after Two Years of Living' — 147
Igea Troiani

Scale in the twentieth century and beyond — 157

Ethos pathos logos: architects and their chairs — 159
Jonathan Foote

'Halfway between the electron and the universe': Doxiadis and the Delos Symposia — 170
Simon Richards

Little boxes — 182
Gerald Adler

Scale and identity in the housing projects of Coderch — 194
Michael Pike

Politics and the deliquescence of scale: the Columbaria of Brodsky and Utkin 206
Michael J. Ostwald

Bibliography *218*
Index *233*

Illustration credits

Excursus 1
1	Edmund Sumner	12
2	Ed Reeve	13
3	Sue Barr	14
4	Sue Barr	14
5	Sue Barr	14
6	Edmund Sumner	15
7	Edmund Sumner	15
8	Ed Reeve	15
9	Ed Reeve	16
10	Ed Reeve	17

The role of small-scale images by Wenceslaus Hollar
1	© The Trustees of the British Museum	25
2	© The Trustees of the British Museum	26
3	Image taken from Wikimedia Commons	26
4	© The Trustees of the British Museum	28
5	© The Trustees of the British Museum	28
6	© The British Library	29
7	Courtesy of Garwood & Voight	32

Mildendo and Masdar
1	Lithograph by Gordon Browne (Swift 1886: 7). Project Gutenberg	35
2	Lithograph by Gordon Browne (Swift 1886: 7). Project Gutenberg	36

'Examining the knots . . . counting the bricks'
1	Courtesy of the Ruskin Foundation (Ruskin Library, Lancaster University)	47
2	Courtesy of the Ruskin Foundation (Ruskin Library, Lancaster University)	50
3	R. Ackerman	51

The worm's eye as a measure of man

1	*Left*: Royer 1960: Plate 2; *right*: Choisy 1873	59
2	Choisy 1873	60
3	Choisy 1899	63

Excursus 2

1	Courtesy of MVRDV	66
2	Courtesy of MVRDV	66
3	Courtesy of MVRDV	67
4	Courtesy of MVRDV	67
5	Courtesy of MVRDV	67
6	© Rob 't Hart	68
7	© Rob 't Hart	68
8	© Rob 't Hart	69
9	Courtesy of MVRDV	71
10	Courtesy of MVRDV	71
11	© Provast	72
12	© Provast	72
13	© Provast	72
14	© MVRDV/ADEPT	73
15	© MVRDV/ADEPT	73
16	© MVRDV/ADEPT	73
17	© Rob 't Hart	74
18	© Dariusz R Cyparski	75
19	© Chris Wright	75
20	Courtesy of MVRDV	76

Scales of interaction

1	Courtesy of Patience Bagenal	89

Measuring up

1	Courtesy of the artist	124

Scaling haptics – haptic scaling

1	Don Fogg	130
2	Carlos Mourão Pereira	131
3	Carlos Mourão Pereira	133

Scale adjustment in architecture and music

1	Richard Coyne	138
2	Richard Coyne	140

Excursus 3

1–12 © Troiani/Original Field of Architecture		148–153

Illustration credits

Ethos pathos logos
1. Sheraton (1793) — 160
2. Courtesy Sistema Bibliotecario del Politecnico di Torino, Biblioteca Centrale di Architettura – Sezione Archivi di Architettura, Fondo Carlo Mollino — 166
3. Courtesy Sistema Bibliotecario del Politecnico di Torino, Biblioteca Centrale di Architettura – Sezione Archivi di Architettura, Fondo Carlo Mollino — 166
4. Fulvio Ferrari. Courtesy Museo Casa Mollino — 167
5. Courtesy Sistema Bibliotecario del Politecnico di Torino, Biblioteca Centrale di Architettura – Sezione Archivi di Architettura, Fondo Carlo Mollino — 168

'Halfway between the electron and the universe'
1. © Constantinos and Emma Doxiadis Foundation, from *Ekistics* 132 (1966) — 177
2. © Constantinos and Emma Doxiadis Foundation — 178
3. © Constantinos and Emma Doxiadis Foundation. Taken from Constantinos Doxiadis, *The Two Headed Eagle*, Athens: Lycabettus Press (1972) — 180

Little boxes
1. Gerald Adler (2009) — 185
2. John Whybrow (1967). Reproduced by kind permission of Robert Maguire — 186
3. RIBA Library Photographs Collection — 191
4. D.A.C.A. Boyne. Photograph in the possession of the current owners of Kentlands, Alasdair and Margaret Paterson, close friends of the Boynes — 192

Scale and identity in the housing projects of Coderch
1. Michael Pike — 197
2. Michael Pike — 199
3. Michael Pike — 201

Politics and the deliquescence of scale
1. D. James Dee, Courtesy Ronald Feldman Fine Arts, New York / www.feldmangallery.com — 213
2. D. James Dee, Courtesy Ronald Feldman Fine Arts, New York / www.feldmangallery.com — 215

Contributors

Gerald Adler runs the BA (Hons) architecture programme at the University of Kent, where he is Deputy Head of School. His Ph.D. was on Heinrich Tessenow, and his book on the British architectural practice Maguire & Murray is forthcoming. He is an active member of both the Architectural Humanities Research Association (AHRA) and the Heinrich-Tessenow-Gesellschaft.

Timothy Brittain-Catlin is Senior Lecturer and Director of Research at the Kent School of Architecture, University of Kent. He is the author of *The English Parsonage in the Early Nineteenth Century* (Spire Books, 2008) and *Leonard Manasseh & Partners* (RIBA Publishing, 2010). He has written for *The World of Interiors* for more than 20 years.

Hilary Bryon is an Assistant Professor in the School of Architecture + Design at Virginia Polytechnic Institute and State University. She holds a Ph.D. from the University of Pennsylvania. Her ongoing research includes a thematic analysis of the use of parallel projection as a form of architectural representation over the last 200 years.

Richard Coyne is Professor at the University of Edinburgh and an architect researching and teaching in design theory and digital media. He is author of several books with MIT Press, of which the most recent is *The Tuning of Place: sociable spaces and pervasive digital media*. He has published *Derrida for Architects* with Routledge.

Michel da Costa Gonçalves is an architect and co-founder of RARE architecture (with Nathalie Rozencwajg). After graduating from ENSALP in France and gaining a Masters degree at the Architectural Association School of Architecture, London, he has worked at Architecture Studio on projects in London, Beijing, Athens and Mecca, as well as collaborating with Shigeru Ban. In addition to practice, he has been Unit Master at the Architectural Association since 2008.

Nathalie de Vries is an architect and co-founding director of the globally operating architecture and urban planning firm MVRDV (with Winy Maas and Jacob van

Rijs), based in Rotterdam and Shanghai. MVRDV is known for projects such as the Expo 2000 in Hanover, the Logrono Eco-City in Spain and the Gyre building in Tokyo.

Gordana Fontana-Giusti is an architect specialising in architectural theory, who has been involved in establishing the postgraduate studies and research at Kent School of Architecture (KSA) since 2007. Prior to that, she was at the Architectural Association School of Architecture, London and at Central Saint Martins, London. She is the author of the *Complete Works of Zaha Hadid* (with Patrick Schumacher, Thames and Hudson 2004).

Jonathan Foote is a Ph.D. candidate in architectural design research at Virginia Tech's Washington-Alexandria Architecture Center in Alexandria, Virginia, USA. His current Ph.D. dissertation research examines the role of full-size drawing in the translation of drawing to building in sixteenth-century Florentine architectural practice. In addition to his scholarly work, he pursues workshop-based research as the faculty leader of various furniture and design/build projects.

Ann Heylighen is Associate Professor at K.U. Leuven, Department of Architecture, Urbanism and Planning (ASRO). She studied at K.U. Leuven and ETH Zurich, did research at Harvard and Berkeley, and received a starting grant from the European Research Council. Her work explores the spatial experience of people living under different living conditions as a source of design knowledge in architecture.

Stephen Kite is Reader at the Welsh School of Architecture, Cardiff University. Major publications include *Adrian Stokes: an architectonic eye* (2009) and, with Sarah Menin, *An Architecture of Invitation: Colin St John Wilson* (2005). His recent research examines the evolution of Ruskin's 'watching' of architecture, in the context of Italy.

Helen Mallinson teaches history and theory in the Faculty of Architecture and Spatial Design at London Metropolitan University. She completed a doctorate at the London Consortium on the history and philosophy of air in the seventeenth century as part of a wider investigation into the limits of 'space'.

Elise Noyez is a Ph.D. Researcher at V.U. University, Amsterdam. She holds Masters degrees in architecture and engineering (2008) and visual arts, media and architecture (2010). Her doctoral research focuses on the photographic representation of artists, but her interest also goes towards the relation between artworks and their architectural surroundings.

Michael J. Ostwald is Professor and Dean of Architecture at the University of Newcastle (Australia) and an Australian Research Council 'Future Fellow'. His Ph.D. is in architectural theory and history and his higher doctorate is in design mathematics. He is on the editorial boards of *Architectural Theory Review* and the *Nexus Network Journal*.

Michael Pike is an architect and Studio Lecturer in Architecture at University College Dublin. In 2003, he formed GKMP Architects with Grace Keeley. Their work has received a number of awards and has been published and exhibited internationally. He is currently working on a Research Masters in housing design.

Simon Richards is author of *Le Corbusier and the Concept of Self* (Yale 2003) and Lecturer in the Department of History of Art and Film at the University of Leicester. His book on the ongoing discourse of environmental determinism in modern and contemporary architecture, *Architect Knows Best*, is under contract with Ashgate.

Nathalie Rozencwajg is an architect and co-founder of RARE architecture (with Michel da Costa Gonçalves). After graduating from the Architectural Association School of Architecture, London, she has worked with Erick van Egeraat (EEA) and Architecture Studio on projects in London, Beijing, Athens and Mecca. In addition to practice, she has been Unit Master at the Architectural Association (AA) since 2004.

Janet Sayers is Professor of Psychoanalytic Psychology at the University of Kent in Canterbury. Her books include *Mothering Psychoanalysis* (Penguin 1992), *Freudian Tales* (Vintage 1997) and *Freud's Art* (Routledge 2007). She is currently completing her ninth book, *Art and Psychoanalysis: Melanie Klein and the story of Adrian Stokes*.

Adam Sharr is Professor of Architecture at Newcastle University (UK), Principal of Adam Sharr Architects, editor of *arq: Architectural Research Quarterly* (with Richard Weston) and editor of the Thinkers for Architects series published by Routledge.

Fiona Smyth is an architect and Ph.D. candidate at University College Dublin (UCD). Prior to beginning her Ph.D. in 2006, she worked for a number of established architectural firms in Dublin. As both an architect and a musician, her research in recent years has focused on how these disciplines work together through acoustic interaction. She has taught at UCD Architecture since beginning her current research and has presented her research at a number of national and international conferences. She is a research fellow at UCD Urban Institute Ireland.

Igea Troiani is a modern architectural historian, architect and independent film-maker.

Peter-Willem Vermeersch is a Ph.D. student at K.U. Leuven, Department of Architecture, Urbanism and Planning (ASRO). His research is framed by the project Architectural Design In Dialogue with Disability (AIDA). His Ph.D. focuses on the spatial experience of people with visual impairments, and possibilities for architecture and the architectural design process.

Fay Zika is Assistant Professor in Philosophy and Theory of Art, Department of Theory and History of Art, Athens School of Fine Arts. Her research interests include colour theory, the senses and cross-modal associations, nature and gardens, identity and gender issues, the relation between philosophy, science and art, and the relation between aesthetics and ethics.

Acknowledgements

We would like to thank the AHRA for giving us the opportunity to host the seventh international conference on the subject of 'scale', which was launched by David Chipperfield in November 2010 at the University of Kent. We are grateful to all those who took part in this enjoyable and successful event, and in particular to Jonathan Hale, the editor of this series of books, and Igea Troiani, the current chair of AHRA, both of whom supported this enterprise from its inception. We would particularly like to thank our keynote speakers: Nathalie de Vries, Hannah Higgins, Nathalie Rozencwajg and Robert Tavernor.

Many people have contributed to the creation of this volume. We would first like to thank all those who sent us their papers. We are especially grateful to those who helped this edition reach its final state: Mohamed Gamal Abdelmonem, Andrew Ballantyne, Peter Blundell Jones, Iain Borden, Mark Dorrian, Suzanne Ewing, Susannah Hagan, Vaughan Hart, Andrew Higgott, Mari Hvattum, Sarah Lappin, Simon Pepper, Peg Rawes, Alexandra Stara, Teresa Stoppani, Jeremy Till and Stephen Walker.

We would like thank Professor Don Gray, Head of the Kent School of Architecture, and Professor Karl Leydecker, Dean of the Faculty of Humanities, University of Kent, for their critical support throughout.

CREAte, the Centre for Research in European Architecture, at the Kent School of Architecture, played the key role in organising the conference and putting this book together. We would like to express our particular thanks to Miss Victoria Friedman, who has been central to this project. We also wish to acknowledge the contributions of Louise Billingham, Howard Griffin, Morgan Grylls, Dele Ojo, Jeanne Straight and Brian Wood.

We are grateful to Routledge for their continuing support of AHRA *Critiques: Critical Studies in Architectural Humanities*, and in particular to our commissioning editor Georgina Johnson-Cook.

Gerald Adler
Timothy Brittain-Catlin
Gordana Fontana-Giusti
Canterbury, September 2011

Introduction

Gerald Adler

Scale seems to be such a commonplace in an architect's armoury that it is very much taken for granted. And yet, if you are an architect, cast your mind back to your first week at architecture school, when you were turning that much-calibrated tool, the scale rule, in your hands, as if it were part of some masonic ritual. Or, if you never trained as an architect, you might have pondered the inscrutability of statements concerning a design being 'in scale' with its particular context. Scale seems to be more pertinent to the plastic arts, so that the intentional ordinariness of the embracing lovers in *The Meeting Point* (Paul Day, 2007) beneath the clock at St Pancras Station, London becomes banal owing to the giant size of the sculpture.

In terms of buildings and sites, scale is crucial in providing the right setting, physically and psychologically, for human encounter and well-being. In a landscape such as that of the Palace of Versailles, there are spaces of both intimacy and grandeur – the Baroque seems particularly adept at accommodating people singly and en masse. And while the modern landscape has its moments of intimacy – the work of the Scandinavians Carl Theodor Sørenson (1893–1979) and Sven-Ingvar Andersson (b. 1927) comes to mind, not to mention that of Peter Aldington (b. 1933) closer to home – it is the sheer size of, say, West 8's projects that typifies its oeuvre (Weilacher 1996; Treib 2002).

Changing ideas of scale

The 'right scale' was a recurring phrase we learned in architectural history, whether contemplating Bramante's Tempietto in Rome ('correct'), Boullée's Newton Memorial ('monumental') or Speer's Germania *Grosse Halle* ('grotesque'). It also used to be a fundamental building block of design education, so that books like Eugene Raskin's *Architecturally Speaking* (Raskin 1954) functioned as set texts for students, as useful adjuncts when it came to designing, as Banister Fletcher was when comparing scale relationships between the parts of a classical temple.

There have been two fundamental changes in our understanding of architectural scale over the last few decades. First, the growing medialisation of the discipline of architecture, as well as its popular reception, has meant that we have become distanced from actual size relationships. Whereas William Curtis's *Le Corbusier: ideas and forms* (Curtis 1986) analysed the Swiss architect in 'real space', Beatriz Colomina in *Privacy and Publicity: modern architecture as mass media* (Colomina 1994) saw Le Corbusier as a canny exploiter of the media of film and photography, spellbound by the image of (scaleless) architecture devoid of people. Second, the effect of the computer has been to minimise scale differences in the act of design (computer drawings may be scaled up or down with no increase or diminution of detail), and to distance the architectural object from the actual size of elements in its environment. In other words, it has tended to privilege architecture freed from site-contextual considerations.

These changes in architectural perception, reception and activity have been driven by social and technical 'advances', but have also been paralleled by new thinking in the arts and humanities. While the conference from which these selected papers derive had a plethora of sub-themes, such as 'Scale, landscape and utopia' or 'Scale and the post-humanist age', we have been far simpler in this collection. 'Scale in art and perception' comprises papers that deal primarily with non-architectural understandings of scale, whose authors also tend to come from other disciplines; it is book-ended by two sections that take a plainly chronological split in their dealings with architecture: 'Scale before the twentieth century' and 'Scale in the twentieth century and beyond'. Our hope is that the more discursive – and extra-curricular – understandings of scale from the perspectives of the other arts, and from the disciplines associated with perception, will illuminate the contribution of the twentieth century to scale, and act as a watershed between it and the preceding centuries. Taken together, these sixteen chapters and three photo-essays offer a broad understanding of scale in relation to architecture, deepening the subject, and widening its scope.

Scale and reality

One question present at the conference but rarely voiced explicitly – the big elephant in a diminutive room – was whether humans could provide the measure of design. This question relates to the dialectic of 'polite' architecture – the numinous church, the exquisite art gallery, the comfortable house for a discerning client – with its obverse, the frequently crass, mass-produced provision of dwelling units, factory sheds and office barracks. The dichotomy between the two modes of design has been with us forever; the difference with Modernism is that the values of mass production have been aestheticised to a greater extent. However, it seems that scale has tended to conform to rather simplistic characterisations, either side of the political and artistic debates pertaining to relative size, such that Mark Fisher sees the appropriation of large scale by powerful industrialists as necessarily detrimental to society, whereas Owen Hatherley views the redemptive power of the large-scale, planned environment as a largely unrealised aim of the Modernist project (Hatherley 2008: Fisher 2009).

Questions of scale tend to mirror similarly framed ones pertaining to the 'real', so that different sections of the intellectual and artistic spectrum will attach the epithet 'real' to opposite ends of the scale continuum. The architect and teacher Michael Benedikt has argued for a pragmatic 'felt' architecture, where human scale is a crucial determinant of a comfortable and meaningful environment (Benedikt 1987). This can seem like a rearguard action, an attempt to corral architecture within the safe confines of tradition, and yet it can act as a corrective to the ever-increasing size of buildings, and the alienation wrought by the growing difficulty of comprehending scale relationships between parts of buildings, and of one part of the built environment to another. This has real political and social traction in today's world of ever-increasing giganticism. However, it is not realistic merely to wish the virtual world away: it is an indisputable part of lived experience across the globe today, and has been a central aspect of Modernist aesthetics for a century now.

Cyclical scale

Hermann Muthesius's famous saying, that he designed '*Vom Sofakissen zum Städtebau*' ('From the cushion to town-planning'), might be reversed today, so that the first term denoting the largest scale takes precedence. Indeed, '*Vom Stadtplan zum Essbesteck*' ('From town-plan to cutlery') was how Christof Wieser put it, echoing the title of an exhibition on contemporary Swedish design held in Zurich in 1949 (Wieser 2008). Wieser identified the tendency towards small or large scale in architecture as a cyclical matter that lingers on today: the same issue of the Swiss journal that detailed Wieser's thesis also featured the Zollverein School of Management and Design at Essen, an enigmatic cube designed by SANAA (Kazuyo Sejima and Ryue Nishizawa 2003–6). It also looked back at MVRDV's Amsterdam housing block 'Parkrand' (2002–7), a massive 'superblock' that reiterates, in scale terms at least, the 'supersize' of housing developments such as Sheffield's Park Hill flats (1957–61) a generation earlier. When the architect Ralph Erskine designed a similar extent of public housing a decade later at Byker, Newcastle-upon-Tyne (1969–75), the scale characteristics of the famous 'housing wall' were reversed, and inhabitants were able to identify their own dwellings within the superblock and neighbouring low-rise housing.

We are familiar with representations that are (usually) scaled down: drawings or models. Architect and teacher Paul Emmons reminds us of that absurdity: the *full-size* map. This is one of Jorge Luis Borges's celebrated fictions, where he discusses a map 'whose size was that of the Empire, and which coincided point for point with it' (Borges 1998). For Emmons, Borges's surreal map 'helps us to understand the delirious condition of scale drawings gone awry that occurs in CAD where buildings are represented at "full scale"'. (Emmons 2005: 227). The limitations of CAD, that it 'forego[es] the senses to assume scale is solely in the mind' is a reminder that phenomenologically based critiques and tactics have their place in architectural production (Emmons 2005: 232). This ludic attempt to locate scale between the twin poles of the real and the virtual is not new: in 1931, the Polish scientist Alfred Korzybski

(Gubler 2008: 10, 27n; citing Korzybski 1973: 38) stated that 'a map is not the territory'. In order to draw a distinction between the scaling apparatus (in architectural terms, the drawing or model) and the territory to be scaled, he went on, 'If the ideal of the map could be correct, the map would include, at a smaller scale, a map of the map, a map of that map, and so on *ad infinitum*'. Jacques Gubler, author of a monograph on the work of the Swiss architect Jean Tschumi, draws on Korzybski's insights in identifying the technique of zooming, one borrowed from cinematography, finding it aptly descriptive of the scaling design processes in the twentieth century, from the time of the *Neues Bauen* onwards (Gubler 2008: 10). He asks:

> [. . .] doesn't architecture proceed from an empirical model – one that nevertheless does not renounce the use of theoretical models? Euclidean geometry and its graphic emanation, perspective, constitute a theory of representation linking Vitruvius to Alberti and Piero de[lla] Francesca to CAD software.
> (Gubler 2008: 10)

Has there been a similar swing in the size of books on architecture? As doorsteps go, *S, M, L, XL* (Koolhaas and Mau 1995) takes the biscuit, followed not far behind by MVRDV's *KM3* (2005). (The penchant for long strings of letters to denote titles of books and magazines, or indeed firms of architects, is itself an index of burgeoning scale in the public reception of design practice.) Perhaps the size of countries is in inverse proportion to that of their books? Michael Benedikt not only made his argument succinctly, but also did so in a format that allows the book to be carried in a jacket pocket. Perhaps today's proliferation of internet images, where pictures come cheap, accounts for such publishing sensations, to use the word in its phenomenal sense. Having said that, the recent publishing ventures of the Architectural Association (*Architectural Words*), Routledge (*Thinkers for Architects*) and RIBA Publishing with the Twentieth Century Society and English Heritage (*Twentieth Century Architects*) represent a welcome return to the pocket-format paperback. This brings us to a consideration of the literature on architectural scale.

Scale writings

> 'Near' is a place to which I can get quickly on my feet, not a place to which the train or the air-ship will take me quickly. 'Far' is a place to which I cannot get quickly on my feet . . . Man is the measure. That was my first lesson. Man's feet are the measure for distance, his hands are the measure for ownership, his body is the measure for all that is lovable and desirable and strong.
> (Raskin 1954: 36, citing E.M. Forster's *Collected Tales*)

Primers for design students used to feature scale prominently: Eugene Raskin's *Architecturally Speaking* (1954) may still be found on our bookshelves. For Raskin, scale was one of those ubiquitous qualities of environment, belonging (with proportion and rhythm) to a humanist design vocabulary. This embedding of an understanding of scale within architectural design practice persisted through books such as Pierre von Meiss's *Elements of Architecture* (1990). Scale was dealt with from a practical perspective in Charles Moore's *Dimensions: space, shape and scale in architecture* (1976), but its coming of age in terms of contemporary theory and practice was marked by the publication of *S, M, L, XL* in 1995, where the *lack* of scale, particularly of places peripheral to traditional cultural centres, was celebrated (Augé 1995). Scale was covered, particularly in its architectural–historical context, in Richard Padovan's *Proportion* (1999), and also in Robert Tavernor's *Smoot's Ear: the measure of humanity* (2007), where competing systems of measurement, and their implications for scale, were discussed. What is telling is that where the metric system of measurements has been adopted, the commonly used measures remain uncannily close to the old ones based on the human frame: the metre, for instance, is to all intents and purposes an English yard. So even where great abstractions purportedly rule our observations of the world, we feel most comfortable with ones that have an intimate connection with the human body.

> Metric truths are measures – human conceptions – stripped bare by reason. Evident in the ironic responses to the empire of science during the twentieth century is an expression of the need to connect directly with the mysteries that surround us, to reveal and associate with the anthropomorphic that is manifest in nature. This need will not be eradicated by science: balance demands that it will become more pronounced. Our bodies require a positive relation with the natural world, and measuring the world with and through our bodies is essential to civilized – human – existence. It is doubtful that the balance will be redressed quickly, though the obstinacy of the United States, and its regard for human liberty, may yet supply an antidote.
> (Tavernor 2007: 189)

Tavernor calls upon the twentieth-century philosopher of pragmatism, Richard Rorty, for a simple poetic image to emphasise the point: 'After the scales are rubbed off a butterfly's wing, you have transparency, but not beauty – formal structure without sensuous content' (Tavernor 2007: 188–9, citing Rorty 1989: 152). In architectural terms, we find an analogy here with the approach of the Swiss architect Peter Märkli (b. 1953), who conceives of his work in terms of sculptural masses; he has collaborated with the figurative sculptor Hans Josephson, and his finished buildings show a clear debt to human figuration, with all that implies for scale relationships of part to part. An early project, for two single-family houses at Trübbach/Azmoos (1982), shows this trait most clearly:

> Because the site is sloping we had a lengthy discussion about plinths. I didn't want to have a plinth, so I came up with an alternative – an illusion. The amphora-shaped columns of the terrace look like they're standing on a plinth because they taper towards the base. They're a little bit stocky because the massing is critical to the architectural expression. Without the columns, the main facade wouldn't work. It's about centring the mass within the facade.
> (Mostafavi 2002: 64)

Increasingly, new digital media have forced critics and practitioners alike to re-examine scale. Hannah Higgins (2009) looked at a plethora of cultural manifestations of scale in *The Grid Book*, and it last featured implicitly in the second *AHRA Critiques* volume, *From Models to Drawings: imagination and representation in architecture*. Alberto Pérez-Gómez is sceptical of today's ubiquitous reliance on the computer in architectural representation, taking in all aspects from inception, design exploration, client meetings and construction information. For him, the process of creation prevalent in architecture today assumes that a conventional set of projections, at various scales from site to detail, adds up to a complete, objective *idea* of a building. It is this assumption of the ideal as real, a conceptual inversion with roots in early Western modernity, that constitutes the first stumbling block (Pérez-Gómez 2007: 12).

The rot set in with Jean-Nicolas-Louis Durand's *Précis des leçons d'architecture* (1802–9). In many respects today's practitioners of parametrics reject scale, seeing it as an outdated, humanist measure of architecture: Patrick Schumacher from Zaha Hadid Architects is a good representative of this stream (Schumacher 2010). For him, and others, Pérez-Gómez's contention that '[p]erception is our primary form of knowing and does not exist apart from the a priori of the body's structure and its engagement in the world' serves to deprive humans of autonomous agency and to limit creative activity in a world that is, after Nietzsche, 'human, all too human' (Pérez-Gómez 1983: 3; Nietzsche 1909).

This book is the seventh in the *AHRA Critiques* series. It seems to have moved a long way since the first volume, *Critical Architecture*. Its editors aimed to bring together the two – apparently – separate activities of design and criticism. The selection of papers in the present volume presumes no such split, as *Scale: imagination, perception and practice in architecture* continues to challenge the accepted meanings, uses and interpretations of the term 'scale'.

Scale before the twentieth century

The section 'Scale before the twentieth century' is preceded by a photo-essay on the scale considerations of a twenty-first-century design within a pre-modern context. **Nathalie Rozencwajg** and **Michel da Costa Gonçalves** of RARE architecture question the dichotomy between scale and complexity. Fragments of detail from a listed building undergoing conversion become leitmotifs of spatial organisation and facade design. The computer facilitates a continuum of scale, with ornament its smallest manifestation, and the building as a whole – its urban form – its largest.

This switch from micro to macro, from close observation of detail to summative rendering of an entire urban mass, is summarised by **Gordana Fontana-Giusti** in her chapter on Wenceslaus Hollar. This Bohemian engraver made his famous depictions of European cities in the seventeenth century and these were subsequently used and appreciated by polymaths such as Robert Hooke in England. The accuracy and calculation that went into the remaking of London after the Great Fire were indebted to Hollar's meticulous depictions. In what might have been subtitled 'the best of times, the worst of times', **Adam Sharr** compares and contrasts two cities of equal size: Norman Foster's project for Masdar and Jonathan Swift's fictional depiction of Mildendo. He uses Fred Dallmayr's 'currency of equivalence' to question the appropriateness of this architecture of scale correspondence, contrasted with the West's political and economic 'superiority' in its relationship with local, non-Western context (Macfie 2000).

Fascination with small-scale detail seems to be a central fact of the arts in the Victorian period; it serves as an index to the painter Richard Dadd's madness. Maddening detail, with all the fussiness of doilies and antimacassars, was surely what the Modernists were rebelling against. John Ruskin's two lessons on watching architecture, 'at the larger scale a sense of breadth and mass, and at the smaller a closer reading of surface texture', are incorporated in **Stephen Kite**'s scale reading, prescient about some of the scale tactics deployed by modern architects, in particular by Ludwig Mies van der Rohe.

The final chapter in this section is one that forms a bridge to the sections on perception, and the final section addressing scale since the twentieth century. **Hilary Bryon** traces the development of perspectival drawing, from its mutations at the hand of William Farish in the early nineteenth century to Auguste Choisy's rendering of axonometric space at the end of the century. It is well known that the development of the worm's-eye axonometric successfully combined tectonic understanding with plan organisation; what is demonstrated in this chapter is how the limitations of the conventional isometric or axonometric drawing were overcome in terms of human scale relationships, enabling us to imagine ourselves to be the 'worm in the bud', as Viola hides her female presence from Duke Orsino in Shakespeare's *Twelfth Night*.

Scale in art and perception

Nathalie de Vries precedes the next section with the photo-essay on her practice work with MVRDV architects. Working diagrammatically, she shows how an architectural scheme in a *tabula rasa* context can have internal logic, and make sense in material and experiential terms. Her understanding that scale does not merely reside in the visual is explored in the chapters that follow in this section, no less so than in **Fay Zika**'s chapter, 'Colour scales'. The artist and critic David Batchelor's point the fact that '[a]nalogical colour is colour, digital colour is colours' has profound implications for architects and their new working methods (Batchelor 2000: 105). Certainly, modern colours are actually constructed pointillistically, as arrays of discrete dots, and we frequently see buildings rendered, and perceived, as such: look at the coloured tiling on the entrance facade of Caruso St John's Museum of Childhood, London (2002–7), or the brightly coloured endgrain to the plywood fin mullions at Robbrecht en Daem's Bruges concert hall (1999–2002): as our eyes pan round, from an oblique monochrome view, we begin to see a candystripe 'barcode' effect. We seem to have returned to Goethe's 'search for serial relationships in nature, emphasising border experiences' (Watson 2010: 205). The sequence of differently coloured enfilade rooms in Goethe's town house at Weimar expresses this most succinctly.

We move from light to sound. **Fiona Smyth**'s chapter on the rediscovery of pre-Reformation music in the early twentieth century aligns with the scientific, quantitative investigations – both in the academy and in practice at large – of the architectural profession. There is a sense that twentieth-century architects were trying to get beyond the received wisdom of academic history, which saw the High Renaissance as its apotheosis, and return to the 'purity' inherent in earlier building: a kind of Pre-Raphaelite movement that found its expression in 'pure' music, devoid of the lush colours of romanticism.

Janet Sayers's chapter on Adrian Stokes is a timely reminder of this Freudian art historian, who had a practical influence on British architecture. His aim – that architecture should offer 'integrated bodily form to the ego' – is still very much with us today, and has filtered into the mainstream of design. The influence of architect and theorist Dalibor Vesely (b. 1934) on a generation of students at Cambridge is testimony to the power of this strain of architectural humanism (Vesely 2004). Staying with the emotions, **Helen Mallinson** finds the current fad for the 'parametric relation between objects' problematic because 'all objects are rendered the same'. Her chapter carefully differentiates the sublime from the beautiful, and the fact that objects are felt emotionally before they are understood intellectually.

Architects feel most comfortable with sculpture when it comes to considering art disciplines relating to buildings. Recent conceptual art, by virtue of its intimate relationship with place, has the power to question our assumptions about the size and shape of space. When we, the viewers, step into the frame, then human bodily scale is instantly at stake. **Elise Noyez** makes this point in her study of the work of Roman Ondák and Mel Bochner.

Where is the faculty of space located in the human being? Conventionally a visual matter, **Peter-Willem Vermeersch** and **Ann Heylighen** present their research team's findings of how blind designers work, and suggest that sighted architects could develop more multi-sensory work by adopting such practices. The kind of incremental design procedures suggested by Vermeersch find support from **Richard Coyne** in his chapter on scale adjustment. What is at issue here is not the striving for perfection; it is rather how to deal with the gritty imperfections that clients, sites and materials present.

Scale in the twentieth century and beyond

The final section looks at a variety of architectural responses to scale in the twentieth century, preceded by **Igea Troiani**'s photo-essay linking the small-scale domesticity of her own house in Oxford with wider contemporary matters. The photos show a concern for 'the everyday' that equates the design to the anthropological turn in mid-twentieth-century Modernism, epitomised by the *Team Ten Primer* (Smithson 1962). This leads to **Jonathan Foote**'s disquisition on architects and their chairs, where the scale of construction evolves out of the pragmatic world of daily practice. Both chapters are instances of the pervasive influence the French philosopher of the everyday, Michel de Certeau (1925–86), continues to have on design thinking.

'Halfway between the electron and the universe' is a beautifully apt characterisation of where we need to locate ourselves. Here, **Simon Richards** examines the work of Greek architect Constantinos Doxiadis, and that of the Delos symposia he ran from the mid-1960s to the mid-1970s. Doxiadis attempted to preserve the small – the 'S' of Rem Koolhaas's S, M, L, XL sequence – and he embedded it within his idea of global city networks. Twentieth-century architecture frequently finds this 'S' – the smallest, most intimate scale – battling for presence among monumental odds. **Gerald Adler** resuscitates John Summerson's 'aedicule', which he used for art-historical purposes in his 1940s essay 'Heavenly mansions', and applies it retrospectively as a spatial category to architecture in the latter half of the twentieth century. The focus, as it was with Summerson, is on churches, but the lessons are far wider. The scale possibilities inherent in mid-twentieth-century design are the subject of **Michael Pike**'s chapter on the Catalan architect José Antonio Coderch. This close reading reveals a 'contextual' architect before the term became widespread, alive to the particularities of Barcelona, as well as the wider international culture in which Coderch was steeped.

The final chapter by **Michael J. Ostwald** offers a disquisition on a particular episode in late Soviet design: the phenomenon of 'paper architecture'. While the aedicule was advocated by Summerson as a humanising scaling device, the Russian architects Alexander Brodsky and Ilya Utkin used scaled-*down* versions of Soviet state architecture for subversive effect, borrowing philosopher Jacques Rancière's (b. 1940) theories about visibility and power.

Excursus 1

The scale of the detail

Michel da Costa Gonçalves and Nathalie Rozencwajg, RARE Architecture

Articulating nested scales, the design diversity of Town Hall Hotel in East London reveals a specific inverted bottom-up design process whereby a layered and non-compositional approach relies on local and particular needs to define the textured conversion of the listed building into a luxury hotel, conference centre and fine dining restaurant and bar. Lodged at various scales, coordinated design strategies offer a seemingly paradoxical differentiation and coherence required to insert several new functions within a physically and stylistically heterogeneous structure. The simultaneous consideration of different scales from the outset illustrates how the preconception of hierarchy can be inverted while maintaining a coherent whole. The reinvented building stands as a distinctively new entity where advanced design, modelling and manufacturing techniques reinvigorate a local icon in one of London's emerging cultural clusters.

Remarkable for its local historical value but lying unoccupied and modified by less preservation-oriented times, the 7,500 m^2 structure presented an eclectic assemblage of various constructions and stylistic periods encompassing the original 1910 Edwardian building, extended in 1937 in a hybrid of neo-classicism and Art Deco. Typical for public buildings of this period, it presented a strong contrast between the unified grand stone-clad facade of the original 1910 Edwardian Town Hall and its eclectic assemblage of various subsequent constructions along convoluted plot lines.

The overall faceted form emerges from a careful assimilation of environmental factors and a fluid adjustment to the discontinuous existing structure. Rights of light and natural light intake, as well as original layouts, shape the volume, absorbing old cavities and new technical elements. The resulting profile, responding to heritage concerns, disappears from certain angles coinciding with original perspectives while being prominent from others. The mediation of accumulated local constraints translated as vectors progressively build the malleable surface of the triangulated extension. Negotiation of contextual information is resolved by hierarchic assessment looped into the smaller scale in the skin's texture. Rather than a top-down compositional approach, it is this sum of site-specific requirements that generates the extension's design. These iterative adjustments of global geometry and local transformation, assembled through the balance of environmental constraints and functional needs, also inform the skin's porosity.

Figure 1
Town Hall Hotel with new extension by RARE, from Cambridge Heath Road.

The bespoke laser-cut skin mediates internal organisation and context through its performative ornament regulating solar gain, views and privacy. A set of associative steps enabled the translation of required performances through the proliferation and scaling of a nominal small square along guiding curves, established at key height lines in relation to the overall shape, internal layout and technical requirements. A selective process controlled intersection and hierarchies according to the desired degree of openness through means of overlap, scaling and level of intricacies that constantly evolve over the 300 linear metres of the facade. From within, the skin creates a protective envelope, which filters and edits the surroundings. Ever-changing shadows create a moiré effect of reflections, which enrich the spatial experience. From outside, the depth of its special coating generates nuances of colours responding to changing light conditions. Contrastingly, at night, the mysterious silhouette reveals evolving life within.

The formal grammar of the skin extracts and develops an existing Art Deco pattern found on site, and thus merges new functional and environmental considerations with historical referencing. The scale of the ornament is expanded beyond its decorative quality to define the extension's image and functionality: the skin performs.

Achieved through the iterative production of various physical and associative digital models, our design process preserved the constant link between the urban scale and the envelope's geometry and openness. It is the detail that defines the guest's views of the context through diffracted multiple frames. As such it is the parameterised

Figure 2
The new wing at Town Hall Hotel by RARE.

Figure 3
View of the new wing, roof extension and cladding at Town Hall Hotel.

Figure 4
Detail of new skin juxtaposed to Edwardian facade at Town Hall Hotel.

Figure 5
Detail of the new wing's cladding at Town Hall Hotel.

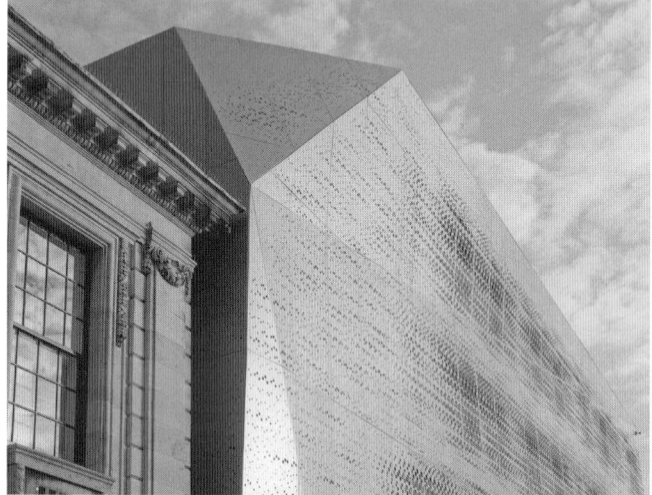

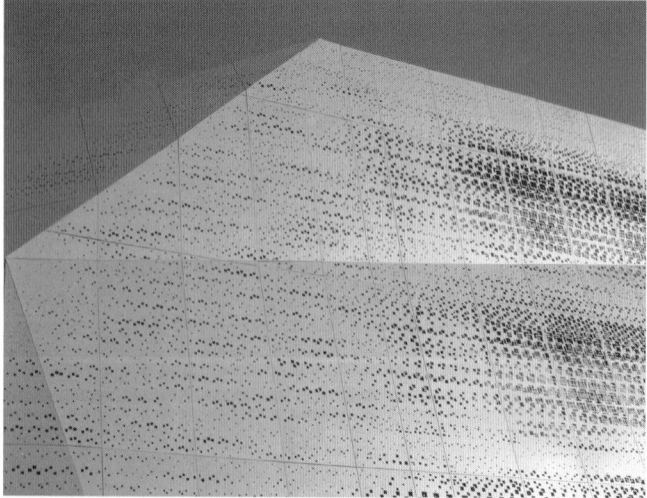

Figure 6
Spatial furniture in Edwardian Suite at Town Hall Hotel.

Figure 7
View from inside of sunlight through new extension's skin at Town Hall Hotel.

Figure 8
Detail of brass rail and decorative ventilation outlet in the lap pool at Town Hall Hotel.

Excursus 1: The scale of the detail

Figure 9
View of a closed DCS panelled kitchen unit at Town Hall Hotel by RARE.

proliferation of a simple component that generates contextual relationships. The inverted scale functions as adaptive architectonics, but in turn it is also the pattern – the ornamental feature, or the lower order of scales, if we use classical terminology – that defines the overall perception.

Stemming from these conceptual and digital tools, further abstractions of existing features generated a new ornamental vocabulary, inserted throughout the building as a means to articulate between spaces and eras. The results produced patterns and materials with a variety of qualities, aesthetically as well as functionally assessed, to provide a range of internal elements such as interpretative marquetry, ventilation outlets, service enclosures and glass manifestation. The computer-aided development and manufacturing of these elements reintroduced the idea of uniqueness – our digital craft. Here scale controls economic value as a direct factor of machining time; the scale of the cuts, scores and milling is inherently correlated to the cost of production.

Amid overall building design and material manufacturing, an intermediary scale inversion appeared in exceptionally featured rooms that demanded a specific preservation strategy. Their potential to become studio apartments presented us with a further opportunity to question the order of scales, whereby it is furniture that defines the space and functions at the scale of the rooms. Spaces are solely defined by these self-contained islands, distributing functional zones though a minimal and evanescent expression of continuous white surfaces with varied textures: matt, glossy, glittering or deep. Simultaneously ingenious containers and spatial divisions, they achieve, by contrast, a fusion between the original grandness and high-end contemporary facilities.

Excursus 1: The scale of the detail

Figure 10
View of the bathroom, brass-detailed corian steps and restored original decorative elements at Town Hall Hotel by RARE.

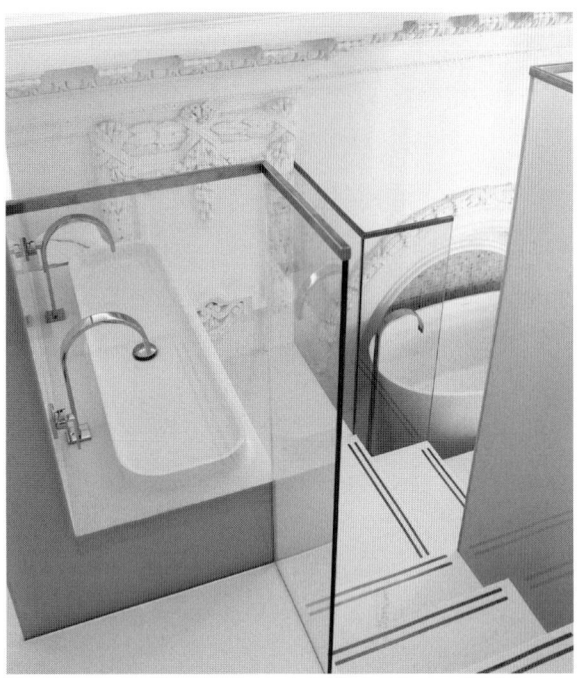

Articulating this diversity of structures, functions and styles, the project unifies old and new through a considered take on the eclectic original design and ornamental features. A new coherence is inserted by the articulation of local and sometimes minute elements forming the overall organisation from the small-scale up. As an opportunity to suggest a non-linear process, the inversion and nesting of scales generated an outcome exceeding the preconceived role of the scale of the detail. Most importantly, the bottom-up approach entailed the generation of a new type of overall coherence to the project – an organisational composition.

Scale before the twentieth century

The role of small-scale images by Wenceslaus Hollar

The rebuilding of London in the late seventeenth century

Gordana Fontana-Giusti

This chapter examines the architectural work of Wenceslaus Hollar (1607–77) in terms of its scale of representation, focusing on the role this opus has maintained in relation to architecture and the cities of the seventeenth century. It concentrates on the significance of small-scale images and argues that the craft that Hollar brought to England was critical for the development of architecture and urban design in London in the aftermath of the Great Fire. The chapter argues how early modern architectural representation brought together rich and nuanced cultural, geometric and empirical understandings of scale. The connection to late seventeenth-century urban design (and the work of Robert Hooke in particular) will be addressed, as it is still a lacuna in the architectural history of London.

Hollar and Prague

After leaving Prague at the age of twenty, etcher and engraver Wenceslaus Hollar lived in Strasbourg, Frankfurt and Cologne. According to the note presented on his best-known self-portrait, drafted by Jan Meyssens, Hollar was 'initially drawn to miniature painting' but was dissuaded from studying it by his father, who wanted his son to pursue a career in law. The young man settled for the graphic art of etching instead. As a son of a high-ranking official and a member of the Bohemian nobility, Hollar could have had access to the works of artists assembled by Rudolf II in the collection at Prague Castle. Rudolf, the Holy Roman Emperor (1552–1612), who was patron to Tycho Brahe and Johannes Kepler, had built the northern wing of the palace for his collection. The collection included works by Dürer, the Bruegels, Van Leyden, Paul Bril, Tintoretto, Veronese and the cabinet of curiosities that later became the model for other collections of a similar kind.[1] The King of Bohemia was one of the first monarchs to have private collections of art in the sixteenth century. The *Kunstkammer* (modelled in part on the Italian *studiolo*) was itself the microcosm of the visible world that was supposed to direct its owner towards a virtuous life.

At the beginning of the seventeenth century, Prague was probably the most exciting European capital. It was the meeting point between people working in the arts and the emerging mathematical sciences. In this context, Wenceslaus Hollar had developed a strong sense of visual culture and an understanding of the specific visual demands of his time. This is evident in his focusing on the medium of prints, which included the portrayal of diverse phenomena, where his love for precision could thrive. The sources upon which Hollar drew included the miniature paintings of Joris Hoefnagel (1542–1600) and his son Jacob (1575–c.1630), Netherlandish artists employed in Prague, the art of Jan van de Velde, and the works of Rembrandt and Jacques Callot. The Prague thirteenth-century school of miniatures was another important stimulus on Hollar, as were the works of Albrecht Dürer, whom Hollar had imitated from an early age.[2]

Documentary, detailed and lyrical, Hollar's images are seen as containing an aura of empathy. The small scale has probably contributed to this perception. A small drawing or a print becomes an object of intimacy that can be taken everywhere. It is a personal item, unlike big tableaux, which are about places, large rooms, light and display.

Hollar and the seventeenth-century visual paradigm

Unease in regard to the old, and restlessness in respect of new investigations, were reflected in the seventeenth century's attitude, which had increasingly attached greater value to observation and reflection in contrast to flights of subjective vision. In other words, this was the time of transition of attitudes and mentalities (*mentalités*).[3] In his own manner, Hollar pioneered the emerging change and visual experimentation.

The position of the visual arts was altering across Europe. Eight years senior to Hollar, Spanish painter Diego Velázquez (1599–1660), known for his experimental enquiries into the nature of painting, is a case in point. His painting *Las Meninas* (1656) has been central in determining attitudes about the nature of pictures, their role in society, in relation to individuals and different social strata (Foucault 1991). In a single gesture of going behind (and around) the canvas, Velazquez has opened up a new territory for the art of painting, taking the *ars pictura* from the realm of resemblance-making into the domain of reasoning.

Richard Pennington, the author of the most recent and complete catalogue of Hollar's work, argued that Hollar had been involved in exploring his interest in space, three-dimensionality and depth throughout his professional engagement (Pennington 1982). The liveliness and the depth of his images come from the fact that even when working at large scale, such as complex constructions of panoramic city views, Hollar completes his work with closely observed and clearly defined detail (Brothers 1998: 4). This move is not a grand gesture as in Velázquez's *Las Meninas*, but it makes a vital link to the viewer. Hollar seems to be guided by the desire to transmit his view most directly to the observer.[4] In a century notable for the establishment of art collections, botanical gardens and scientific collections of animals and plants, the demand for systematically drawn and engraved images became pervasive. The images reproduced in folios and books became essential in spreading emerging connoisseurship and knowledge. Having been part of medieval illuminated manuscripts as hand-drawn meditative images, miniatures became prominent again – as prints.[5]

The epistemological role of these miniatures needs to be acknowledged, as they were linked to the category of microcosm that was essential in controlling the exuberant proliferation of similitudes that governed knowledge in the sixteenth century and first half of the seventeenth century. It is likely that Hollar had understood his images as this kind of microcosm – a claim that can be supported by the nature of his framing, his precision and by his Prague background. For Hollar, it was essential that the relation of this microcosm to the macrocosm of the world (including architecture) should be preserved accurately, as it was a guarantee of the otherwise unstable limitless knowledge. As such, the quality of the miniature drawings and prints by Hollar marked the limit of knowledge and pushed the confines of its possible expansions.[6]

Hollar's representation of space

Hollar's landscape series began with Prague and its environs. These views were compact: the surrounding scenery acted as a frame, a curtain enclosing the small-scale representation of the urban form in the distance. The views of Strasbourg followed, becoming more developed and expressive, conveying Hollar's softness of articulation in unfolding the length of the view.[7] The small landscape drawings that precede the prints are the intimate expressions of Hollar's personality, as drawing was his first medium and the creative mode in which he attained perfection.

Hollar's compositional counterpoint between the city in small dimensions and the overall portion of landscape is characteristic. He had adopted the technique employed by the painters ('painter's algorithm'), where distant parts of a scene were drawn before the parts that were nearer – *repoussoir* – a technique that produces a feeling of depth.[8]

Commentators agree that the nine years spent in Germany were important for Hollar's personal development, and in particular the period spent at the Merian studio.[9] Comparing the quality of Hollar's work before and after his stay there, it is evident that this employment greatly contributed to the enrichment of Hollar's technique. The practice required fast, accurate work of high quality, and not individuality or artistic inclination (Pav 1973: 104). By taking part in this enterprise, Hollar acquired the topographical techniques for panoramic city prospects and bird's eye views.

Hollar incorporated these techniques into his own style of representation. It gradually became highly original and new, combining topographical knowledge with an artistically driven manner of representation comprising curiosities, softness and compassionate interpretation.

Hollar had travelled up the Rhine to Mainz, Delft and Rotterdam. The Düren drawings that followed are considered among the best examples of Hollar's work. They evoke emotional harmony with a landscape based on realistic study. The large view of

Cologne (1636) represents in many respects the peak of Hollar's achievement in topographical drawings.[10]

The emergence of small-scale detailed representations should be considered beyond their artistic context. They need to be viewed within a broader field of vision, including the discipline of optics and related experiments that characterised seventeenth-century scientific developments. One such milestone, which increased the possibilities for magnification, was Kepler's advancement of Galileo's telescope in 1611.[11] Although single-lens magnifiers had been in use in the mid-fifteenth century, it was the invention of the microscope that had revealed previously hidden miniature worlds. The seventeenth-century developments of the telescope on the one hand and the microscope on the other had extended scientific knowledge and inspired the scrupulous illustrations of the structure of plants, animals, birds and insects as produced by artists such as Hollar. In this respect, it could be argued that the seventeenth century decisively addressed the question of scale (Edgerton 2009: 155–68).

Travels (including Hollar's own) and the increased movement of people contributed to the circulation of new ideas and to the 'sharpening of vision'. The educational 'touring' around Europe was not only about gaining knowledge and acquiring crafts, it was also about training the eye. Hollar had learned how to observe the differences between states and principalities, and how to adjust the manner according to the dominant mores.

Arrival in England

Hollar's involvement in England began in 1635 when he met the Earl of Arundel, who was on a diplomatic mission in Europe. The English diplomat was an aspiring art collector, who, after seeing Hollar's work, made him an employment offer. The earl planned an etched catalogue of his collection and needed a skilled engraver, as the art of etching had not been fully developed in England (Brothers 1998: 4).[12]

Hollar arrived in London in 1636 and was soon to acquire many commissions.[13] His English patrons included the Earl of Arundel (a member of the Privy Council), Charles II and the Duke of York, later King James II. Hollar had benefited professionally from these connections, leading him to secure royal favour around 1641, following the death of Van Dyck, who had been the court painter.

Hollar's work had been gaining ground, as global trade was shifting towards the Atlantic nations. London became the place of exciting encounters, exotic goods and coffee shops.[14] The critical enquiries and debates that were previously taking place throughout Europe were now to be found in London. They had prompted the establishment of scientific assemblies such as the Royal Society (1662), dedicated to the promotion of science and knowledge. Hollar had famously etched the Royal Society history book front page designed by John Evelyn.[15]

Hollar's interests were wide and included the representation of animals and plants, as well as ladies' fashion and significant events of the time. This made Hollar quite original and unique. His *The Several Habits of English Women from the Nobility*

Figure 1
Winter, by Hollar, from *The Four Seasons*, 1643, with the Royal Exchange, London in the background. (Pennington. 609, 253 x 180 mm)

to the *Country Woman*, 1638–40, is an exceptional visual study into female costumes that resulted in the production of rendered masterpieces of this genre. Hollar's *Theatrum Mulienarum* (1643) is equally attractive. Women were portrayed in their local costumes as they came from across Europe: England, the Netherlands, France, the German principalities, Bohemia, Italian cities as well as Greece, the Balkans, Turkey and Persia. Notable are *The Four Seasons*, representing women in the clothes designed for each season. Here the women were situated in a specific spatial/urban context: *Winter* famously stood on a pedestal with the London Royal Exchange in the background (Figure 1).

This kind of artistic representation stands in contrast to the more 'masculine' aspect of Hollar's work on maps, as in the well-known 1644 map entitled *The Kingdom of England and the Principality of Wales*. This map was reputedly used by Cromwell during the Civil War as he regarded it the best and the most detailed of all maps of Great Britain. One of the clues for this variety of interests is the relentless eye of the miniaturist. It seems as if Hollar's eye cannot stop absorbing while it penetrates into the entirety of the fabric of seventeenth-century life, people, places, animals and plants.

Scaling of London

Hollar was fascinated by London, its topography, its prospects on the Thames, as well as by its surroundings, such as Islington, Lambeth, Surrey and Greenwich. Several of the smaller London views show the quality of Hollar's delicate line, notably the six

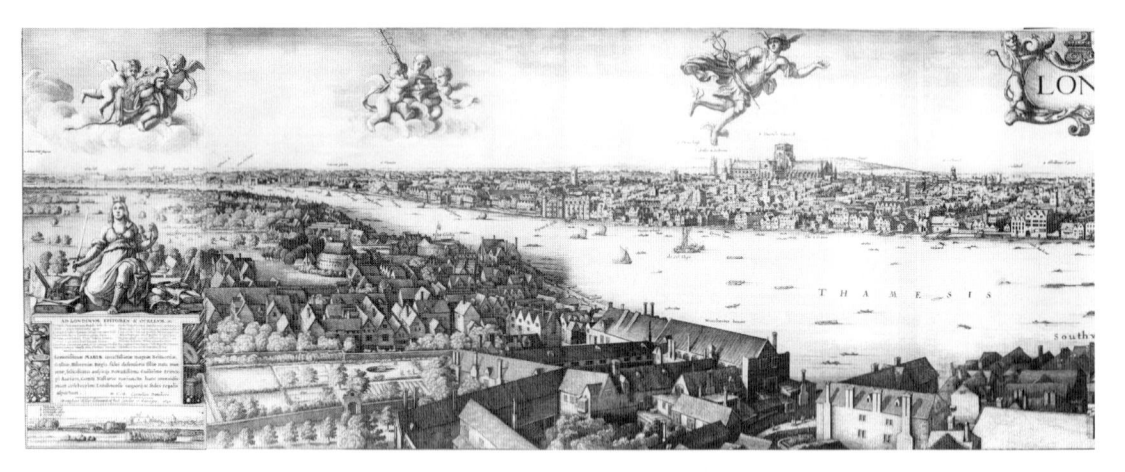

Islington Views and the *View of London from the Top of Arundel House*, while the long view of Greenwich rendered in 1637 became paradigmatic for its choice of viewing point, which remains relevant for subsequent architectural schemes up until today (Figure 2).[16] The Richmond view depicts the royal party in miniature scale. Views along the Thames from Whitehall and Lambeth Palaces are precise and revealing of the historical edifices along the Westminster and Strand area.

    Hollar's best known view is that of seventeenth-century London drawn before the Great Fire, originally published by Cornelius Danckerts in Amsterdam in 1647, while Hollar was in exile. This view is a construct made of a number of smaller views that Hollar had kept as drawings, assembling them together into an outstanding composite presentation observed at a 180° viewing angle from the top of St Mary Overy, presently Southwark Cathedral (Figure 3).[17] This iconic view of London is probably Hollar's most copied and disseminated work.

    Although Hollar drew on small sheets of paper (depending on genre they ranged in size between approx. 50 x 70 mm and approx 250 x 500 mm), his printed city plans and views also appeared on a grand scale. Hollar's (c.1658) *West Central District of London* (only known from two copies, one held in the British Museum, the other in the Folger Collection, Amherst) is a good example of the ambitious combination of the

Figure 2
View of London from Greenwich by Hollar, 1637.
(P. 997 145 x 831 mm)

Figure 3
Long View of London from the Top of Southwark Cathedral at Bankside by Hollar, 1647.
(P. 1014, 6 plates each print 462 x 392 mm)

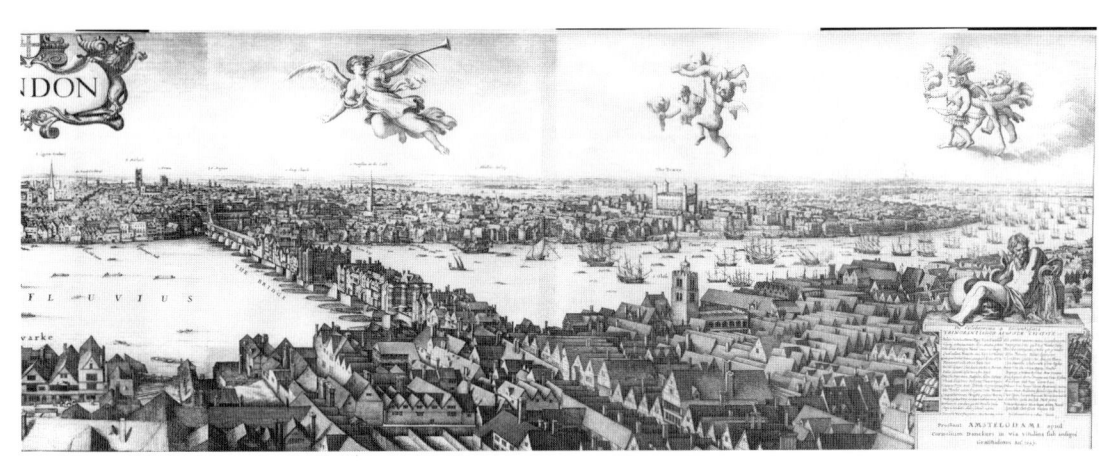

practical aims of a map and an attractive delineation depicting the houses and gardens of the city (Figures 4 and 4a). London squares such as Covent Garden (Figure 4) and Lincoln's Inn Fields are rendered from above, thus complementing the separate terrestrial views of the same squares (Figure 5). The view is full of details (Figure 4a) etched in Hollar's style, combining a well-structured bird's-eye view with architectural features (Hind 1972: 15). This view is wide, with vanishing points beyond the scope of the print, thus giving the appearance of an axonometric. The composition could thus be seen as a precursor of axonometric representation.

Richard Godfrey has argued that *West Central District of London* could have been a sample piece for a larger view of London that Hollar was planning to do in the 1660s, when he had issued a flysheet of *Propositions Concerning the Map of London and Westminster*. This map was supposed to be of a significantly bigger scale (10 ft x 5 ft) and was to express 'not only the Streets, Lanes, Alleys, etc: proportionally measured; but also the Buildings (especially of the principal Houses, Churches, Courts, Halls; etc) as much resembling the likeness of them, as the Convenience of the room will permit' (Godfrey 1995: 25). The ambition, the quality of the rendering and the available evidence would suggest that Godfrey could have been right, implying that *West Central District of London* is an unfinished masterpiece. Overall, Hollar produced 2,733 pieces,

Figure 4
West Central District of London, bird's-eye view. (P. 1002, 338 x 451 mm)

Figure 4a
Detail of the Covent Garden area, c.1658.

Figure 5
Lincoln's Inn Fields perspectival view by Hollar, 1660s. (P. 998A, 85 x 389 mm)

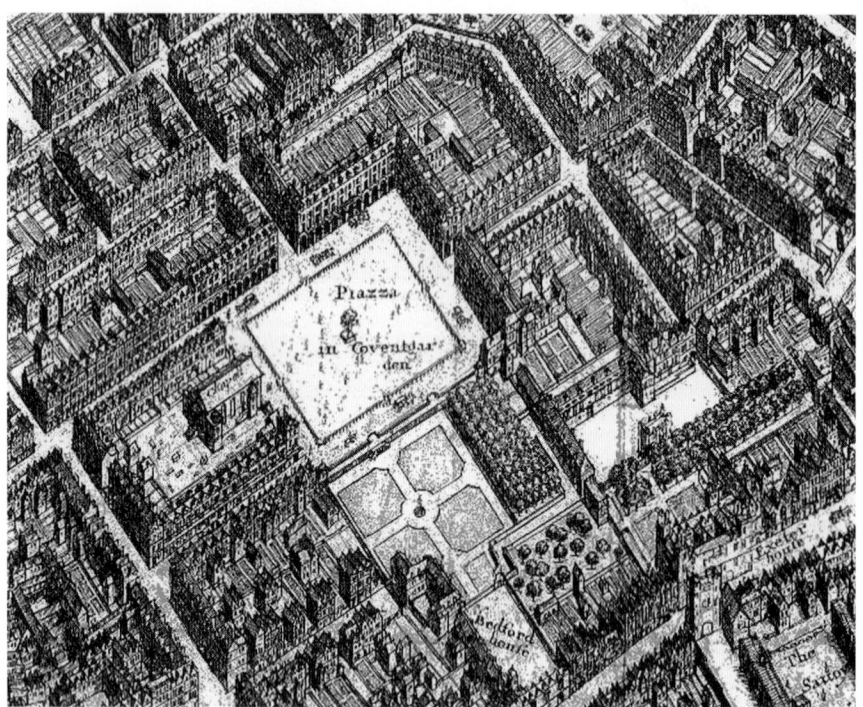

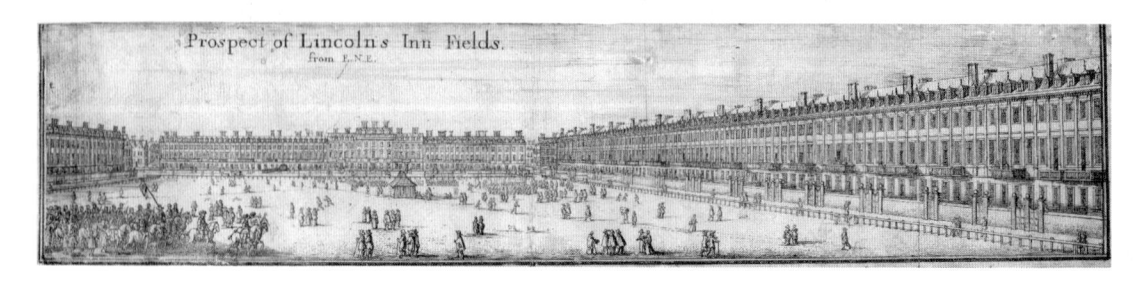

including numerous representations of English churches, monuments and cities published for the folios of William Dugdale and John Ogilvy (Pennington 1982).

The city after the fire

The lifelike renderings of London before and after the fire made Hollar an invaluable source of information for the City of London authorities as they responded to the claims in the aftermath of the disaster. City officials instructed Hollar to make an exact survey of the city as it stood after the fire. Hollar's maps were thus the definitive record of the Great Fire, representing the burned-out districts as white spaces (Figure 6).

As many as 436 acres of the medieval city had gone, but the fire also created an opportunity to make a new grand, planned city with better amenities. Charles II was determined to create a city that would reflect London's status. Within days of the fire, five proposals appeared, including the well-known scheme by Christopher Wren, the less known by Robert Hooke, the proposal by Richard Newcourt to rebuild each parish as a single block, Valentine Knight's city plan ringed with canals, and the courtier and diarist John Evelyn's scheme comprising a series of elegant boulevards.

Figure 6
Hollar's plan of London showing burned areas of the City in white, 1666. (P. 1004, 268 x 345 mm)

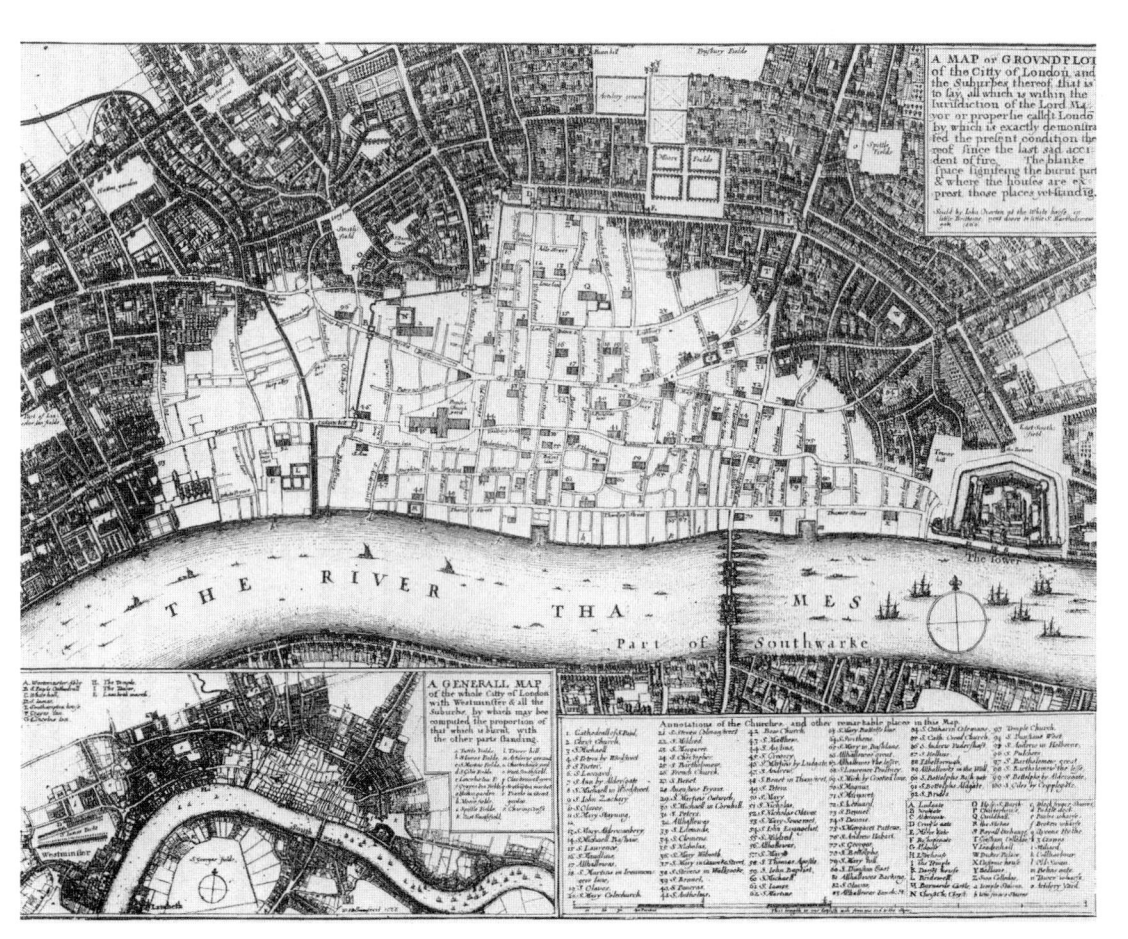

The scientist, polymath and architect Robert Hooke proposed a modern grid layout with gently meandering streets.[18] The organic layout of Hooke's scheme looked as if it had been inspired by the microscopic images as presented in his 1665 book *Micrographia* – a beautifully produced edition, seminal in its use of drawings as an integral element of scientific rhetoric.[19]

The king favoured the scheme by Christopher Wren, whose scheme was closest to Charles's vision of a European-style grand capital with piazzas, long straight avenues and magnificent views. Despite the king's wishes, all the grand plans were abandoned as there were no funds to compensate the owners of the city plots. Instead, individual owners had to be allowed to rebuild their own houses, and the old medieval street plan was kept in its outline. This approach favoured Hooke's flexible and meandering cellular grid, which was able to negotiate new buildings with the old plan. This was also one of the reasons why Charles II had asked Wren and Hooke to jointly oversee the rebuilding of the city (Cooper 2003).

A closer examination of Wren's and Hooke's work shows how they used Hollar's prints and drawings to further their own designs. Wren's drawings, such as the amalgamated depiction of St Paul's Cathedral kept at the British Museum, comprises the rendering of St Paul's as executed by Hollar, while his positioning of the Greenwich Observatory and the Royal Naval Hospital seem to have been derived in relation to and along the axis of symmetry of Hollar's Greenwich view, respectively.

Hooke is known for his engineering and scientific skills; the fact that he was an architect with a good visual and aesthetic sense is often forgotten. Hooke had an artistic education with Peter Lely, and is the author of drawings that have recently been traced back to Hans Sloane's eighteenth-century collection. Hooke was neglected for a long time due to his dispute with Isaac Newton (Hunter 2010: 251–60). Architectural scholarship on Hooke is scarce, but it is certain that Hooke was Wren's main collaborator on the Monument, the Greenwich Observatory and St Paul's Cathedral.[20] Hooke's precise structural considerations and understanding of materials were applied in the building of the dome.

Even if Hooke's and Wren's grand original projects were not carried through as conceived, their planning, surveying and the overall vision were incorporated in the principles of urban design as negotiated with the City of London. Jointly, they contributed to the emergence of a temperate but significant redesigning of the city after the disaster. The rules for this subtle transformation to the urban fabric that were established by Hooke and Wren have carried on until the present day. These regulations enabled London to transform itself several times, without having to endure major ravaging such as had happened in Paris in the nineteenth century, or in Vienna when the Ring was built. The interventions to the urban fabric negotiated by Hooke are not to be underestimated because they built upon the existing plan. The post-1666 system of regulations in urban design may not have suggested a monumental scheme, but the new design emerged in its own right. The novel buildings had to be different, made of more sturdy materials, fire-resistant and structurally sound. The medieval wooden structures of limited height and span were replaced. In doing so the buildings were morphologically altered as the lengths, heights and other ratios were subjected to the required structural changes. The urban design components were kept in terms of their overall character and disposition – the 'neighbourliness' of their elements, indicating the transformation of a topological kind.[21] The new topology was based on Hooke's interpretation of the old city plan that was superimposed and correlated with the newly required safe distances between the buildings. The documentation that was used in this process was provided by Hollar. In his diaries, Hooke (1935) refers to Hollar on several occasions, stating that he had appreciated his 'scientific method' and the scale of '100 to an inch', which had reportedly been favoured by Hooke himself.[22] The selection of the 'right' scale was therefore an important criterion and an indication of a particular approach.

Hooke's contribution to the rebuilding of London deserves reappraisal within the history and theory of architecture. The subtle topological transformation that was implemented in the City of London depended upon the precision of mathematical, artistic, practical and experimental knowledge that Hooke possessed. While Wren had an overall vision for the metropolis, acquired while travelling in France, Hooke's proficiencies included expertise in drawing, measuring, handling experiments and understanding materials. Wren depended on Hooke in respect of these skills.[23] Hooke was thus not an ordinary assistant: he was intellectually equal to Wren and an architect in his own right.[24] Hooke negotiated the design with the owners of the plots while complying with Wren's (and his own) future vision of the new city. The subtle geometry of Hooke's originally proposed plan with its organic cellular structures most probably continued to guide his vision and his negotiations.[25] The author of *Micrographia*, who used to sit behind the microscope and observe microorganisms and cells, was now designing urban structures on a scaled-up macro level (Figure 7).

The present configuration of the City of London is therefore a product of this complex vision, negotiation and scaling-up. This skilful leap contributed to the shaping of an organic urban morphology based on Hollar's unassuming but detailed depictions, and brought to life by Hooke's interpretation, understanding and foresight.

It is possible to conclude that Hollar's 1637 long view of Greenwich had introduced a new aspect of vision to London. This was followed by the other views produced by Hollar that gave London its iconic set of aspects anchored largely along the Thames. Hollar's etchings won this acclaim because they were, according to Evelyn, 'copied from life and hence more deserving of appreciation than those which rather depict chimerical curiosities and things non-existent in Nature' (Evelyn 1995). Evelyn, like Hooke, Wren and other connoisseurs and scientists of the time, collected Hollar's prints. Moreover, Hollar and Hooke shared a profound curiosity on the level at which they approached the world. They both observed phenomena in minute detail with a curious, sensitive and insightful eye. Hollar explored, loved and celebrated the miniature scale format in his images (Hunter 2010: 251–60). Their most powerful legacy is the versatility and resourcefulness that, among other things, stimulated the production of architecture and urban planning.

The miniature's ability to communicate to different people, disciplines and discourses sheds new light on the nature of architectural design, knowledge and debates in the late seventeenth century. By virtue of their compactness, empathy and adaptability, drawings and prints by Hollar circulated widely. They increasingly populated the emerging

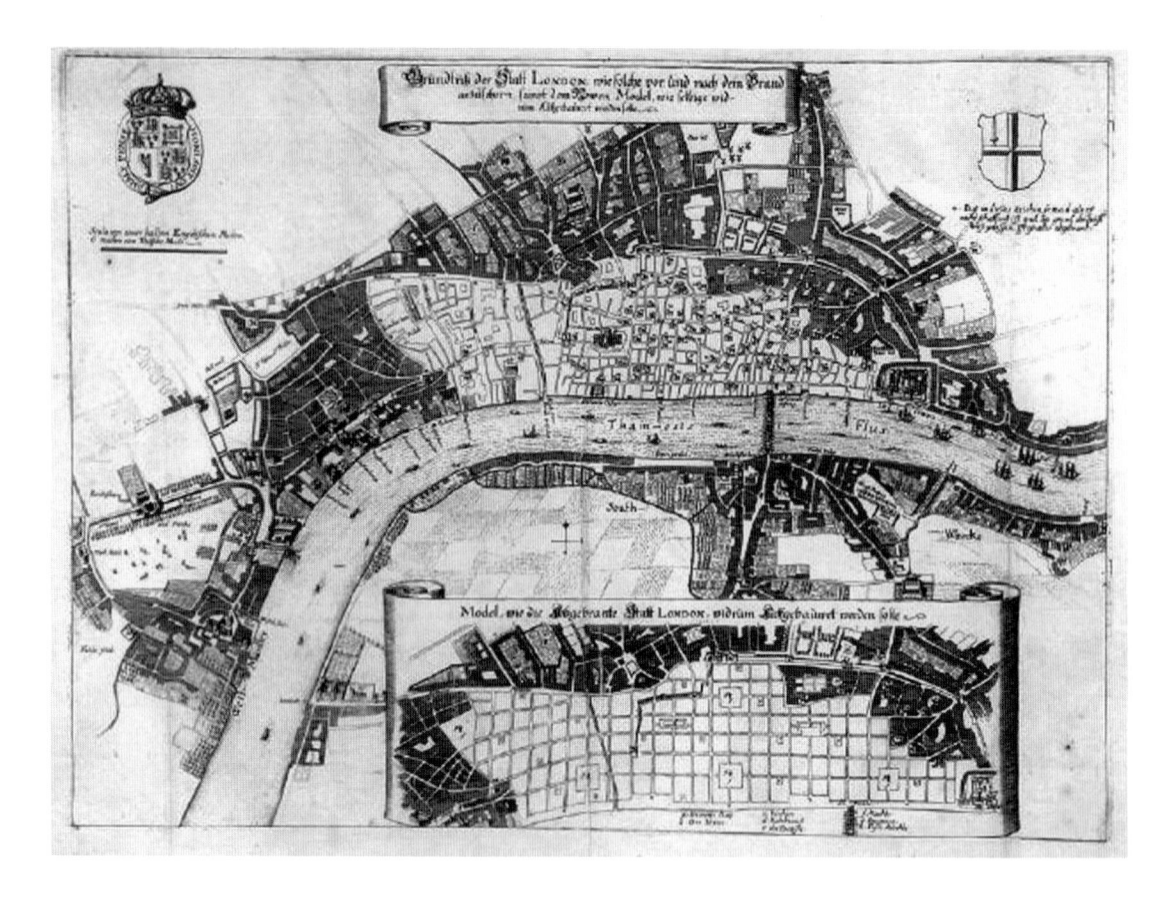

Figure 7
The image inserted into Merian's plan is Hooke's plan for London, c. 1670.

scientific texts, thus becoming intimate with the realm of the new sciences. They grew to be part of the world of learning, underpinned by the same epistemological ground as the scientific writings of the time. In turn, they began to mould, change and determine the basis of scientific texts. In this way, illustrations by Hollar acquired and affirmed their position of consequence in relation to knowledge, architecture and urban planning of London and beyond.

Notes

1 During the Thirty Years War, works of art were looted by the Swedes in 1648. The last rebuilding of the castle was by Queen Maria Theresa in the eighteenth century.
2 The works addressed here are Hollar's Christ, Madonna, self-portraits and landscapes.
3 This is in the Annales sense of the term.
4 John Aubrey, one of Hollar's three biographers (with Evelyn and Vertue), had traced Hollar's love for drawing to his early age, when Hollar was a 'precise delineator of the scenes' (Aubrey 1898). Detached and disciplined, he was an excellent illustrator despite the fact that he had never had a systematic training.
5 The term *miniature* comes from the Latin *minium*, red lead, used in a picture in medieval illuminated manuscripts; the early codices have been miniated. The generally small scale of the medieval pictures has led to an etymological confusion of the term with minuteness and to its application to small renderings. Source: www.enotes.com/oxford-art-encyclopedia/miniature (accessed November 2010).
6 On this matter, see more in Foucault (1991: 32).

7   This kind of print dates back to Dürer and his followers, the so-called German 'little masters' (Brothers 1998: 3).

8   *Repoussoir* (French, 'to set off'): a figure or object in the foreground is 'set off' from the principal scene, thereby increasing the sense of depth. Source: www.enotes.com/oxford-art-encyclopedia (accessed November 2010).

9   This period in Hollar's life remained unclear. Pav has corrected some errors. He has clarified Hollar's movements inside Germany (1627–36) and has traced Hollar's development from the early drawings of the Stuttgart period to the more mature works of Cologne in 1636 (Pav 1973: 96).

10 Hollar's representations are mainly executed as etchings, although the difference between the etched and the engraved is imprecise in seventeenth-century sources. Hollar himself was inconsistent, according to Van Erde (Van Erde 1971: 4). Vertue states that all Hollar's works were executed by etching, adding that he has well adapted that manner of engraving to them (Van Erde 1971: 142).

11 The important events at the time included the invention of Galileo's telescope in Venice. This was an improvement of the systems developed in the Netherlands (see Steadman 2001). Galileo published the work, including his observation on the sun and the moon, provoking anger within the Catholic Church, followed by the 1633 trial. His *Dialogue* was outlawed for centuries.

12 For more on Arundel, see Springell, who corrects Aubrey's and Vertue's report. Springell maintained that Hollar went to Merian's studio directly after Prague (Springell 1963: 136–7). However, the argument made by Pav about Hollar being with Merian in 1630–31 is more convincing.

13 Hollar's role in respect to Arundel is not entirely clear. He was a member of Arundel's household and as a nobleman maintained his independence. Arundel's life circumstances were exceptional. Both his grandfather and his father had come to disastrous ends. Arundel travelled to Italy in 1614 with Inigo Jones as a companion. In 1616, he publicly repudiated Roman Catholicism by embracing the Church of England and in 1621 he was appointed Earl Marshal of England. See Griffiths and Kesnerova (1983: 29).

14 The seventeenth century saw an increase in the scale of international travel and commerce, opening up of colonial markets, establishing enterprises such as the East India and South Sea Companies.

15 In 1662, a group of scholars from Oxford (Christopher Wren, Robert Boyle, John Wilkins, Robert Moray and William Brouncker) proposed a society 'for the promotion of Physico-Mathematicall Experimental Learning'. This body received its Royal Charter from Charles II, and The Royal Society of London for the Promotion of Natural Knowledge was formed.

16 Even today, the views from this point are considered when granting permission to the tall buildings in the City of London. Source: Tavernor, Robert. Scale Conference, Canterbury, November 2010.

17 The original prints can be found at the British Museum, British Library and the Museum of London; the composition was subsequently reprinted and copied by various artists.

18 The diversity of Hooke's activities and knowledge that gave him the nickname 'Leonardo of London' has presented a problem in attempts to assess his life and work. He was a Curator of Experiments to the Royal Society.

19 This scheme was mentioned by Marsh and Steadman (1971).

20 Recent scholarship includes the works by Lisa Jardine, Alan Chapman, Paul Kent, Michael Hunter, Michael Cooper.

21 On topology, see Marsh and Steadman (1971).

22 Already in the seventeenth century, Hooke had a vision of the decimal scale.

23 This was the reason why the king was in favour of Hooke. Another reason was that, politically, the king needed a good relationship with the City of London.

24 Hooke designed the Bethlem Royal Hospital (Bedlam) in Moorfields in 1675, and Ragley Hall, Warwickshire. Hooke was the Gresham Professor of Geometry. The City, having appointed Hooke as Gresham Professor and having preferred his plan for rebuilding to that of their usual surveyor, sought from him a vital contribution during the years 1667–74 (Cooper 2003).

25 This was intuited by Marsh and Steadman. In regard to Hooke's own scheme, the authors stated that Hooke had 'mapped his ideas of the city into the cell of the sponge'. They thus credited him with designing the first cellular city. Hooke had recognised the 'cell' as the smallest unit of life, thus introducing the term into its usage in biology (Marsh and Steadman 1971: 33).

Mildendo and Masdar

A tale of two cities

Adam Sharr

Jonathan Swift's *Gulliver's Travels*, first published in London in 1726, is arguably the definitive meditation on scale (Swift 1994). It has been read as a satire on governing elites, and on the meaning of civilisation and sanity. It has also been read as an anticipation of science fiction and a forerunner of the modern novel. The text is a parody of travellers' tales and colonialism. There have been many imitations and sequels, and multiple adaptations for radio, film and television. The book is structured in four parts, each part describing one voyage by the protagonist, Lemuel Gulliver, from his native England to 'remote nations of the world'. Scale is the central theme of parts one and two – the journeys to Lilliput and Brobdingnag – which satirise power, colonialism and the practices of gentlemen tourists.

The trip to Lilliput is the most famous of Gulliver's four voyages and children's books have been published under the title *Gulliver's Travels* that contain only the story of this journey. This chapter discusses the capital city of Lilliput, named Mildendo. Echoing Swift's enthusiasm for dialectical pairings, I will explore Mildendo's affinities with another city: Masdar, the eco-city, or so-called 'global clean technology cluster', recently designed by the architects Foster + Partners.[1] My aim is to tease out, beyond the superficial similarities of these two cities, an argument about architects, colonialism and the importance of scale.

Mildendo

Lemuel Gulliver is a professional; a surgeon who considers himself knowledgeable, reasonable and civilised. 'My hours of leisure', he recounts, 'I spent in reading the best authors, ancient and modern [. . . and] in observing the manners and dispositions of the people [. . .]' (Swift 1994: 3). After being shipwrecked, Gulliver wakes on the shores of Lilliput, finding himself lashed to the ground with tiny ropes (Figure 1).

He discovers that he is surrounded by diminutive people whose scale he later calculates to be one-twelfth of his own (Figure 2). These people are in perfect

Mildendo and Masdar: a tale of two cities

Figure 1
I lay all this while in great uneasiness. Lithograph by Gordon Browne, in Jonathan Swift, *Gulliver's Travels*.

"I lay all this while in great uneasiness."

Figure 2
The common size of the natives is somewhat under six inches high. **Lithograph by Gordon Browne, in Jonathan Swift,** *Gulliver's Travels.*

"The common size of the natives is somewhat under six inches high."

proportion with the animals and fields of the province. At first, the Lilliputians are wary of Gulliver, treating him simultaneously as a threat and a spectacle. But, as reward for his honourable behaviour, they feed him. He learns the language, makes peace with the emperor and earns his liberty. His first request on being set free is to see the metropolis Mildendo. Gulliver records his visit in the supposedly objective tone of many early travel writers. Stepping over the city wall, he finds that:

> The garret windows and tops of houses were so crowded with spectators, that I thought in all my travels I had not seen a more populous place. The city is an exact square, each side of the wall being five hundred feet long. The two great streets, which run across and divide it into four quarters, are five feet wide. The lanes and alleys, which I could not enter, but only view them as I passed, are from twelve to eighteen inches. The town is capable of holding five hundred thousand souls: the houses are of three to five stories: the shops and markets well provided. The emperor's palace is in the centre of the city, where the two great streets meet.
> (Swift 1994: 40)

This visit to Mildendo marks the zenith of Gulliver's celebrity in Lilliput. Soon, he becomes embroiled in the province's war with the neighbouring island of Blefuscu. Following the defeat of the Blefuscutians, he refuses to comply with their subjugation and becomes the victim of a court plot. On the eve of being sentenced to blindness, he spots a drifting rowing boat and effects his escape.

The geometrical figure of its footprint suggests that Mildendo is a planned settlement. Its axial organisation anticipates Baron Haussmann and his layout of grand urban boulevards for both military enterprise and civic display. The palace at the centre of the city records in urban form the hierarchies of state authority, literally and metaphorically putting the populace in its place outside the centre of power. While the city may be sized at 1:12 to the rest of the world, the structure of its urban design is familiar.

Masdar

The construction of Masdar – designed by Foster + Partners – has recently begun. It will, superficially at least, be scaled at 1:1 to the rest of the world. It is located in the city state of Abu Dhabi, the largest of the seven United Arab Emirates (UAE) and their capital. The state is ruled by the Abu Dhabi Emiri family and *Fortune* magazine claims that it is the richest city in the world. Masdar is to be located 17 km from downtown Abu Dhabi. It will, reports the website of Foster + Partners, 'eventually be home to companies, researchers, and academics from across the globe, creating an international hub for companies and organisations focused on renewable energy and clean technologies'.[2]

The project for Masdar has certain similarities to Swift's mini-metropolis. So far, both cities are known to the world through words and drawings. Masdar is also organised as a perfect square, enclosed by a city wall. Its population is projected to grow to the same as that of Mildendo: 500,000. It will also be densely packed with buildings of around five storeys separated by lanes and alleys. Like the Lilliputian capital, it has two cross-axes, supplemented by three boulevards that meander across the city's rectilinear grid in the manner of Broadway in New York. According to the publicity, Masdar will be 'zero carbon and waste free', so, like Mildendo, it will be at the centre of its own self-sustaining system: its own 'economy', in the oldest sense of that word.[3] Mildendo is centred around the emperor's palace, and the computer renderings of Masdar also show significant buildings at its centre, although the brief for these structures has not yet been publicised.

Whatever Masdar has in common with its diminutive fictional counterpart, there is more that separates them. Its design can be styled as 'eco-tech', responding to environmental problems with technological solutions. It will bristle with innovative devices: photovoltaic arrays, vacuum blankets to keep out heat and a driverless Personal Rapid Transit system.

This new future is, we are told, to be informed by lessons drawn from the regional Arab past and its image. According to its architects, the design for Masdar is inspired 'by the architecture and urban planning of traditional Arab cities', incorporating 'narrow streets; the shading of windows, exterior walls and walkways; thick-walled buildings; courtyards and wind towers; vegetation; and a generally walkable city'. Its virtues are promoted in terms of functional efficiency and environmental technology:

> The design provides the highest quality living and working environment with the lowest possible carbon footprint [. . .] There will be green parks separating built-up areas, not only to capture and direct cool breezes [. . .] but also to reduce solar gain and provide cool pleasant oases throughout the city. The intelligent design of residential and commercial spaces will reduce demand for artificial lighting and air conditioning. Carefully planned landscape and water features will aid in reducing ambient temperatures, while enhancing the quality of the street; the elimination of cars and trucks at street level not only makes the air cleaner for pedestrians but also allows buildings to be closer together, providing more shade but allowing maximum natural light.[4]

Whatever one may think of the waste created by the building of a new 'waste-free' city – and the energy required both to build it and to sustain its green spaces in desert conditions – the rhetoric is impressive. As BBC Radio 4's 'Costing the Earth' programme reported in March 2010: 'The genius of Masdar [. . .] will be combining twenty-first-century engineering with traditional desert architecture to deliver zero-carbon comfort'.[5]

Two cities and two travellers

There are tempting parallels to be drawn between Mildendo and Masdar that help us to reflect on Foster + Partners' design in the context of *Gulliver's Travels*. First, following Swift's satire of colonial attitudes, the eco-city can be read in relation to Edward Saïd's thinking on *Orientalism* (Saïd 1978). Saïd famously examined Western academic and artistic depictions of the East in the eighteenth and nineteenth centuries. He found these depictions to be ideological constructions of 'the Orient', as imagined by outsiders, which became instruments of colonial power. He surveyed the continuing pervasiveness of the values they record.

The design for Masdar emerged from a strand of Western modern architecture, epitomised by Foster + Partners, which seeks rational technical solutions to design problems, attempting to optimise function, structure, construction and environmental response (Wainwright 2011). Antony Vidler has shown how this thinking refers to the idea of the vernacular in support of its values (Vidler 2009). In particular, certain strands of Modernist architectural historiography have sought to distil climatic design principles from so-called Middle Eastern vernaculars. Western Modernist authors have tended to caricature the Arab city as an assembly of three particular tropes: narrow shady streets, windcatchers and intricate timber shades. This pervasive caricature is repeated from Reyner Banham's technological descriptions of *The Architecture of the Well Tempered Environment* (Banham 1984) to Bernard Rudofsky's romantic photographic inventory in *Architecture Without Architects* (Rudofsky 1984). It is precisely these tropes that Foster + Partners repeat in the design of Masdar. But any local specificity that these architectural elements once had becomes subsumed into a generic Arabness by the logic of eco-technological modern architecture. Saïd criticised the 'Hindoo' styling of Brighton's Royal Pavilion, which, he argued, comprised an exoticised veneer over an

English architecture. Likewise, Masdar is technological, capitalist, Western architecture that has been 'orientalised' with windcatchers, narrow shady streets and intricate timber shades. It dresses up in Arab costume an architecture whose values are thoroughly modern, Western and technocratic. There seems to be little attempt to re-think these values for Masdar according to Eastern practices, cultures and customs.

Another tempting parallel can be drawn between the figure of Lemuel Gulliver and that of Norman Foster. Both are, to some extent, fictional characters. We know Gulliver through what purports to be a sincere and truthful account of his voyages, although he is apparently the creation of Jonathan Swift. Meanwhile, Norman Foster is to be found only in media-managed snapshots, profiles and sound-bites manufactured to promote the architectural practice of Foster + Partners. He is even elusive in his recent authorised biography written by the journalist Deyan Sudjic (Sudjic 2010). To all intents and purposes, the man has been subsumed by the corporation that bears his name. The extent of his personal contribution to the projects of Foster + Partners remains difficult to discern. Whether Foster has visited the site at Masdar (or, indeed, whether he has had any involvement in the design at all) is unknown. In the context of Swift's Gulliver, it is tempting to speculate whether he really exists.

For the purposes of this chapter, I imagine a fictional protagonist named Norman Foster arriving in Abu Dhabi in his business-class aeroplane seat. It is fully reclined and he is strapped in with a seatbelt in a more comfortable imitation of the arriving Gulliver strapped to the shores of Lilliput. Like his counterpart in the other fiction, this imagined Foster is also the epitome of the professional gentleman tourist. He addresses his hosts with the utmost respect, seeking to behave with honour, to demonstrate his literate civilisation. He is the embodiment of rational values, keen to return to England with sincere observations of the place and the dispositions of its people that can inform the creative endeavours of design. In *Orientalism*, Edward Saïd notes how the tradition of Western literature 'created' the Orient through the manufacture of stereotypes. The Westerner is seen as being 'essentially rational, developed, humane, superior, authentic, active, creative and masculine, while the Orient (the East, the other) (a sort of surrogate, underground version of the West or the self) is seen as being irrational, aberrant, backward, crude, despotic, inferior, inauthentic, passive' (Macfie 2000: 4). The imaginary Norman Foster, returning to London from Masdar, might appear to perpetuate these stereotypes. The professional architect with scientific modern architecture in mind brings technocratic Western values to bear wherever he travels (and usually it is 'he'). Like Gulliver, star architects become a spectacle in the land they visit. The aura of the global brand that they embody makes them a kind of giant, their stature in proportion to the cost of their professional expertise. Their expensive consultancy rates command authority and, as such, their discourse exerts power and their cultural superiority is perpetuated.

The currency of equivalence

In the light of Edward Saïd's work, these are, to some extent, easy criticisms. It is easy to pick on Masdar for its exoticised technocratic Modernism and it is easy to pick on an imaginary Norman Foster for embodying the supposed rational superiority of Western technocratic values. But it is important to remember that Saïd's work has itself been criticised, not least for its tendency to pose the Orient and the Occident as opposites always locked in confrontation. Fred Dallmayr, for example, refers to Saïd's 'facile invention of formulas', suggesting that constructs such as 'Eurocentrism or anti-Eurocentrism' are often cast in simplistic terms (Dallmayr 2000: 366). Another criticism is relevant here, concerning Arab agency. In Saïd's account of *Orientalism*, Arabs are frequently stripped of agency, becoming almost passive in the face of repression and domination by colonial Westerners. The story of Masdar as it is published in the English language news media and architectural media repeats this tendency. The client is curiously absent. The organisations and individuals are hardly named, let alone credited with any of the project's ideas or impetus. Their agency is undeniable but their voice is drowned out by the media power of their globe-travelling consultants.

Dallmayr – following Saïd, but with criticisms of Saïd's work in mind – reflects on what he calls the 'currency of equivalence' that the West exports. This 'currency of equivalence', he argues, equates the free flow of capital with ideas of freedom and technical rationality. Financial capital and cultural capital (Bourdieu 1986) here consolidate their power through a universalising positivist rhetoric. This rhetoric constructs a continuity between the technocracy of the military industrial complex, the utilitarian bureaucracy of (conventional) management theory, the rational authority of the professional expert, and supposedly universal ideas about (a certain kind of) democracy. The design for Masdar, 'inspired by' so-called Arab architecture, can be located squarely in this project of equivalence. Its generic rhetoric of 'highest quality living', 'reducing solar gain' and 'carefully planned landscape and water features' could apply to any development anywhere in the world, whatever its geographical or political circumstances. Despite the rhetoric of local distinctiveness and the application of generic 'Arab' architectural tropes, Masdar's technocratic values chime with those of global eco-technology, construction management and mass media. Following Dallmayr, Masdar can be seen as part of the ongoing export of supposedly superior Western values, as satirised by Swift and exposed by Saïd.

Superficially, Mildendo is at scale 1:12 in relation to the rest of the world and Masdar is at 1:1. However, their respective scales seem more complex and shifting. It has famously been calculated that the average American uses twelve times as much energy, and the average European uses four times as much, as one Chinese person. The average resident of Abu Dhabi is not included in this calculus, although one might imagine that this rich state's air-conditioning demand puts its residents near the top of the list. In this respect, the designers of Masdar aim, admirably, to reduce the scale of the city, in terms of its carbon footprint. But the sense of superiority embodied in the design's technocratic rationality also expands the intellectual space it takes up. Its ratio is thus enlarged, somehow, in relation to its locality.

The endurance of Swift's story has exaggerated the size of Lilliput in popular consciousness way beyond its scale. Many people are more familiar with Mildendo than they are with other cities whose existence is more physically tangible. Likewise, through its association with the global design brand of Foster + Partners, Masdar has a metric in the global news media that outstrips its proposed size, or its present stage of construction.

Meanwhile, the computer renderings of Masdar are curiously scaleless. Its ideal geometry in relation to the open space of the desert, and its proportions, could seemingly be enlarged or reduced at will. Are its sides 500 metres or 2 kilometres long? The images yield little. Like Lilliput, as found by Gulliver, everything in the images of Masdar appears in perfect proportion in relation to itself. But it remains difficult to reach any meaningful appreciation of its size.

The strange scalelessness of Masdar's imagery mirrors the eco-city's curious position in relation to the locality and its cultural heritage. Mildendo appears in clear relation to its own locality and culture, and for this reason its scale is easily measured. Masdar, on the other hand, is scaled to Dallmayr's 'currency of equivalence' as exported by the West, which equates technical rationality with freedom and the free flow of capital.

Scale operates by relation, measuring one thing against another (as indicated by the colon that appears in any mathematical notation of scale, such as 1:5, 1:12, or 1:100). Equivalence, however, allows no discernable relations. Everything is always more or less the same as everything else. Things are always in proportion, but never in scale. This equivalence is familiar in global architecture. The same motifs recur worldwide, like those mentioned earlier: 'highest quality living', 'reducing solar gain', 'carefully planned landscape and water features'. And the same architects recur in so-called signature projects worldwide, their consultancy purchased for aggrandisement, irrespective of brief or site. For a signature building, any of the familiar signatures is effectively equivalent to another: Zaha Hadid, Jean Nouvel, Renzo Piano, Norman Foster. Scale, in this sense, is not so much a tool for anticipating design through drawing or an idea about relative bigness or smallness. It is, instead, distinguished as a metric with potential to counter the project of pervasive equivalence.

To appreciate scale is to appreciate relations; to acknowledge and differentiate the motions of disparate cultures, ideas, and flows of capital and power. It is to appreciate other people, other places and other architectures in their own right rather than understand them simply as ciphers of what is already familiar. Lemuel Gulliver's tale frequently finds Mildendo to be continuous with the England that he knew, despite its small size. He understood differences largely in relation to what was similar, preferring to document habits, values, urban structures and social structures that chimed with those of his own milieu. Similarly, Masdar's design – like the rhetoric that accounts for it and the images that represent it – finds the economic, cultural and physical landscape of its Abu Dhabi site to be largely continuous with that of England, Europe or America. The specificities of the place and its histories, the conditions of Masdar's immigrant construction workers, and the exclusive profile of its future residents, go largely unspoken in the fulfilment of a project couched in a language and a graphic that remain reassuringly familiar to Western power, trade and capital. The scalelessness of the city plan merges with the scalelessness of the computer renderings, somehow emptied of human relations despite the photographic figures cut and pasted in from elsewhere (Till 2009). The political relations implicit in these renderings are covered over by the rhetoric and the image of equivalence. While the consultants have drawn their ideas 'to scale', they have neglected the proper relations of scale, rendering the unfamiliar largely continuous with the familiar. Masdar's aspiration towards sustainability is admirable. But this is the sustainable architecture of global developers, financiers, project management firms and building product manufacturers, driven by the values that unite their flows of trade, capital, language and ideas. Paying attention to scale – as the opposite of pervasive equivalence – might suggest an alternative approach to sustainability: one that is capable of dealing in specificities and contingencies, rather than collapsing richly disparate lives and cultures into a single reductive drawing plane.

Notes

1   Refer to www.fosterandpartners.com/Projects/1515/Default.aspx (accessed 16 November 2010).
2   Refer to www.fosterandpartners.com/Projects/1515/Default.aspx (accessed 16 November 2010).
3   I am grateful to David Leatherbarrow for introducing me to this interpretation of 'economy'.
4   Refer to www.fosterandpartners.com/Projects/1515/Default.aspx (accessed 16 November 2010).
5   *Costing the Earth*, BBC Radio 4, broadcast 29 March 2010, 21:00.

'Examining the knots ... counting the bricks'
John Ruskin's innocent eye

Stephen Kite

Meditating on the awesome imagination of the Romantic artist J.M.W. Turner, in the first volume of *Modern Painters*, the English art critic and social reformer John Ruskin (1819–1900) asserts:

> The higher the mind; it may be taken as a universal rule, the less it will scorn that which appears to be small or unimportant; and the rank of a painter may always be determined by observing how he uses, and with what respect he views the minutiae of nature. Greatness of mind is not shown by admitting small things, but by making small things great under its influence. *He who can take no interest in what is small, will take no interest in what is great* . . .
>
> (Cook and Wedderburn 1904–13, vol. 3: 491, Kite's emphasis)

Ruskin's obsession with the small in scale, and the fragment – at once rooted in the modes of fracture of the picturesque, and presciently Modernist – continues to fascinate us moderns. A striking example comes from the Venice Architecture Biennale of 2010, where the British Pavilion in the Public Gardens was renamed 'Villa Frankenstein' (recalling John Ruskin's despair at the 'Frankenstein monsters' of London villas and public houses inspired by his praise of Venetian architecture). Within the Pavilion, his Venetian pocket-books of 1849–50 were displayed – brought 'home' from the Ruskin Library, University of Lancaster, to the city they record so minutely. A timber amphitheatre (a 'Stadium of Close Looking') was also constructed, on whose tiers the youth of Venice were encouraged to draw the small-scale (fragments of stones, shells, tiles, bricks, glassware and the like), practising that work of close seeing that Ruskin encouraged in all social groups, which was, in his deeply empirical method, the only basis of full understanding (British Council 2010). As he declares in one of his most forceful passages: 'The greatest thing a human soul ever does in this world is to *see* something, and tell what it *saw* in a plain way. Hundreds of people can talk for one who can think, but thousands can think for one who can see. To see clearly is poetry, prophecy, and religion, – all in one' (Cook and Wedderburn 1904–13, vol. 5: 333).

Describing Ruskin's fieldwork in Venice in the winter of 1849–50, Wolfgang Scheppe writes of:

> the visual analysis of thousands of details, corresponding to thousands of drawings. No one before or after has ever undertaken such an effort: a vast mosaic completed over long wanderings of observation and recording deduces the form of work as a conceptual whole from the close looking at a myriad of physical particles of materialised labour. In the stones of Venice, Ruskin read the city of society.
>
> (Scheppe 2010: 38)

The pressure of such undertakings would advance Ruskin's ultimate descent into madness. But there were also many moments of closure when Ruskin would write 'Done' on a sheet or note, to mark its fixing as text or image – hence the title *Done. Book* that Scheppe gives to his record of this Biennale show. Certainly, my chapter ends with Ruskin in Venice – but no later than 1841; the major work of 1849–50 and 1850–51 lies beyond the horizon of these pages, though I have written on this later period elsewhere (Kite 2007, 2008, 2009b). Here, the aim is rather to trace earlier roots of these practices of precision in observation, of this minituarist-like envisioning of architecture, which becomes the greater knowledge of cities and their societies through the small-scale. Hence, for Stephen Bann:

> Throughout [Ruskin's] intense communion with the spirits of past Italy, he was attempting to recover an image of historical wholeness from the disorder, fragmentation and sheer anomaly of the contemporary Italian environment. How was this image to be secured? . . . It had to be through the strategy of synecdoche – through the precise description of the detailed drawing that gave imaginative access to a whole greater than its parts.
>
> (cited in Hewison 2009: 120)

Ruskin's synecdochic reading of the whole through the part can be discovered on many levels. His evangelical mother had instructed him in the typological unpacking of biblical texts verse by verse; this is extended in his symbolical reading of architecture as language, as in the 'Lamp of Memory' of *The Seven Lamps of Architecture*, a method linked by a number of commentators to Victor Hugo's presentation in *Notre-Dame de Paris* (1831–32) of the cathedral as a material inscription of human thoughts, to be read stone by carved stone (Bullen 1992). Against accounts of the fragment that overstress the avant-garde, John Dixon Hunt reminds us of the roots around 1800 of those picturesque modes of vision in which the earlier Ruskin, particularly, is saturated, such as the enjoyment of the aperspectival potential of the broken parts of ruins and the fascination with architectural miniaturisations such as follies (Dixon Hunt 2004). These are new visual worlds to be discovered through the chance encounters of embodied movement, rather than pre-ordained presentations to the fixed gaze; for an itinerant of Europe, and of many a Venetian passage and *campo*, this peripatetic dimension to Ruskin's discovery of architectural part-objects is very important.

Viewing vignettes of art and life

In fact, John Ruskin first imagined the architecture of Italy through the small-scale in J.M.W. Turner's tiny vignettes to Samuel Rogers's *Italy: a poem* – a thirteenth birthday present given to him on 8 February 1832. As Ruskin recalled: 'The book was the first means I had of looking carefully at Turner's work; and I . . . attribute to the gift, the entire direction of my life's energies' (Cook and Wedderburn 1904–13, vol. 35: 15). With the 1822 painting by James Northcote in mind, Rosalind Krauss opens her *The Optical Unconscious* with a portrait of 'little John Ruskin, with his blond curls and his blue sash and shoes to match, but above all his obedient silence and his fixed stare', noting his ability, in a childhood lacking toys and much *physical* affection, to give an analytical attention to things (Krauss 1993: 1). And Ruskin remembers how he could pass his days 'contentedly tracing the squares and comparing the colours of my carpet; – examining the knots in the wood of this floor, or counting the bricks in the opposite houses', as he would one day count the bricks of Venetian palaces (Cook and Wedderburn 1904–13, vol. 35: 58). In *The Stones of Venice* (1851–53) Ruskin describes such habits as a close 'watching' of building:

> And as for these Byzantine buildings, we only do not feel them because we do not *watch* them; otherwise we should as much enjoy the variety of proportion in their arches, as we do at present that of the natural architecture of flowers and leaves.
>
> (Cook and Wedderburn 1904–13, vol. 10: 15)

Using Ruskin's sketches and notebooks – held in the archives of the Ruskin Foundation (Ruskin Library, University of Lancaster) – this chapter focuses on his 'watching' of architecture from childhood, up to his first major Italian tour of 1840–41, aged 21. Yet Ruskin was not always alone, for he read the Bible daily with his evangelical mother, Margaret Ruskin (Cook and Wedderburn 1904–13, vol. 35: 128). These early experiences of romantic reading, analytic attention and Biblical instruction already inscribe the distinct threefold character of Ruskin's imagination, as Denis Cosgrove summarises: 'Romantic thought that was enhanced by early travel through mountain scenery, a scientific training in accurate observation that was encouraged by his art teachers, and a religious experience that stressed the symbolic interpretation of things' (Cosgrove 1979: 46). As with the Turner vignettes, or the knots in the wood of his nursery floor, in these formative years we shall begin to discover the importance of the small-scale in his readings of architecture – fragments that indeed imbricate the romantic, the scientific and the symbolic. This use by Ruskin of the small-scale to emblematise the whole – his 'synecdochic method' – is of most consequence in the city whose stones inspire his greatest obsessions with building (*Stones of Venice* 1851–53). As J.B. Bullen points out, 'not only are the contending forces located in a single place, Venice; they are focused, as in a burning glass, within a single art – architecture. The flux of human events is arrested in art; the chronicle is memorialised in stone' (Bullen 1992: 56). From this standpoint the thousands of fragments Ruskin would come to record, beyond the juvenilia examined here, capture something more than mouldings; they supervene a linear recording of history in their ambition to arrest cultural, symbolic and physical interactions in a material *presentness*.

Ruskin's *First Sketchbook*

Ruskin's *First Sketchbook* is described exactly in his autobiography *Praeterita*:

> My quite first sketchbook, an extremely inconvenient upright small octavo in mottled and flexible cover . . . filled with outlines, irregularly defaced by impulsive efforts at finish, in arbitrary places and corners, of Dover and Tunbridge Castles and the main tower of Canterbury.
>
> (Cook and Wedderburn 1904–13, vol. 35: 77)

On this drawing (RF 1189) of the soaring central tower of Canterbury (completed by John Wastell in 1503) Ruskin later wrote: '. . . Canterbury, 1832. / my first, as ever was – study / of architecture . . . .' In a 13-year-old hand – within ruled lines outlining the perpendicular Gothic framework – he picks out the quatrefoils marking the stages of the tower, and the intricate outlines of its pinnacles (Figure 1). Moving closer to the cathedral, Ruskin made a study of part of the south porch (RF 1188). Here his detailing of niches with their vaults-in-miniature, and their finials and crockets, again shows a precocious sensibility to architectural detail for a 13-year-old, and more sense of organic life in the architecture than evidenced by the tower study. As Ruskin himself later pointed out in *Praeterita*: 'I got little satisfaction and less praise by these works; but the native architectural instinct is instantly developed in these,– highly notable for any one who cares to note such nativities' (Cook and Wedderburn 1904–13, vol. 35: 78).

Here are already two modes of representation that will frequently recur. First, the Canterbury tower corresponds to a frontalising mode wherein the building's architectural elements are laid out with a certain objectivity – a later example is the notable 1845 watercolour and bodycolour sheet of *The Casa d'Oro, Venice*, made at the threshold of the period when Ruskin embarked on his study of architecture with a new seriousness. Here, the celebrated traceries fill out the ruled outlines of a sheet left one-third blank; in their *non-finito* aspect, such lacunae augment the collage-like modernity of Ruskin's drawings. At 'the Ca' d'Oro' it is possible that the building work of G.B. Meduna's drastic 'restoration' of the *casa* prevented Ruskin's progress; at other times he seems to just suspend work on a sheet when his intense scrutiny fades, perhaps through fatigue or nervous exhaustion, or simply other calls on his restless imagination. So, at Canterbury, only the left half of the upper stage of Wastell's masterpiece, *Bell Harry*, is delineated by Ruskin; the right of the sheet is left blank. Whereas, second, the porch fragment initiates those myriad studies of architectural detail where Ruskin places himself close to the building's fabric; his visual craving is excited, and minute detail is recorded with an energised line in a close-cropped image. As John Unrau has remarked, as Ruskin

Figure 1
John Ruskin,
Canterbury,
1832.

'approaches to within a few feet of a fine medieval . . . building, [his] visual appetite seems to grow' (Unrau 1978: 119).

Ruskin also recollects 'a really good study, supplemented by detached detail, of Battle Abbey' (RF 1142). This is probably the sheet Ruskin later noted as 'Battle abbey – JR. Sketch on the spot 1831 Aged 12', where the abbey gateway is outlined in elevation, and the parts of its battlements and elements are numbered and lettered in cross-reference to 'detached detail' at the side of the page – very analytical for a 12-year-old. This information of part and whole may have been pulled together to produce the stiffer, painstakingly detailed, three-quarter view of the gateway (RF 1143). Both drawings confirm an early and intense appetite for the particular. In the pages of this *First Sketchbook*, it is also revealing how architecture and the natural sciences are interleaved; thus there is 'My First tree! From nature', as Ruskin later noted on a sketch of particularly twisty branches. Then, there are 17 closely written pages of pencil notes on geology with headings such as 'Garnet', and 'Arsenical Cobalt' – the first drafts of the mineralogical dictionary that Ruskin began at the age of 12. The influence of this passion for the materials of the earth on the character of his close reading of architectural detail cannot be overstressed; these stones needed to be closely examined, and pored over, to unlock their particular mysteries (see Hilton 2002: 17).

Ruskin came to loathe mathematical repetition in architecture, such as the perpendicular Gothic of parts of Canterbury Cathedral, but his love of the textures typified by the first ruin he ever drew – St Radegund's Abbey, west of Dover – foreshadows the 'Lamp of Memory' of *The Seven Lamps of Architecture*. As he remembers: 'the first "remaining" of Antiquity I ever sketched, when a boy of fourteen, spending half my best BB pencil on the ivy and the holes in the walls . . .' (Cook and Wedderburn 1904–13, vol. 27: 492).

Under drawing masters like Charles Runciman, and later James Duffield Harding, Ruskin was taught, like many of his social class, to draw as a gentleman–amateur, and later regretted his lack of artistic imagination: ' I never saw any boy's work in my life showing so little original faculty, or grasp by memory. I could literally draw nothing, not a cat, not a mouse, not a boat, not a bush, "out of my head" . . .' (Cook and Wedderburn 1904–13, vol. 35: 75; Walton 1972: 8). Certainly, Ruskin never became a Turner, or even a David Cox, but his gifts as draughtsman, and visionary, would lead him far beyond this milieu of the gentleman–amateur. By the 1850s, Ruskin would encourage in the adult that directness of seeing of the infant gazer at carpets, and knots in planks, when he calls for

> our recovery of what may be called the *innocence of the eye*; that is to say, of a sort of childish perception of these flat stains of colour, merely as such, without consciousness of what they signify – as a blind man would see them if suddenly gifted with sight.
>
> (quoted in Crary 1992: 95)

In the context of this later key formulation of vision, Jonathan Crary identifies 'a major reconfiguration of the observer' in the earlier nineteenth century, around the time that the teenage Ruskin was sketching Dover Castle, and its neighbouring abbeys and ruins in that awkward small octavo *First Sketchbook*. Vision, argues Crary, now requires 'an interrogation of the physiological make-up of the human subject'; it escapes 'the timeless order of the camera obscura' – or, indeed, any other certainties – to become located 'within the unstable physiology and temporality of the human body' (Crary 1992: 66, 70). Moreover, as noted, this is now the body of the picturesque walker engaged in real movement who, in ruins like these castles and abbeys, delighted in the time-wrought disintegration of the well-integrated object, enjoying the play in parallax of fragments of interior and exterior (see Collins 1965: 26–8). Amateur sketching, like young Ruskin's, flourished in this enthusiasm for direct contact with natural and architectural topography, producing a steady demand for instruction manuals such as those authored by Samuel Prout (1783–1852).

Following Prout

In the spring of 1833, Ruskin's father brought home a work by this important topographer – his *Sketches in Flanders and Germany*. Inspired by this volume, the family decided to see the sites of Prout's lithographs for themselves. On this tour, Ruskin first saw the Alps and Lake Como. In April 1835, his parents again took him to the continent on a tour, which culminated in his first visit to Venice in October. For Collingwood, Ruskin's first biographer, he made a choice on this second continental journey 'to imitate the imitable' by following Prout rather than attempting to 'idealise his notes in mimic Turnerism' (Collingwood 1893: 51). Now, he is 'as ready with his pencil as he had been with his pen', and there follow many laborious architectural studies imitating Prout's broken line.

The observation of this tour is more probing and critical, yet remains a displaced activity in its self-conscious referencing of travel engravings, as in his *Part of St Mark's Church and the Doge's Palace* (RF 1055; Figure 2). In this stiff study, the perspective goes awry and the upper treasury wall of St Mark's looks more like timber panelling than marble revetment. Ruskin's casual attitude to detail was the reverse of the man who later 'watched' for every moulding. As he later confessed:

> All carving came nearly alike to me, so only that it was rich. I cared only for 'curlie-wurlies and whigmaleeries', and was as happy in the fifteenth century as in the tenth.
> I used only such rude and confused lines as I had learned to imitate from Prout, and left their places blank in my sketches, to be filled up 'out of my head' at home.
> (Cook and Wedderburn 1904–13, vol. 35: 622–23)

Ruskin learned to emulate Prout's style through the tried method of copying whole drawings, such as the facsimile he made in 1833 of the Hotel de Ville, Brussels. More importantly, he also followed the 'progressive method' of Prout's manuals. This was the typical system of the teaching books of the time, whereby the student progressed from

Part of St Marks Church, and entrance to Doges Palace,
VENICE.

the small-scale to the larger (see Bicknell and Munro 1988: 12). Prout's books are mostly architectural, building from doors, steps and cottages to larger wholes; thus his *A Series of Easy Lessons in Landscape Drawing* (1820) is 'arranged progressively from the first principles' (Figure 3). At the beginning, the student is confined to looking at one thing; a single gate-post stone, or a few blocks upright or inclined – drawn in Prout's distinctive glyphs of worm-like wiggles and broken lines, well describing that 'golden stain of time' which for Ruskin is the magic of the picturesque (Cook and Wedderburn 1904–13, vol. 8: 234). Then follow plates of architectural fragments such as Gothic and Romanesque arches. In further engravings, these elements conjoin into vignette compositions – two broken arches and a belfry for example – which take their place in a landscape setting.

In *Modern Painters* (1843), Ruskin praises Prout's feeling for 'locality and life' in his depictions of Venice, in contrast to the generalising images of Canaletto. In Prout's work 'we feel there is something in the subject worth drawing . . . That house is rich and strange, and full of grotesque carving and character – that one next to it is shattered and infirm, and varied with picturesque rents and hues of decay . . .' (Cook and Wedderburn 1904–13, vol. 3: 256). Ruskin's drawing of the Casa Contarini Fasan, made in Venice in May 1841, represented the zenith of his imitation of Prout's language of

Figure 2
Part of St. Mark's Church and entrance to Doge's Palace.

Figure 3 (opposite)
Samuel Prout, plates from *A Series of Easy Lessons in Landscape Drawing*, 1820, R. Ackerman.

John Ruskin's innocent eye

the picturesque particular. 'Though full of weaknesses and vulgarities', as he wrote, Ruskin thought his own drawings of this period had 'also much good in them' (Cook and Wedderburn 1904–13, vol. 4: 342–3). On the Contarini palace sheet there is certainly close observation, but less grasp of the reality of the architecture's anatomy. Writing forty years later, Ruskin claimed that he 'knew absolutely nothing of architecture proper' at this point, he 'had never drawn a section nor a leaf moulding', but nonetheless he 'drew with an acuteness of delight in the thing as it actually stood'. In the following year, he continues, he 'began trying to do what I could not, and have gone on ever since, spending half of my days in that manner' (Cook and Wedderburn 1904–13, vol. 35: 296).

The vortex of Turner's imagination would shatter such picturesque enframing, drawing Ruskin centripetally into a more tactile and emotive engagement with building and the natural world. Later, he could balance his passion for Turner against what Prout had given him:

> Turner saw things as Shelley or Keats did; and with perfectly comprehensive power, gave all that such eyes can summon, to gild, or veil, the fatalities of material truth. But Prout saw only what all the world sees, what is substantially and demonstrably there; and drew that reality in his much arrested and humble manner indeed, but with perfectly apostolic faithfulness.
> (Cook and Wedderburn 1904–13, vol. 14: 396–97)

Therefore, it was still through the frame of the picturesque that Ruskin viewed France and Italy when he embarked on a major tour with his parents at the end of September 1840. However, in the early 1830s Ruskin had also become aware of another acute observer of architecture – the topographer David Roberts (1796–1864). In contrast to Prout's manner, Ruskin comments how Roberts's 'drawing of architecture is dependent on no unintelligible lines or blots, . . . the main lines of the real design are always there, [and] . . . his sense of solidity of form is very peculiar . . .' (Cook and Wedderburn 1904–13, vol. 3: 223). The language of the diary of this tour is of one seeking out 'subjects' or 'picturesque motifs'. Thus, at Florence 'there is really not a single piece of this whole city thoroughly picturesque' (Evans and Whitehouse 1956: 111). But the Forum at Rome, where the party arrived on 28 November, 'is certainly a very good subject', and on 5 December he notes, 'passed fountain of Trevi, which I must get: it will be a good subject for exaggeration' (Evans and Whitehouse 1956: 120).

More positively, the habits of attention to a city he described as 'picturesque, down to its doorknockers' led to a closer absorption with the surfaces of architecture as Ruskin succumbed to the palimpsests that Rome presents at every turn: that archaeology of Sigmund Freud's psychic entity where the 'remnants of ancient Rome appear as scattered fragments in the jumble of the great city that has grown up in recent centuries' (Freud 2002: 8). This enthralment with the fragment that would intensify as his 'synecdochic method' evolved is marked in a passage of the diary describing 'that architrave smashed at one side and built into a piece of Roman frieze, . . . – projecting over a mouldering wooden window, supported in its turn on a bit of grey entablature, with a vestige of inscription . . .' (Evans and Whitehouse 1956: 118).

Scales of register

So, in terms of watching architecture, two key lessons come out of the 1840–41 tour: at the larger scale a sense of breadth and mass, and at the smaller a closer reading of detail and surface texture. Initially, there is no ambivalence about Venice: 'May 6th. VENICE. Thank God I am here! It is the Paradise of cities' (Evans and Whitehouse 1956: 183). But the drawing soon becomes a mixed experience: on 8 May he complained of feeling 'excessively sulky and bored about my drawing to day – could not get on; drew like a child, and did not like the general effects of the narrow canals [. . .] My romance is going' (Evans and Whitehouse 1956: 184, 185). The romance *is* going – along with the trust in the picturesque. For *The Stones of Venice*, he will need to acquire those new registers of small-scale analysis that the better drawings of this tour tend towards. Thus 'The Court of Ducal Palace' synthesises Roberts's sense of mass and breadth with the minute observation of Prout. These developments are a complex story that belongs to 1845 – his first journey to Italy *without* his parents – and the years thereafter.

It has not been the aim here to rashly predicate the range of an optical thinker of Ruskin's stature solely on the work of the early years. But his visual habits do seem to proceed from an early threefold inculcation of romantic/picturesque, scientific/analytical and symbolical/religious world-views, progressively assimilated through the small-in-scale and the fragment: in the romantic worlds encompassed in a Turner vignette contemplated in a drawing room corner; in the natural science of scenery and geology and its carving out in the details of the Gothic imagination; in the typologies of Biblical *lectio* and the scanning of the scriptures phrase by phrase, as one might read meaning into the cumulative measures of a medieval facade.

As noted above, the 'Casa d'Oro' drawing, and this palace's invasive 'restoration' of 1845, point to a serious turn in Ruskin's watching of architecture. At the same time, the new rail-causeway of 1845–46 had obscured the romantic lagoon setting of Venice; this presage of industrialisation comes at the same critical moment when Ruskin resolves to lay aside the picture work of his *Modern Painters* project in the face of the imperative need to record Gothic buildings apparently doomed to imminent destruction. Beginning then in 1845, and yet more forcefully in the *Stones of Venice* fieldwork of the winter of 1849–50, Ruskin learns to adapt the analytic detailed instincts of the natural scientist to his acute tectonic and symbolic readings of architecture as he probes beyond the suggestibility of the picturesque. Like an Old Testament Jeremiah, Ruskin wants to provoke and disturb; his readings of stone fragments mingle the mathematical and metaphorical, to become admonitions of good and evil.

Acknowledgements

I am grateful for the assistance and wisdom of Stephen Wildman, Rebecca Patterson and Diane Tyler in my archive research at the Ruskin Library, University of Lancaster. I also wish to thank the British Academy, whose grant monies enabled aspects of the archive research and related fieldwork in Italy.

The worm's eye as a measure of man

Choisy's development of axonometry in architectural representation

Hilary Bryon

Scale, and consequently proportion, as related to representation, has a long tradition of being related to the human body. With the Renaissance, humanist depictions of architectural space were innovatively delimited using linear perspective, in which the rendered image is fixed to a viewer's eye. Perspective remained the primary mode of pictorial representation late into the nineteenth century until another post-humanist, rationalist mode of pictorial representation challenged its authority: the axonometric.[1] Axonometric projection is a specific form of parallel projection in which the projectors are perpendicular to the plane of projection. Unlike perspective projection, in which the projectors meet at a fixed point in space, parallel projectors are said to meet at infinity. The three axes of an axonometric projection are uniformly measurable and precisely scaled relative to the axis system's angle of inclination to the picture plane. Many architectural critics assert that meaningful architectural representation was eroded by the technical instrumentality tied to a representation generated by the positivism of science.[2] Descartes's philosophy, and his Cartesian geometry, is thought to have objectified the subjective view of the world, so that the individualised, inhabiting, 'embodied' viewer was forced into the position of passive, 'disembodied' observer (Pérez-Gómez and Pelletier 1997: 313). This chapter counters that position with a critical consideration of the history of axonometry and proposes that Auguste Choisy's inventive development of the worm's-eye view parallel projection is a meaningful, immersive measure of man. Indeed, Choisy uses the subjectivity of his worm's-eye view to impart a sense of our own bodily scale within the measured, spatially materialised boundaries of architecture.

Parallel projection: isometry to axonometry

The invention of a modern, post-humanist form of architectural representation – the axonometric – was spawned by William Farish's presentations of mechanical philosophy at the University of Cambridge during the early nineteenth century. Farish devised a kit-of-parts modelling system, and a coincident drawing system, to demonstrate the principles of Newtonian mechanics. Farish's drawing system, called 'isometrical perspective', was developed in order to record the temporary demonstration apparatus. Farish publicly introduced his formal discourse 'On Isometrical Perspective' to the Cambridge Philosophical Society in 1820, and the essay was published in their *Transactions* in 1822. Farish observed that while plans, sections, and elevations are measured and accurate, they do not allow a construction to be understood as a three-dimensional entity in space. Conversely, common perspective distorts the reality of the object, since parallel lines are not represented as parallel and there is no measurable scale. Farish's isometrical perspective combines the useful attributes of orthographic and perspective projections.

Isometric literally means equal measure, and Farish indicated that the term describes a cube represented so that the three principal faces make equal angles with the picture plane, and consequently all have the same scale. The author acknowledges that isometric perspective is not a perspective, but corresponds to the function of a perspective by rendering a pictorial view. The eye of the artist is placed at an indefinite distance, rather than at a fixed vanishing point; thus, the projectors are parallel. Farish assumed a bird's-eye view that also instils a sense of distance. Regardless of his expressive terminology, Farish understood isometrical perspective as a 'species of orthographic projection'; the projection is on a plane perpendicular to the diagonal of a cube (Farish 1822: 5–6). In terms of architectural representation, the successive developments of this new form of projection lead to a modern spatial visioning system with determined scale.

Farish's method was taken up by German engineers, geometers and mathematicians. In 1844, Julius Weisbach published the critical geometric, trigonometric evolution of isometry towards axonometry in 'Die monodimetrische und anisometrische Projectionsmethode (Perspective)'. In addition to building on the many isometrical methods successive to Farish, Weisbach expanded on the nomenclature and theories of crystallography proposed by Carl Friedrich Naumann in 1830. Naumann's theory linked the inherent axial structural forms of crystals to their appropriate graphic representations.

Weisbach established a projective axis system by theorising that points could be projected by their coordinates on axial planes (Meyer and Meyer 1863: 13, n1). Thus, the orientation and reduction of the axes did not have to stay isometrically inclined and equally reduced. The coordinate axes could be reduced in scale relative to their angles of inclination; Weisbach qualified these scaling conditions as monodimetric (in the case in which two axes are equally reduced) or anisometric (in which all three axes are differently scaled). While Weisbach differently coordinated the space of the isometric, he did not use the term axonometric to encompass the newly defined axial projections. This appears to have occurred eight years later, in 1852, in a work by the Meyer brothers of Freiburg.[3]

The Meyers proposed in their *Lehrbuch der axonometrischen Projectionslehre* that Weisbach's measured and scaled axis system, comprising isometric, monodimetric, and anisometric projections, be named axonometry, and that the method be called axonometric projection. Whereas Weisbach's work was exclusively theoretical, Meyer and Meyer comprehensively explored axonometric projection's theory and practice through its history, aesthetics, geometry, mathematics, process and application. They advanced a method by which to construct axonometric projections in space; the representation is bound to axiality. Their axonometric drawing method is demonstrated by first determining the desired orientation of the axonometric axes, and by consequence the orientation of the rotated or revolved object in space.

Like Naumann and Weisbach before them, the Meyers advocated that the nature of the object should influence the orientation of the axis system to the picture plane, and thus to its representation. To establish the orientation of the axis system, the object is imagined as to how it naturally falls into the picture, or projection, plane. They clearly asserted that maintaining this natural aspect would more closely approximate the image as one receives it to the eye, the first prerequisite for image-making (Meyer and Meyer 1863: v). The vertical axis coordinate plane typically stays vertical as it is equated to gravity; it measures height. The perpendicular, horizontal planes naturally correspond to the plan; these coordinate planes are parallel to its length or width. They observe that the easily constructed and accurate isometric system can be an awkward representation for some objects due to its prescriptive, inclined, often bird's-eye view (Meyer and Meyer 1863: vi). The natural relation of the object to the eye is not considered in the isometric due to its completely systematic application. The Meyers believed that a more complete expression is offered by the monodimetric and anisometric axis systems, which support a closer interaction between observer and object through the selective rotation of their axes.

The Meyers elaborate that establishing a *point of view* in axonometry does not conclude with the selection of an axis system. Within the same axis system and scaled ratio of reduction, there can be various points of view. The inherent revolving spatiality of the parallel, axonometric axis system allows reversibility; they state that 'one can also exert an inverse bias with this axis system, so that the observer may see into the system as at an angle or from below' (Meyer and Meyer 1863: 50).[4] Accompanying figures of monodimetric representations of a cube demonstrate the potential for transpositions within the same axis system and the same ratio via the axonometric lines; first they are articulated forward, then backward. It is within the context of a perspective and monodimetric comparison that we see the Meyers' only up-view representations. The reverse axis, the same monodimetric relation as that conveyed in the aforementioned demonstration cube, is used to convey a comparable image to an up-view perspective of an Ionic entablature. The Meyers conclude that the two rendered impressions are similar, but the tectonic, axonometric view is more multivalent than that tied exclusively to the eye.

Finally, the brothers maintain that the axonometric method is not only a means by which to manifest an image of real bodies in a single picture, but that the picture has the same effect as the object itself (Meyer and Meyer 1863: v). Meyer and Meyer contend that the axonometric is truly spatial. Points, lines, surfaces and bodies as located in space are projected onto one picture plane (Meyer and Meyer 1863: 1).[5] The scaled values of true form and size are juxtaposed in space. Under axonometric projection, the figurative representation on the plane of projection allows one to understand the true spatial nature of bodies. Meyer and Meyer liken this spatial view of parallel projection to that of conic perspective. The Meyers convincingly argue that central perspective, called the 'painter's perspective', finitely restricts the image to the eye; whereas axonometric projection, by virtue of its true parallelism in infinite space, 'allows the eye to hover at each single point', and is thus liberated and imaginative (Meyer and Meyer 1863: 1).[6] One can perceive that the invented views fabricated by axonometric projection are contingent on a different, modern conception of the object and man in space.

The Meyers' work was followed up by another study by Julius Weisbach (1857). While much of the material closely parallels that of the Meyers, there is a note of originality: the demonstration of the projection of axonometric shadows. This application firmly establishes the axonometric's place as a method of representation, and not merely a mathematical or geometrical operation.[7] The interjection of shadow links axonometry to the world of optic projection, thus embodying the subjective scale of man as a measurable quality within the mathematical space of parallel projection.

The bird's-eye view

The Meyers' articulation of varied points of view is a critical turn tied to the axonometric's development. The bird's-eye view had been an implicit convention of early parallel projections; the overview tied by Farish to isometric projection was preceded by that of oblique projection.[8] During the sixteenth century, the mechanisms of war depended on measured precision and the art of fortification became the vehicle for oblique projection's first analytical articulation.[9] Military (from the plan) oblique projections were conceptually tied to an overview of the horizontal plane through the orthogonal plan and its volumetric extrusion. The Germans alternatively referred to the cavalier (from the face) oblique projection as a *Vogelperspektive*, a bird's perspective. The practice was maintained with the invention of isometry. Farish's convention assumed the perspective normatively from a bird's-eye view and this premise was maintained by his followers, including Jopling, who maintained a bird's-eye view as he positioned geometric solids within a static isometric cube-frame (Jopling 1842: 18–20). The underside is depicted by rotating the object, not the bird's-eye position of the observer. In most cases, the bird's-eye view was assumed. Weisbach and the Meyers all commented on the alien up-standing view accorded to isometrical projection. The early convention of parallel projections, oblique or isometric, held the observer at a distance, defining the object by a summary overview.

Revolutions in space: framed from below

The up-view parallel projection evolved as a natural extension of axonometry's rotational freedom and the need to overtly posit a point of view. Axonometric space allowed architectural spaces to be technically scaled and materialised relative to a positioned observer. The geometric shift from the isometric cube to the axes of coordinates stimulated reinterpretations of all parallel projections, axonometric and oblique. The potential of this spatial, rotational freedom relative to architectural representation was first extensively investigated by the French engineer Auguste Choisy during the late nineteenth century. In his first published work, *L'art de bâtir chez les Romains* (1873), one can see the manipulation of axonometry's varied but specific axial revolution and its inherent reversibility.

Choisy had a clear intention in this book to express graphically the spatio-tectonic nature of Roman vaulted construction; however, he could not tectonically and spatially explicate the effect of Roman vaults from above. Choisy observed that the primary material structure of Roman vaulted construction consisted of an 'encased framework in a mass of masonry' (Choisy 1873: 3).[10] Tectonically speaking, the lower, inside surface is where the embedded framework, this essential component, is structurally expressed, as well as the enclosing space of the vault itself containing the body of man. The necessitating nature of the Roman tectonic, combined with the spatio-geometric potential of axonometry, appears to have led Choisy to revolutionise the tectonic vision of parallel projection via a view from below.

The *Romains* was the result of meticulous, measured, minute observation of physical and textual sources, from which evolved Choisy's theory of form. We gather an impression of Choisy's early field methods through his sketches in his 'carnet de mission de 1867': two pages depict the bridge of Narni in Umbria (Figure 1, left). The focus of the sheets seems to lie in the relation of the discrete stones to a composite whole. The individual travertine blocks are measured, carefully positioned within the scaled assembly, and shown rising into an arc. The stacked stones are seen from below, as undoubtedly seen by Choisy, from the ground. Written on the underside of the enlarged detail in the lower right corner is the word *dessous*, or underneath. Here one sees the tectonic origins of axonometry's worm's-eye view. The material matter of architecture rises to delineate a habitable space. The fully developed worm's-eye views will make that tectonic space manifest.

The compiled sketches essentially revolve around the springing of the arch, collecting views in a 180° rotation around the object. These views of the pier coalesce in the *Romains* into one pictorial, yet precisely scaled, oblique projection, and a diagram superimposing horizontal sections of the vault ribbing (Figure 1, right). The clean extraction of such tectonic fundaments will come to define Choisy's earliest work. In Choisy's sketches and drawing, we can see the relationship between this constructive logic and the worm's-eye view. The observer inhabits the space under the vaults of the Roman engineers; the structure builds from the earth to the sky to delimit architectural space. The up-view is phenomenally paramount.

Among the many graphic attributes, the most consistent device in the plates of the *L'art de bâtir chez les Romains* and its successor, *L'art de bâtir chez les Byzantins* (1883) is the use of the worm's-eye view parallel projection. In the *Romains*, the up-view is applied to all forms of parallel projection: isometric, dimetric and trimetric axonometrics, and oblique projections from the plan and elevation. There appears to be no system. The types and angles of projection are diverse. Perhaps following the

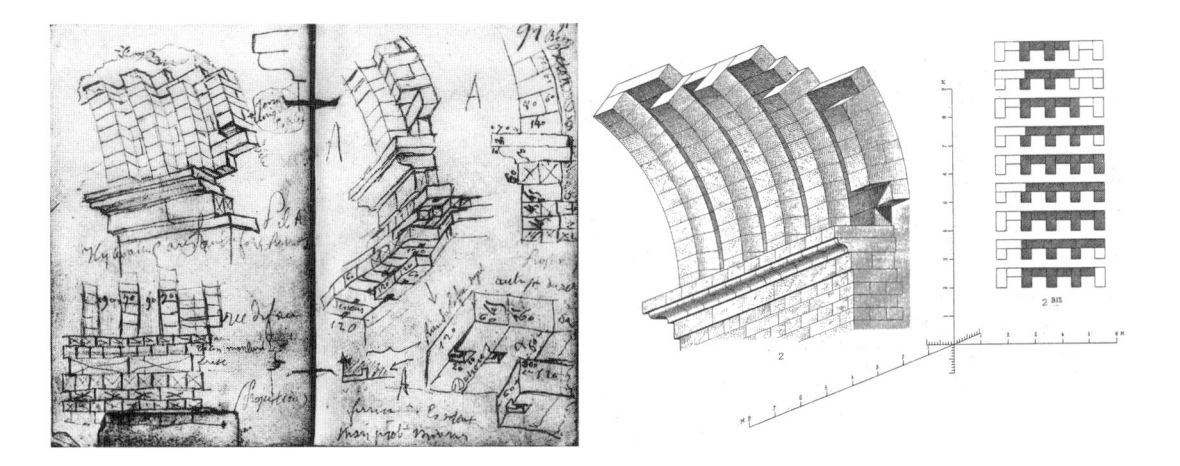

Figure 1
Left: bridge of Narni in Umbria from Choisy's sketchbook, 1867 (Royer 1960: Plate 2). *Right*: oblique projection from the elevation (Choisy 1873: Plate XVI, detail).

recommendation by the Meyers, Choisy adjusted each viewing angle to that which best expressed the object to the observer. The up-view encloses the viewer in the space of the vault and Choisy's first step to achieve this is to establish the directions of the projections of the axes. Fundamentally, this subjective decision orients the viewing angle of the object. Subsequently, the relative reductions of the scales of each inclined axis are determined via projection. The resultant representation is a true measure of the object, and man, in space.

Choisy suggests that his parallel projections serve an intentioned dialectical purpose by positing the vaulted artefacts as concrete realities and as a mental construct (Choisy 1873: 'Note sur le mode de représentation adopté'). Multiple graphic qualities frame a dual reading of these images. The realm of the discovered, extant and documented ruin is upheld through the depiction of overgrown vegetation, shadows and, in a few instances, representations of sky or ground. The shadows evoke a picturesque variety expressing the remnant as a focal point and located to one moment in time. Such environmental renderings reflect one of Choisy's self-imposed rules, 'to make known the antique construction by personal observation of the monuments' (Choisy 1873: 84–5).[11] Other graphic details also point towards the found condition of the monuments. The arches and vaults are limited to fragments, like the ruins themselves. In some cases, each side of an arch springs into the air, but is truncated, no longer connecting to its counterpart (Figure 2). Such shards evoke a complete entity, thus animating the past. The monuments are also depicted denuded of decoration, and so the material essence is excavated for study. The rendered surfaces of this material structure are shown with delaminating surfaces, protruding bricks and, in one or two cases, frayed, crumbled edges. Despite the fact that Choisy did not reproduce the actual state of the ruin, his drawings demonstrate through these atmospheric treatments an inherent natural beauty found in the structural remains of architectural form.

Concurrently, some of the same drawing components portray the core relic as a prospective model. The ideal realm of the structure of the past is scaled, in part, by Choisy's use of construction lines. The latent rational structure of the remnants of the past is delimited and extrapolated with such graphic tracings. These lines variously

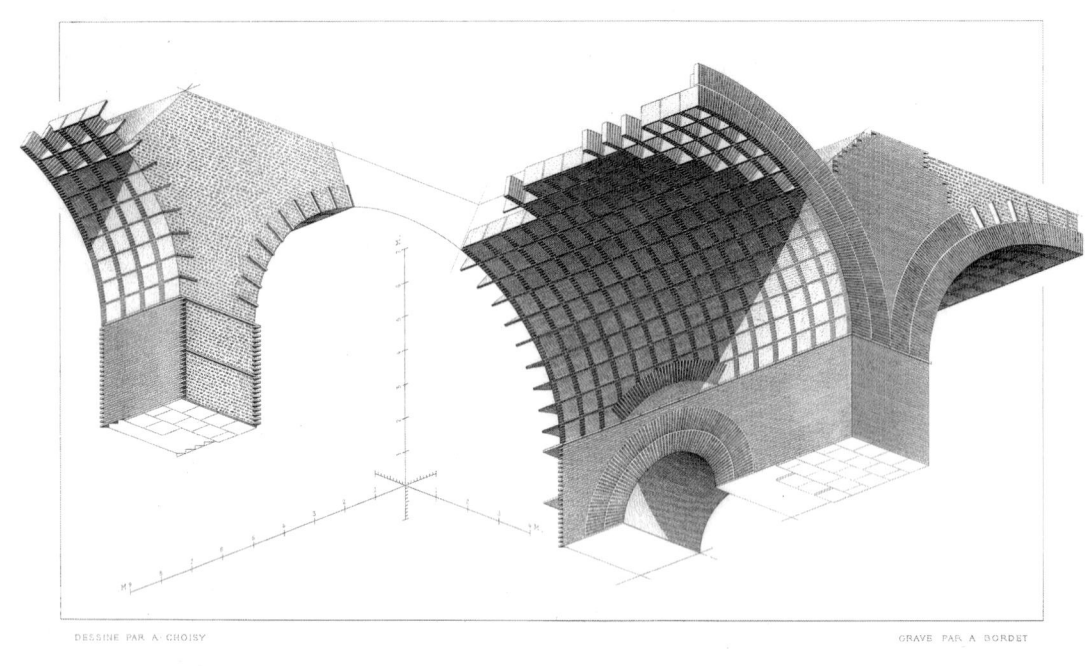

PALATIN

abstract geometric, material, graphic and quantitative information, and are also instrumental, constructive elements. The found remnant is largely dissected in a clean, pure manner; sectional cuts are typically blank voids delineated by hard edge lines. At times, the rendered material surface wraps into the sectioned plane, yet the material element, typically brick, is distilled to its outline. The graphic extension of the material is always partial, but each material element is always maintained by its standard dimension. Shadow lines banish ambiguity and embody qualitative space within the orthogonal constructs. Other lines, sometimes dashed, extend into space to render an outline of a complete tectonic structure. The materially ruptured vaults of the Palatine Hill are completed through delicate trajectory lines connecting across the spatial gap. These traces geometrically conceptualise the determinant growth of the particular constructive process. Still other lines circumscribe the pure circular geometries ordering many of the vaulted forms. Of course, each representation is accompanied by axial scales of measure. These intersecting lines correspond to and scale the three dimensions of the object. Pragmatically, the establishment of the three-dimensional scale is the initial act of the drawing's projection, but within the static frame of the finished drawing, the axes blatantly posit the architectural artefact as inseparable from its measured, material three-dimensionality. Juxtaposing these axial lines of infinite space with the essential tectonic core also advances a conceptualisation of a progressing constructive extension into three-dimensional space. The abstracting nature of these various regulating lines is instrumental in modelling the prospective, ideal constructive scale of the archaeological artefact.

Figure 2
An up-view, diametric axonometric projection (Choisy 1873: Plate I).

The drawn and traced boundaries of the artefact are informed by the necessary structure. The essence of the system exposes each building's pure core. Choisy individualises the graphic technique to overtly reveal the varied complex of constructive scales in the tectonic fundament: from individual material elements, combinatory systems, structured assemblages, to functional arrangement. The material element is an ideal unit. A tile or brick, measured and put into place by the hand of man, is always drawn as a complete constructive part. Even when the rendered material surfaces are delaminated, the peeled-away layers always respect the material unit. This accentuation of the essential material constituent is also manifest through selective, spatial protrusions, with small elements operating at a subsequent scale, structuring various constructive systems to fulfil formal arrangements. The extent of the represented core assembly is complete when the complete spatial order is inferred. The formal plates of the *Romains* and *Byzantins* offer a simultaneous vision of the structural fragment in a state of retrospect and prospect; the essential core is concurrently a sited ruin, as seen in the documentation of the extant, materially scaled remains, and a potential mechanism, as indicated by scalar units of construction and lines of abstraction, including first and foremost the fundamental axial scale of infinite measure.

The worm's-eye view

After the 1873 and 1883 publications of the *L'art de bâtir* series, a great part of Choisy's research efforts were devoted to the development and production of his most noted work, the *Histoire de l'architecture* (1899), a historical account of architecture from prehistory to the early nineteenth century.

Choisy's sketches from 1885 reveal the nature of the evolution in his use of parallel projection for the *Histoire*. His travels that year are represented by sketches of the churches of Saint-Etienne of Nevers, Saint-Savin on the Gartempe and Notre-Dame-la-Grande of Poitiers. Within the pages of the *Histoire*, all three buildings similarly represent a stage in the formal progression of Romanesque architecture. However, there are noticeable differences among their sketched representations. The sketch from Nevers is raw. Both the textual and the graphical notations are smudged by an error and reflect a correction. The line work of the sketch is loose, perhaps even inaccurate. The viewpoint is from below and the view conveyed is of the apparent scene, like that of the visitor standing in the nave or perhaps sitting at a pew and looking up. The sketch shows an on-site impression of the structure.

The other, paired sketchbook pages from 1885 contain a study of Saint-Savin on the left page and Poitiers on the right, facing page; both sketches approximate to canonical isometrics. Furthermore, they are both up-views, like the sketch from Nevers. Unlike Nevers, the viewpoint is more analytical; it moves below the horizon line and the constructive elements are suspended in space. Under this aspect, these two sketches, of Saint-Savin and Poitiers, are unique. They clearly hint at the synthetic potential of the worm's-eye view as ultimately realised. There are no other extant sketches that so closely correspond to their future, final composition as published in the *Histoire* 14 years later.

One can easily speculate that these juxtaposed sketches formed a prototype and reflect Choisy's proposed, and ultimate, comparative format for the *Histoire*. Between the sketch and the illustration, the chronological adjacency, viewing angle and level of detail remained virtually unchanged, whereas the form of parallel projection is changed, from isometric axonometric to oblique projection. One can reasonably draw the conclusion that Choisy's transition from axonometric to oblique projection in this case is fully intentional, and that each drawing system was to be used for particular ends in the *Histoire de l'architecture*.

One discerns different intentions behind Choisy's use of parallel projection in the *L'art de bâtir chez les Romains* versus *L'histoire de l'architecture*. Choisy's later drawings appear to challenge their instrumental, geometric, technical lineage and evince a modern view of the spatial simultaneity of architectural phenomena. The worm's-eye view oblique projections in the *Romains* and *Byzantins* typically sprang from a horizontal section above the ground plane, not from a plan. These up-view drawings detailed the technology of the fragment and were limited to explicating particular vaulted conditions built into space. The case of the particular was illustrated. It was not until the *Histoire* that the structural element was posited in direct relation to its composite structure, which is determinant of the whole form. This shift relates to the up-view moving from a more pictorial viewpoint to a completely imaginary position below the horizontal ground plane. Such worm's-eye views still examine structural elements in the *Histoire*, but with regard to their essential contribution within a system explicitly determinate of the whole space.

While the drawings of the *Romains* and the *Byzantins* overtly straddle the function of retrospect and prospect through their scientific control of graphic, analytic methods, so too do those of the *Histoire*. However, an evolved conformity of method was used to scale and discriminate essential differences. Different rendering techniques, more abstract in nature, aid the comparative reading of architectural form. Unlike Choisy's drawings in the *Romains* and *Byzantins*, the oblique and axonometric drawings in the *Histoire* are not projections. The drawing systems have been distilled almost exclusively to military oblique projections or canonical isometrics. This is subtly indicated by the disappearance of the axial, spatial scale for each dimension and its replacement with a single dimensional scale for all three. Furthermore, the illustrative, individualised representations of the *Romains* and *Byzantins* became necessarily abstracted to posit a conceptualised theory: rendered materiality is shifted to a structural framework, the temporal shadows are replaced by academic *poché*, the fragment of the ruin becomes a module of design, and the subjective orientation of three-dimensional axes is supplanted by the repeated system of the worm's-eye view oblique projections. The history of architectural form is all the more imaginatively scaled through rational and scientific techniques.

In using oblique projection, Choisy's new methods transformed the artefact into a graphic tectonic language (Figure 3, left). This was largely achieved when the measured uniformity of the conventional plan was combined with uniformly applied rendering techniques that reinforce the comparative nature of the similarly oriented, successive worm's-eye view oblique projections. With oblique projection, there is simultaneity between the geometric purity of the plan, and its proportions and geometry,

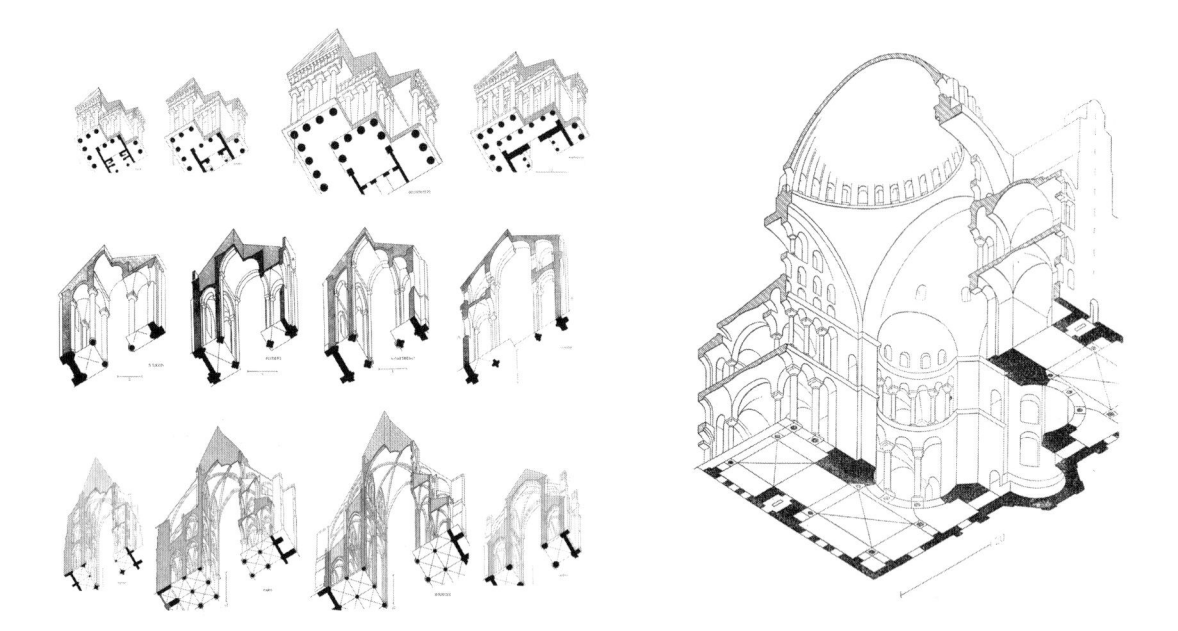

Figure 3
Left: worm's-eye view, plan-based, oblique projections convey the spatio-tectonic progression of Greek, Romanesque and Gothic architecture (Choisy 1899).
Top: Paestum, Olympia, Selinunte, Parthenon (figs 7, 8, 10, 11).
Middle: St Savin, Poitiers, Parthenay, Issoire (figs 11, 12, 13, 16).
Bottom: Noyon, Paris, Bourges, Langres (figs 6, 7, 8, 10).
Right: worm's-eye view, isometric drawing of Hagia Sophia, Constantinople (Istanbul) (Choisy 1899: Vol. II, 49).

as juxtaposed with the spatial organisation of the structure. Not only does the up-view animate the structure above our heads, but the worm's-eye view grounds the architecture to its organising plan. Though the ground plan is invisible to the inhabitant, it determines with precision the quality of the spaces we inhabit. The dissection and abstraction in the *Histoire* became an intellectual method of discursive thought, as a means of hypothesis. The deconstruction indicated construction. The scalar purification of parts, elements, modules, proportions, hierarchies, bays and systems indicates a reverse process, one of building. Thus, Choisy defied the general trend of separating the real from the imaginative. He used the synthetic simultaneity of the oblique projections symbolically, to represent building, in addition to buildings.

Whereas the oblique projections are grounded by their scaled orthographic plans, the few axonometric projections show free, floating images, somewhat detached from the ground plane (Figure 3, right). The building in space and the space of the building are animated via the skewed view of the axonometric ground plan. The axonometric's explicit warped view was intentionally used by Choisy to animate his graphic visualisations. Isometric projections evidence the harmonic totality and uniform spatial extension of the unified structure of domed spaces, such as Hagia Sophia in Salonica and Constantinople. Choisy considered that the whole composition grouped itself around the dome (Choisy 1899: v. 2, 47–8). He wrote of Salonica, 'the whole system of equilibrium is inside; all the dispositions are considered in light of supporting and accompanying the dome: the ensemble, in which each part is subordinate to this principal reason, produces an impression of striking clarity' (Choisy 1899: v. 2, 48).[12] The constructive ensemble and the space under the dome are impressed upon the viewer when the spatial simultaneity of the worm's-eye view axonometric brings us inside. One has the distinct sense that one is within the space, bounded by its concrete surfaces and held by the dome. Unlike the drawing, the body of man is not free-floating; it is relationally contained within the spatio-tectonic boundary by the worm's-eye view.

The axonometric drawing models the spatial and tectonic reality of architecture. The subjectivity of the worm's-eye view pulls the viewer into the space of the building. Such rational, scaled drawings denote the spirit of architecture's essence – the space of the structure and the space of man.

Notes

1 A more detailed, published explication of the distinct history of oblique and axonometric parallel projections can be found in my article, 'Revolutions in space: parallel projections in the early modern era' in *arq*, vol. 12, no. 3–4, 2008.
2 For example, see Pérez-Gómez and Pelletier (1997) and Bois *et al.* (1979).
3 Meyer and Meyer's work was first published serially between 1852 and 1855, *Lehrbuch der Axonometrie:* Lief. I (1852), Lief. II (1853), Lief. III (1855), and eventually published together in 1863.
4 'Dass man auch bei diesen Axensystemen eine Neigung nach hinten vornehmen kann, so dass der Beschauer gleichsam schräg von unten in das System sieht, bedarf seiner weiteren Erwähnung.'
5 'Die räumlichen Grössen (Linien, Flächen und Körper).'
6 'Malerperspective' . . . 'Bei welcher das Auge über jedem einzelnen Punkte stehend.'
7 As asserted by Loria (1921: 419).
8 Oblique projection is an older class of pictorial parallel projection. One trait that overtly divides oblique from axonometric projection is that oblique projection has both two-dimensional and three-dimensional space attributes. Oblique projection presents an aspect of two-dimensional geometric purity as one plane of the object lies parallel to the picture plane. Depth is indicated in an act of oblique extrusion.
9 See Maggi and Castriotto (1564).
10 'Cette ossature empâtée dans le corps des maçonneries.'
11 'Pour rester entièrement fidèle à la règle que je m'étais imposée, de faire connaître la construction antique par l'observation personnelle des monuments . . .'
12 'Tout le système d'équilibre est intérieur; c'est en vue de maintenir et d'accompagner la coupole que toutes les dispositions sont ménagées: l'ensemble, où toutes les parties se subordonnent à ce motif principal, produit une impression d'une saisissant netteté.'

Excursus 2

Scale in recent projects by MVRDV

Nathalie de Vries

Scale is one of the most powerful instruments in spatial design. It is not only a tool to zoom in and out, but a crucial element in choosing the right scale in which design problems should be dealt with in the first place. In this photographic essay, I would like to illustrate contemporary design issues in a connecting scale.

Scale 1: Global urbanisation

In the 'China Hills' project, the question is what new cities in China should look like. By 2020, 60 per cent of the country's population will live in cities, while the urban areas of China cover only 6 per cent of the surface of the country. At the same time, large areas are needed for agriculture, sustainable energy production and afforestation, to deal with the demand for food and combat carbon dioxide emissions. Because of the topography, only a limited amount of space is suitable to accommodate all these demands. In China, a massive growth of new and existing cities is taking place. Some Chinese people think it is time for a shift in thinking about future cities. One of China's biggest development corporations gave us the commission to design the Chinese city of the future. With the help of our survey of the current and future needs, we created 'China Hills'. 'China Hills' are new urban complexes in which necessary elements for vital cities are combined as much as possible.

Scale 2: South Koreans all want to live in an apartment

Massive urbanisation leads to ever-higher densities in cities. The vast majority of the urban population lives in apartments. In Songdo Landmark City, one of the South Korean new towns, tens of thousands of apartments have been built. Fifty years ago, living in an apartment was extremely unusual in Korea. It seems nowadays that there is no other choice as both the government and developers heavily promote apartment living. This leads to the production of endless seas of apartment buildings, often with almost

Nathalie de Vries

Figure 1
China Hills.

Figure 2
China Hills.

Figure 3
Landmark City,
Crown, Songdo,
South Korea.

Figure 4
Landmark City,
Grass, Songdo,
South Korea.

Figure 5
Landmark City,
Valley, Songdo,
South Korea.

Figure 6
Gyre, Omotesando Street, Tokyo, Japan.

Figure 7
Gyre, Omotesando Street, Tokyo, Japan. The public route up the building brings the streetlife up to a higher level and offers panoramic views of the city.

Figure 8
Gyre, Omotesando Street, Tokyo, Japan. Fashion store interior.

identical interiors. If architects want to escape their fate of only designing fashionable exteriors to these towers, they have to find ways to create a good urban design in which the towers can be unified in new types of communities. The methods to escape the uniformity of floor plans have to be researched. In our design for the over 2,000 apartments, we made three different proposals for neighbourhoods. Each neighbourhood is based on a different spatial configuration, together with the housing typologies. In the different options, a way of life can be chosen: the relaxed campus-like grass field in Grass; the urban boulevard in the Valley; and the plaza in the project called Crown. The client has selected this last version for further development.

Scale 3: The building and the street

It is not only housing that is created in ever-greater densities; public and commercial functions are combined and increasingly piled up on top of each other. For the reasons of controlling comfort and safety, a lot of street life is internalised. This, however, leads to less interesting cities and less exciting public street life. In the commercial building 'Gyre' on Omotesando Street in downtown Tokyo, we tried to combine the best of both worlds. Although the building is a small shopping centre, an external route – all the way to the top – connects all functions, varying from small boutiques and restaurants to bakeries and art galleries. This has led to a building that still interacts with the street and where the units have big windows and balconies. The street is spiralling up around the building.

In Oslo, the users of the headquarters of Norwegian DnB NOR bank inhabit the exteriors of the building; on the lower levels, the public spaces are incorporated into the building. Even in a building with high levels of security, people inhabiting the building will be encouraged to interact with the street.

Scale 4: New programmatic clustering in public buildings

Inside (public) buildings, purely public and commercial functions are entangled. Most of these buildings provide useful combinations of functions for busy urbanites, saving time and space. In the Markthal, in Rotterdam, the commercial housing programme shapes the public building, the covered market. At the same time, the building becomes a new covered plaza and passage in the dense urban tissue of the city of Rotterdam. Kube ('House of Culture and Movement') is a project in which a Danish local government authority combines good things for both body and mind. Cultural facilities and physical health are combined in a complex that has both exteriors and interiors. The fun character of the building has been designed as both an advertisement and stimulation for a healthy lifestyle for the community.

Excursus 2: Scale in recent projects by MVRDV

Figure 9
DnB NOR bank,
Oslo, Norway,
south west
aerial view.

Figure 10
DnB NOR bank,
Oslo, Norway,
west passage.

Figure 11
Markthal,
Rotterdam,
The Netherlands.
One hundred
market stalls will
offer fresh food
daily.

Figure 12
Markthal,
Rotterdam,
The Netherlands.
Each apartment
will have a view
towards the market
as well as the
surrounding city.

Figure 13
Markthal,
Rotterdam,
The Netherlands.

Excursus 2: Scale in recent projects by MVRDV

Figure 14
House of Culture and Movement, Frederiksberg, Denmark. Performance zone.

Figure 15
House of Culture and Movement, Frederiksberg, Denmark. Zen zone.

Figure 16
House of Culture and Movement, Frederiksberg, Denmark.

73

Figure 17
Ypenberg, The Hague,
The Netherlands.

Excursus 2: Scale in recent projects by MVRDV

Figure 18
Silodam,
Amsterdam,
The Netherlands.

Figure 19
Balancing Barn,
Suffolk, England.

75

Figure 20
**Didden Village,
Rotterdam,
The Netherlands.**

Scale 5: Houses

Ultimately, we all have to live in a place we call our home. With each housing project, there is usually a task to create an attractive environment. If necessary, the building itself can take up collective functions. We believe it is great if inhabitants are able to point out where they live and if they are able to identify their homes in the street – 'that is our building'. Additionally, in the past years we have observed people's growing interest and awareness in participating and contributing to the customisation of their homes. It is our task as designers to design methods that help people to do so (Figures 17–20).

How can we build denser and more sustainable cities for more and more people and at the same time raise the quality of standards for all and not just for a happy few? How can we make people feel comfortable in mass housing, and still make it possible that choices are offered? Instead of striving to design one perfect floor plan, we should dedicate our time and energy to create more differentiation in order to offer greater choice in mass-housing projects.

Scale in art and perception

Colour scales

Fay Zika

Ludwig Wittgenstein's *Remarks on Colour* opens with an example of two language games: reporting whether a certain body is lighter or darker than another; and stating the relationship between the lightness of certain shades of colour. Wittgenstein draws an analogy: this is like comparing the lengths of two sticks and the relationship between two numbers. The form of the language game is the same: 'X is lighter than Y'. But in the first, it is an external relation and the proposition is temporal; in the second it is an internal relation and the proposition is timeless (Wittgenstein 1978: 2).

Several points are raised by the above paragraph. First, that issues of shade of colour or hue, like those of relative size, are matters of scale – that is, of degree and relative judgement, rather than simple or absolute categories and values. Second, that both involve, on the one hand, empirical judgements (when, for example, we compare the colour or length of two bodies), and, on the other, logical relations: the internal relations between hues are placed on the same side as those between numbers (that is, on the side of logic and necessity rather than on that of contingent experience). Influenced by Gestalt and Bauhaus traditions, in which the value of a unit is determined by its position in a system (Aarsleff 1982; Arnheim 2004), Wittgenstein draws elements from psychology and linguistics in order to maintain a certain necessary structure to our colour concepts, within which every hue can find its place. He is thus led to maintain that the concept of colour presupposes a system of colours (Wittgenstein 1981: 2; Zika 2008).

This chapter centres on the fact that decisions about colour choice – whether in art, design or architecture – presuppose a system of colour, a system that involves a number of issues, primary among which is the possibility of ordering colours and hues in some coherent set of gradations or scale.[1] My aim is to investigate some of the principles that govern certain theoretical or practical approaches to ordering colours, drawing on distinct areas such as physics, psychology, chemical and digital production, linguistics and anthropology. A thread running through the above considerations is the issue of whether colour classifications and scales depend more on culture than nature, thus making communication about colour difficult, or even impossible, across space and time. A further aim of this chapter, therefore, is to attempt to assess how much of our colour ordering depends on natural or cultural constraints, as well as the possibility of reconciling concepts and structures drawn from different areas and interests.

Colour spectrum

I came to philosophy – or rather, I stayed with philosophy – due to a variety of puzzles having to do with colour (Zika 2004). One of them relates to a problem that arose when, as a child, I had difficulty putting colour pencils back in their box. I would start, I suppose, with red, and continue with orange, yellow, olive, green, turquoise, blue, purple. Then what? There were several colours left outside the box that I could not fit into any 'acceptable' order: black and white, greys and browns, the various shades of blending with white – pink, light blue, cabbage green, and so on. There seemed to be an order that was different to the linear ordering provided by the pencil box, and yet I could not figure out what it could be. This childhood puzzle opened up for me a whole area of questioning and investigation. For how do colours and hues get their ordering? How do they end up fitting in coherent scales? According to what principle(s) can they be set out in gradations or degrees?

In trying to put colour pencils back in their box, the obvious place to start looking for a solution seemed to be one of the wonders of nature: the rainbow. When Newton carried out his experiments with prisms and refracted so-called white light into the visual spectrum, leading to the spectral analysis of light, the rainbow apparently stopped being such a wonder (Boyer 1987). It was a phenomenon whose order could be explained, reproduced, analysed and eventually measured. In a famous stanza, the poet John Keats mourned the loss of its magic: 'Philosophy will clip an Angel's wings, / Conquer all mysteries by rule and line, / Empty the haunted air and gnomed mine – / Unweave a rainbow' (*Lamia*: II.229, Keats 1973). But though the mystical wonder of its order seemed to have been lost, locating colour scaling in the rainbow or spectrum did not solve my pencil-box puzzle.

Before considering some other solutions to my puzzle, I want to make a small excursus into the analogy drawn between colour scale and musical scale. Some of the major problems raised by scaling are how to draw the line between different colours and hues, how to separate and name them, how many to distinguish, and on the basis of what criteria. Based on a tradition going back as far as Aristotle (Gage 1997: 227; Gage 1999: 139–43), colour order has often been compared to musical scale, intervals, and harmony. Newton, for example, opted for dividing the spectrum into *seven* colours, equivalent to the seven tones of the Western musical scale (Wasserman 1978: 11; Isacoff 2003: 9–25). The wave theory of light was not yet available to Newton, but when it was established later in the eighteenth century, making light rays of varying refrangibility measurable, it made a big difference to the scientific and philosophical status of colour. As Kant discerned in *The Critique of Judgment*:

> Assuming with Euler that colours are isochronous vibrations of aether, as tones are of the air set in vibration by sound, . . . then colour and tone would

not be mere sensation. They would be nothing short of formal determinations of the unity of a manifold of sensations, and in that case could even be ranked as intrinsic beauties.

(Kant 1969: 66)

The association of colours with vibrations or waves had a number of implications: it enabled their measurement and scaling according to particular wavelengths; this led to the possibility of formalisation of a quality that, until then, was considered secondary, subjective and elusive; the wave nature of both light and sound gave new impetus to the ancient analogy between colour and music, which also pointed to principles of colour harmony (scaling and matching) based on an analogy with musical scales and chords (Gage 1997: 227–46). Others, however, were sceptical of this analogy. Goethe, in his *Theory of Colours*, published in the early nineteenth century, warned against taking the analogy between colour and music too far:

> That a certain relation exists between the two, has been always felt. . . . The error which writers have fallen into in trying to establish this analogy we would thus define: Colour and sound do not admit of being directly compared together in any way, but both are referable to a higher formula, both are derivable, although each for itself, from this higher law. They are like two rivers which have their source in one and the same mountain, but subsequently pursue their way under totally different conditions in two totally different regions, so that throughout the whole course no two points can be compared.
>
> (Goethe 1982: 298–9)

Goethe's point seems to be that, despite the wave-related and graduated nature of both, colour and sound are distinct perceptual qualities with distinct internal structures.

If the linear hue order of the visual spectrum gave rise to the possibility of establishing an analogy with the seven-tone Western musical scale in the eighteenth century, the analogy was given new impetus by the elaboration of the more complex, atonic or dodecatonic musical scale in the early twentieth century. Painters and composers were in close collaboration, producing some of the most fascinating works in both arts of the early Modernist period. Kandinsky, who collaborated with composer Arnold Schoenberg on various projects, wrote: 'Colour is the keyboard, the eyes are the hammers, the soul is the piano with many strings. The artist is the hand which plays, touching one key or another, to cause vibrations in the soul' (Kandinsky 2006: 52). Further support in this direction was provided by renewed interest in the perceptual and physiological mechanism underlying synaesthesia, the rather strange phenomenon whereby the stimulation of one sense gives rise to simultaneous sensation in another sense (without corresponding stimulus), the most common case being that of 'coloured hearing' or 'visual music'. The possibility of transcending the limits of the senses and establishing a mystical unity of experience fascinated artists who, on the basis of colour or sound alone, aspired to the Promethean task of unravelling the laws of cosmic harmony and establishing spiritual unity with the universe.[2] However, synaesthesia, being a rather rare phenomenon, did not provide a sufficiently wide sample of human subjects upon which to base the colour–sound analogy. Additionally, the experience of synaesthetic subjects proved to be highly subjective – each making their own sound–colour connections, therefore not providing a common ground for scaling and harmony. So the possibility of establishing an essential unity between the internal order of colour and sound was once again left aside, though it continues to be a subject of speculation and investigation.

Colour system

As mentioned above, determining colour scale according to spectral order did not solve my pencil-box problem. On the contrary, it corroborated it. For it left black and white in the lurch – an endemic conceptual ambivalence in our culture in which we are always wavering as to whether to include black and white among colours. In the context of a concept of colour dominated by the theory of light, black is the privation of light (therefore, not a colour), white the combination of all light rays (therefore, not a specific colour). Nor did spectral order incorporate the other non-spectral hues, such as browns and greys, and the wide variety of light and dark hues of particular colours.

The development of a colour system, related less to light than to pigment and phenomenal appearance, came from various areas in the nineteenth century, including artists' research and experimentation with pigments and their psychological effects, as well as the rise of chemistry and its relation to the industrial production of paints and dyes (Gage 1997: 153–91). The first move was to 'close' the ends of the visible spectrum into a circle, thus supplementing the perceptual continuum with hues between red and blue, such as purple and magenta. Goethe, for example, wrote:

> The chromatic circle . . . [is] arranged in a general way according to the natural order . . . for the colours diametrically opposed to each other in this diagram are those which reciprocally evoke each other in the eye. Thus, yellow demands violet; orange, blue; red, green; and vice versa: thus . . . all intermediate gradations reciprocally evoke each other; the simpler colour demanding the compound, and vice versa.[3]
>
> (Goethe 1982: 21)

The colour circle or wheel was further developed in the mid-nineteenth century by the French chemist Emile Chevreul, who was called to the Gobelins tapestry factory in order to help improve the brightness of their dyes. In 1854, Chevreul published his *Principles of Harmony and the Contrast of Colours and their Application to the Arts*, in which he put forth the view of complementary colour-matching as superior to any other: opposing colours on the colour wheel (blue–orange, purple–yellow and red–green) reinforce each other if they are placed next to each other (Gage 1997: 174–5; Roque 2009). This was incorporated as 'the law of complementary contrast' by Charles Blanc in his *Grammaire des Arts du Dessin* in 1867 (English edition: *The Grammar of Painting and Engraving*, 1879), an artist's handbook in which he enunciated the view that not only drawing but also colour could be taught on the basis of the 'mathematical rules' of colour provided by Chevreul's system (Gage 1997: 174).

It is important to note that the colour circle was the basis for a number of theories relating to colour contrast, matching and harmony, which are beyond the scope of this chapter. Here, I want to introduce a further move in the comprehensive ordering or scaling of colour; that is, the inclusion of the achromatic hues – white, black and gradations of grey. As opposed to a theory based on light, which does not incorporate black and white as colours, theories based on material and phenomenal aspects of colour need to take these into account. As we saw above, the colour circle 'closed' the linear array of the spectrum by making its ends meet, created a continuum that corresponded more closely to human experience, and provided a space for desaturated hues (mixed with white) along the radii from the circumference to the centre. Would this solve the pencil-box puzzle? No, for there were still several colours left out: black, white, greys and other hues, such as brown (allegedly, a dark orange). The move had already been effected by Goethe's contemporary, the artist Otto Runge, who included the gradation of light to dark by adding a vertical axis to the colour circle, thus producing a number of different colour spheres. The significant step, therefore, was the drawing out of the colour circle into a three-dimensional space: the addition of a vertical dimension covering *brightness* or *lightness*, the gradation from black to white, in order to produce a comprehensive colour array in which all colours that could be perceived by a human observer could find a place. The colour solid consisted of two cones (one inverted) with the saturated (chromatic) hue circle as their common middle cross-section (Thompson 1995: 44–51). The colour solid was elaborated in the early twentieth century by Albert Munsell, who was the first to separate hue, brightness (value) and saturation (chroma) into perceptually uniform and independent dimensions, and to systematically illustrate the colours in a three-dimensional space; it is thus generally referred to as the Munsell Colour System.

The colour solid provided the most comprehensive structure of phenomenological or psychological colour ordering. It was this system or colour space that Wittgenstein had in mind when he talked of the perspicuous 'geometry' or 'logical grammar' of our colour concepts. To return to my original pencil-box puzzle: were it not for its cumbersome shape as far as arranging the colour pencils was concerned, the three-dimensional colour solid provided the required solution to that puzzle.

Colour chart

The emphasis and research that went into developing a consistent colour theory, but also the problems encountered by such an attempt (Zika 2004), has led to scepticism and reaction against such a theoretical approach to colour. A relatively contemporary development away from colour theory and closer to commercial colour practice has been marked by the growing use of colour charts, including in artistic practice. This point is well documented in the catalogue of an exhibition charting the use of colour in art from the 1950s to today (Temkin 2008).

Colour charts came into use by the 1880s, as a direct result of the mass production of ready-mixed paints for household use. The earliest colour charts included glued-in samples, made by applying paint to cardboard or thick paper that was then cut into units for the charts. Their design established a format that, remarkably, has been retained to the present day: a set of individual colour units arranged in rows and columns on a neutral field. The colours are unmodulated by any brushstrokes or other textures, so as to demonstrate how flat the paint will appear on the surface to which it is to be applied. As Ann Temkin points out:

> Unlike that of a spectrum or colour wheel, there is no necessary logic to the sequences of colour ranges – it is simply a nonhierarchical list of what is available. . . . The colour-chart possesses no higher truth than the materials required to make it, and no higher classificatory logic than what the manufacturer deemed useful for builders and contractors, decorators and designers, craftsmen and do-it-yourselfers.
>
> (Temkin 2008: 16)

The colour chart has largely supplanted the colour wheel, which for three centuries embodied the attempt to organise colour meaningfully and hierarchically according to scientific principles. During the course of the past century, those systems have come to be understood as reflecting the human desire for order more than any intrinsic truths about colour. Classifications once considered immutable are now recognised as reflections of personal choice or cultural and historical context (Temkin 2008: 17). As David Batchelor points out in his book *Chromophobia*:

> The colour circle has dominated the understanding and use of colour in art. Based on a geometry of triangulation and a grammar of complementarity, the colour circle establishes relationships between colours and also implies an almost feudal hierarchy among colours – primaries, secondaries and tertiaries, the pure and the less pure. The colour chart offers an escape from all that. It is, in effect, simply a list, a grammarless accumulation of colour units. In the colour chart, every colour is equivalent to and independent of every other colour. There are no hierarchies, only random colour events. The colour chart divorces colour from conventional colour theory and turns every colour into a readymade. It promises autonomy for colour – from other colours and from the dictates of colour theory.
>
> (Batchelor 2000: 104–6)

'Autonomy of colour' is also associated with the new techniques provided by digital media:

> The colour-chart colours have contributed to a further change in the use and understanding of colour. This might be called the digitalization of colour, whose opposite is analogical colour. The colour circle is analogical; the colour chart

is digital. Analogical colour is a continuum, a seamless spectrum, an undivided whole, a merging of one colour into another. Digital colour is individuated; it comes in discrete units; there is no mergence or modulation; there are only boundaries, steps and edges. Analogical colour is colour; digital colour is colours.

(Batchelor 2000: 105)

'Autonomy of colour', in this sense, seems to be going against Wittgenstein's view, outlined at the beginning of the paper, that the understanding of colour requires knowledge of the system of colours. Batchelor's point, however, seems to be an exaggeration since, on the one hand, colours, even within a system, can still be individuated; and, on the other, the fact that colour charts are based on practice rather than theory does not mean that they are not governed by some principle(s) of gradation and organisation. For example, the Pantone colour charts or sets of swatches, even though not a continuum like the colour circle or as holistic in their representation of the human perceptual colour space as the colour solid, are still based on arrays of gradation, and therefore governed by at least some principles of ordering or scaling.

A second point that has been raised in relation to the so-called arbitrariness of colour charts is the fact that it coincides with the rejection of the possibility of achieving universality in our understanding of colour, given the vastly different and often contradictory practices of colour-naming among different cultures. On the other hand, it is maintained that

the colour chart as the foundation of standardization – evident in the success of international colour-matching systems such as Pantone – is symptomatic of a global age in which cultural differences in colour are being eroded no less than those in language and cuisine.

(Temkin 2008: 17–18)

So what is it to be: culture–relative or universal?

Colour naming

A debate over the latter issue has become prominent in another area in which colour order plays an important role, that of linguistic anthropology. Contemporary linguists and anthropologists tend to work with a view of colour as a property of objects or surfaces (not of light), the phenomenal qualities of which may be determined in terms of the three factors mentioned above (hue, lightness, saturation; Lyons 1995: 198). But colour naming differs greatly from culture to culture, and it can also be very difficult to assess which qualities are being selected – for example, hue, which may be the major quality of differentiation in so-called Western culture, may not be so important in other contexts; and colour distinctions may also be related to texture, freshness and succulence, which do not constitute main factors of our colour recognition and categorisation. The traditional view of colour as a subjective quality in Western culture has fitted in well with cultural relativism with respect to colour terms – the view that colour terms differ widely from culture to culture; that languages divide colour space arbitrarily; that this shapes the way their speakers perceive coloured objects; and that this also accounts for the enormous problems in the translation and understanding of colour terms across space and time.

However, the now well-known research of linguistic anthropologists Brent Berlin and Paul Kay, published in *Basic Colour Terms: their universality and evolution* (1969), has challenged linguistic relativity for colour terms and given rise to an ongoing debate. Berlin and Kay were struck by the ease with which common colour terms could be translated between languages from areas as diverse as Tahiti and Mesoamerica. Their research involved speakers of 20 distinct languages asked to categorise samples from a simplified Munsell Colour System. Their results were expressed in what has come to be known as the Berlin–Kay hypothesis: that there are 11 psychophysically definable focal points or areas within the continuum of colour, and that there is a natural hierarchy among at least six of these focal areas that constitutes what they referred to as universal 'basic colour terms'. Languages with only two basic colour terms were discovered to have focal points in the areas of black and white; with three, in the areas of black, white and red; with four, in the areas of black, white, red and either green or yellow; five would add blue; six, brown. There were four more areas (purple, pink, orange, grey), which did not have any apparently distinct hierarchy in their order of precedence.

This constitutes a different kind of order or scale – that in which humans carve up linguistically and categorically/conceptually the phenomenological colour space. The Berlin–Kay universalist thesis has been challenged from within the field of linguistic anthropology, but it has also been defended by further experiments and methodological adjustments. It has also formed the basis of an interdisciplinary attempt to investigate the extent to which cross-cultural regularities can be explained by the operation of the human visual system. The main trend in contemporary neurophysiology supports a view known as 'opponent-process theory', according to which our colour vision is determined by neural channels governed by opponent processes in three basic pairs: one achromatic (black–white) and two chromatic channels (red–green, blue–yellow), covering both the notion of primary hues and the above order of appearance of 'basic colour terms' in a variety of languages. If this can be established, colour terms and categories carving up perceptual colour space, as well as their evolutionary order (the order in which they appear in various languages), would be given a natural basis in the neurophysiological mechanism of the human visual system (Hardin and Maffi 1997).

Conclusion

It looks as if a system of gradations is a necessary component of our understanding of colour. Some of the difficulties involved in achieving agreement between individuals and between cultures in the carving up of human colour space have encouraged the view of perceptual and linguistic cultural relativity. However, there seem to be important areas of convergence, which have stimulated interdisciplinary research on the possibility of common or universal categories and ordering principles, both at cultural and natural levels. Note, for example, the symmetry between the linear order of the visual spectrum and the equivalent order of the phenomenological colour circle or wheel, which is formed by 'closing' the two ends of the spectrum (deep blue and red) and filling in the 'gap' between them with purple and magenta; or the convergence of linguistic–anthropological finds about common colour categories with the corresponding basic colours in the neurophysiological mechanism of the human visual system.

In the closing sections of *Remarks on Colour*, Wittgenstein considers the possibility of understanding people with a colour language and a carving up of colour space very different to our own. He asks: 'Can't we imagine people having a different geometry of colour than we do?' (Wittgenstein 1978: 11; see also 27, 36). 'Imagine a *tribe* of colour-blind people. . . . They would not have the same colour concepts as we do' (Wittgenstein 1978: 4). You may be wondering what the issue of understanding between the 'normally' sighted and the colour-blind may have in common with colour scaling or, more generally, with the carving up of perceptual colour space across cultures and languages. But this analogy has already been effected: reflecting on the difficulties of translating colour terms from ancient Greek into English, a classical scholar ventured the verdict that ancient Greek colour terminology was defective either because the Greeks had little interest in the properties of (absorbed and reflected) light or because they were colour-blind (Platnauer 1921).

Wittgenstein again: 'Is it possible then for different people in this way to have different colour concepts?' His answer is partially affirmative: '*Somewhat* different ones. Different with respect to one or another feature. And that will impair their mutual understanding to a greater or lesser extent, but often hardly at all' (Wittgenstein 1978: 21). What I hope to have shown from the above discussion is that our ability to order colour in systems of degrees or gradations is central to our understanding of colour; and to have elucidated some of the principles that govern this order. These principles may differ widely, depending on the area from which they are drawn – physics or psychology, chemistry or linguistics, digital media or neurophysiology. Finally, despite differences, there may be a species-specific basis for the possibility of understanding and achieving at least partial convergence between cultures in the way in which humans carve up colour space.

Notes

1. Some of the other issues a system of colours may account for, but that are beyond the scope of this paper, are: distinguishing between primary and binary hues; rules of harmony (matching and contrast); different colour qualities resulting from different media; mixing in a variety of media; warm and cool hues; the relation of colours to emotions; colour symbolism in different cultures; and so on.
2. This phenomenon and its artistic repercussions have been thoroughly traced back in three major exhibitions during the last decade, and their equivalent catalogues: Lemoine *et al.* (2003), Brougher and Mattis (2005), Guy *et al.* (2007).
3. Note that 'natural' here does not relate to spectral order but to perceptual relations, 'evoking in the eye'.

Scales of interaction
Aligning the qualitative with the quantitative in music and architecture

Fiona Smyth

The first recorded use of the term 'acoustics' in the English language occurs in Francis Bacon's *Of the Advancement of Learning*, published in 1605.[1] In tracing the application of the word over the succeeding centuries, it was used up until the mid-1800s, mainly in reference to magical and mechanical contraptions and instruments, rather than in allusion to an environment or to a mediating context. In fact, the term, since its inception – in a journey from adjective to noun – has retained connotations of mechanical contraption, magical phenomenon, biological function and finally, since the mid-nineteenth century, of the qualitative.[2]

The latter half of the nineteenth century saw the word 'acoustics' established as it is currently understood in terms of architecture: applied in the context of sounds, maths and the senses, these expressed in reference to space, scale and environment.

The changing conceptions surrounding this and related words saw shifting applications evidenced in literature over the course of the last four centuries, as well as changing focuses and forums. The term 'microphone', first coined by Narcissus Marsh in the seventeenth century, was created in allusion to a device he conceived of as an audio version of a microscope (Marsh 1684: 482), while the term 'acoustician' seems first to have been used – albeit somewhat tentatively – in volume five of the *National Magazine* in 1859,[3] where it was applied in reference to theatre design and architecture (Sutherland-Edwards 1859: 102). The word 'acoustician' was re-used in a similar vein shortly thereafter in the first edition of Grove's *Dictionary of Music* (Hipkins 1879: 54).

The term 'acoustics' remained out of common use, however, and, by 1926, the first edition of Fowler's *Modern English Usage* had classed it alongside other 'outlandish words' (Fowler 1926: 9). The entry went on to speculate as to whether it would ever come into popular use and offered suggestions as to the most appropriate pronunciation of the term, debating whether it should be pronounced after the Greek or the French fashion – with an 'ow' or an 'oo' sound to the second syllable.

Fowler was not alone in his scepticism of acoustics. A paper on the topic and its application within architecture had been presented to the Royal Institute of British Architects (RIBA) some years earlier by a young architect in 1914, and roundly dismissed.

Scales of interaction

Figure 1
Hope Bagenal.

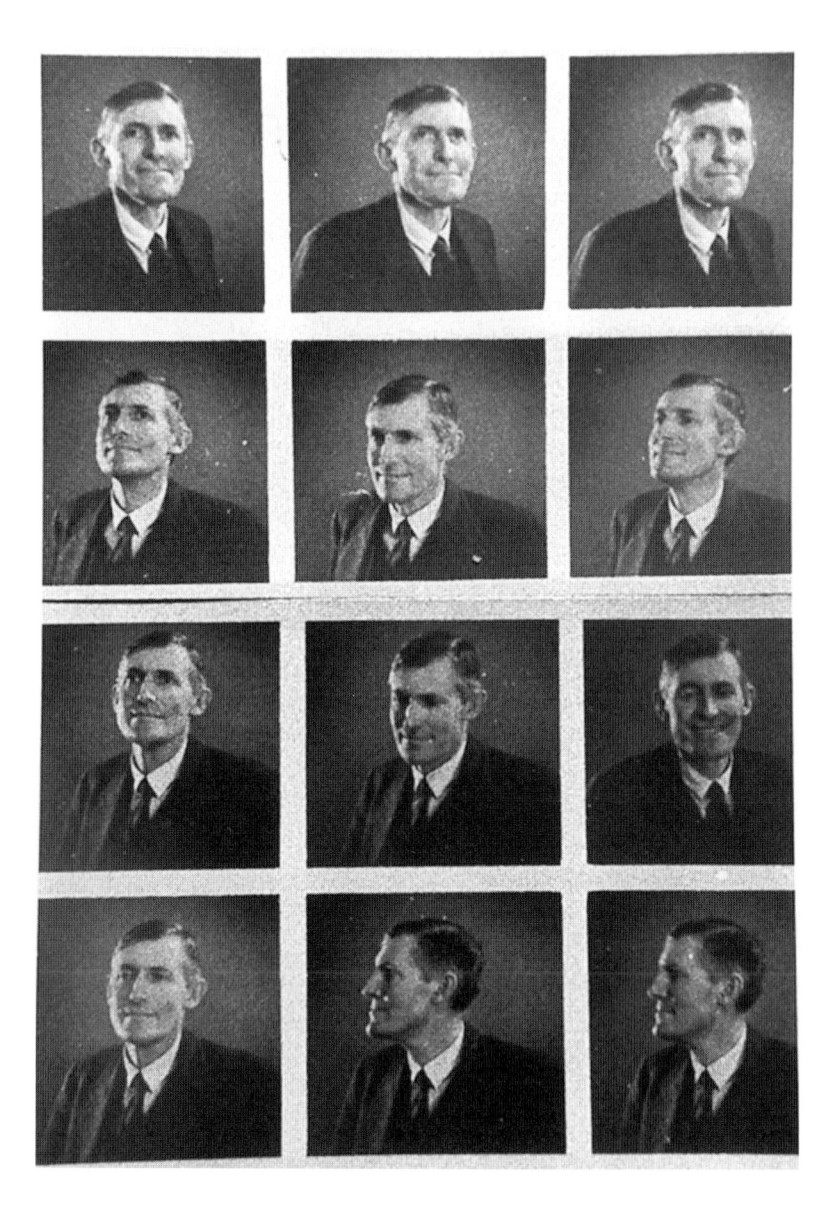

The reaction was such that the paper's author, Hope Bagenal, forbore to discuss it beyond the remark that 'they hated it'.[4] A contemporaneous article published in 1915 in one of the more prominent music journals of the day, entitled 'Acoustics: suggestions on behalf of an unpopular subject' (Elson 1915), would suggest that the diffidence that was directed towards acoustics by doyens of the architectural and literary worlds was mirrored by those in the musical world.

Opinion was turned fully around in the following decade, however, and the early misconstrued paper on acoustics was to become the foundation of a long and fruitful research alliance between physicist Dr Alex Wood at Cambridge and architect Hope Bagenal of the Architectural Association (AA) School, London (Figure 1). The precepts and early musings upon which it was based led to influence and counter-influence between architect and musician, evidenced in recurring themes and references in the writings of Bagenal and of Richard Terry, a prominent musicologist of the era. By 1931, the initial paper, 'Acoustics Relative to Architecture' had formed the architectural basis of the book *Planning for Good Acoustics* (Bagenal and Wood 1931), one of the most seminal and accessible publications on acoustics. It was positively received by scholars and reviewers in numerous disciplines, sparked a career in research, writing and practice, and found a voice in architectural, musical, scientific, craft-based and technological circles alike.

Hope Bagenal held the position of librarian and teacher in the AA School, and was editor of the *AA Journal*. His position in the school left him ideally placed to meet and to interact with like-minded individuals in the architecture world. He had a keen, enquiring mind and was an avid letter-writer. His correspondents included opera singers, academics, poets and architects, as well as the American physicist Wallace Clement Sabine. Sabine, a physicist in Harvard, had completely redirected the field of architectural acoustics at the turn of the twentieth century through his applied research. Application and advice on acoustic design in the preceding century was vague, and often based on dubious rules of thumb. Acoustic thinking, in so far as it existed, had been primarily focused on geometry as the single most influential aspect worthy of consideration, but even advice in this regard it was relatively unsubstantiated.[5] Sabine brought architectural acoustics into the realm of quantitative science, enumerating in terms of practical measurements what had hitherto been speculative and individual issues, in the process spearheading the derivation of mathematical formulae from subjective experience. He quantified the impact of material and texture and charted his findings against time, measured with the human ear.

In contemporary England, Bagenal was at the forefront of the acoustic 'movement'. He encountered Sabine's work – seemingly before anybody else in the country, physicists and architects alike – in two separate articles, both of them American publications directed towards architects.[6] One was a general article on acoustics, which appeared in *Sturgis' Illustrated Dictionary of Architecture and Building*, an American publication edited by the eponymous Russell Sturgis, which was published in three volumes between 1901 and 1902.[7] While the main thrust of the article most properly lies in physics, in a description of the general maths and science of sound, it succeeds in being both precise and accessible in terms of its architectural application, delineating how sound behaves within a *building* with examples focusing on illustrations of surfaces and dimensions rather than purely on mathematical formulae.

The other article was a more particular paper entitled 'Building Material and the Musical Scale' (Sabine 1922), which was published in the American *Brickbuilder*; a copy of *Sturgis* was held in the AA library, but *Brickbuilder* was not. It is unclear where Bagenal might have encountered it, but it certainly piqued his interest as, judging from the dates of the correspondence, he wrote to Sabine almost immediately, and had received a warm, polite and interested response within a fortnight.

Bagenal was intrigued by Sabine's work, and questioned him, notably in his investigations of the acoustic behaviour of different building materials – which he (Sabine) had examined over a range of frequencies – and which, in the *Brickbuilder* article, were expressed in terms of the numbers and letters of the musical scale. Sabine's research at this juncture had reached a point where he was investigating absorption and reverberation across a range of materials slowly and painstakingly, with each material defined and graphed on a note-by-note basis, extending over six octaves. Once the properties and behaviour of one material had been categorically determined, investigations could proceed to the next 'space', usually a new architectural context that introduced additional material to be assessed on foot of the precisely determined material characteristics of the preceding studies.[8]

Bagenal's first *published* paper on acoustics was entitled 'Acoustics of Churches and Choral Music.' It was published at the end of 1919 in the *Architects' Journal* and republished two months later in the *AA Journal*.[9] In this article, Bagenal first put forth his ideas on the reciprocity of developments historically in music and in architecture with notable emphasis on examples of both, which were designed specifically for the liturgy. His argument, with regard to the cathedrals he alluded to, connected music with an architectural space and scale rather than categorising it as embodying the ethos of a cathedral school or particular repertoire. In linking architectural scale with musical response, the paper also outlined his ideas on the tonality of spaces, identifying 'treble A or A flat' as the signature note particular to most of the large churches and cathedrals he had encountered. Later work, particularly the book *Planning for Good Acoustics*, identified the different signature notes specific to churches of differing scales, which followed a comprehensive project he had undertaken to build up a dossier of information characterising the acoustics of a number of large churches and cathedrals throughout England. This was a lengthy study, with a number of the results published in the journal *Music and Letters*, and more of them constituting a fascinating chapter in the book *Planning for Good Acoustics*, which he co-wrote with Alex Wood.

Wood was a Cambridge physicist whom Bagenal had first encountered in 1916–17 while in Eastern General Hospital in Cambridge, recovering from injuries sustained at the Somme. Wood, in his capacity as physicist, had just read Sabine's work, and was intrigued at Bagenal's earlier dissertation on acoustics and his perspective on the topic as an architect. A long and fruitful research collaboration ensued. Bagenal's time in Cambridge also saw him attend a service at King's College Chapel. Music for the service included a movement from Brahms's *Requiem*, under the direction of the noted organist Dr A.H. Mann, a musician distinguished, among other things, for working with and tempering music in the chapel to its very specific acoustic. Bagenal was struck by the manner in which both building and music were enlivened by their interaction, and as part of an autobiographical letter he wrote a beautiful description of how music, through the medium of acoustics, entirely changed his perspective and experience of the space. (Bagenal 2010: 73) In later discussions on signature notes within architecture, Bagenal afterwards wrote that Mann was noted among his peers for transposing works for the choir into a key to suit the tonality of the chapel at King's College (Bagenal 1931: 217).

The 1919 paper outlined these concepts – the foundations of his approach to cathedral and church acoustics. The insight and appreciation displayed in his description of the experience at King's and the concept of viewing an auditorium as a musical instrument in its own right are themes that run through the paper, particularly in his reference to the acoustics of Westminster Cathedral and his comments on the calibre of choral music being produced therein by the cathedral's inaugural director of music, Richard Runciman Terry.

Terry was a renowned musicologist, and a leading figure in the revival of pre-Reformation liturgical music. He was also noted for his ideas regarding the 'key of the church' (Bagenal and Wood 1931: 217), and a sensitivity to acoustics that one of his biographers attributed to his scholarship under the same A.H. Mann of King's College Chapel (Day 1994: 302). In his time as Director of Music at Westminster Cathedral, Terry uncovered and brought to life a huge repertoire of previously dormant music. His choral achievements and the repertoire presented in the sung services were so well regarded that students from the Royal College of Music were instructed to go to Westminster Cathedral to hear the choir and to experience 'Palestrina for Tuppence' (Andrews 1948: 133; Dibble 2002: 268n)[10] – the sum of money in question referring to the price of the bus fare. By the close of the first decade of the twentieth century, both *The Times* and the *Daily Mail* had begun a regular correspondence on the nature, calibre and catalogue of music into which Terry and his choir at Westminster were breathing new life. Bagenal was to refer to Terry and his work on pre-Reformation music on numerous occasions in the succeeding years, alluding frequently to the particular acoustic of the cathedral and the manner in which the architecture plays with the note in varying ways from distinct points of audition. Bagenal's thoughts on Westminster Cathedral regarded the building as nothing less than a musical instrument in its own right, writing at one point that 'the domes, the apse, the side chapels appear to deliver the note as though the organ instead of being at the West End changed its position bodily a dozen times' (Bagenal 1927: 442).

Terry, for his part, also published prolifically, and at the close of the war years, he was writing of the perfection of the cathedral's acoustic in augmenting vocal music, disguising the sparsity of a choir that had been inevitably decimated by the First World War:

> the acoustics of the building are so perfect that the casual weekday visitor, hearing a five-part Mass being sung would hardly realise that the effect was obtained by a single tenor and two basses, in conjunction with the boys.[11]
> (Andrews 1948: 111)

Terry and Bagenal moved in similar circles, geographically, intellectually and professionally, and the influence of each other comes across in their respective writings. Both were based in Westminster at the same time; Bagenal as a student at the AA School when it was based at Tufton Street prior to its move to Bedford Square, and Terry in the cathedral. Both wrote very engagingly and articulately, and published in a broad range of journals outside their immediate disciplines. Bagenal, the architect, addressed the Royal Musicological Association and the Incorporated Society of Musicians, the proceedings of which were both published. A number of his articles from the *RIBA Journal* and the *AAJ* were republished in music journals, particularly *Music and Letters* and *The Musical Times*. Bagenal referenced Terry directly in a number of his articles in music and in architecture journals alike, as well as in correspondence that appeared in the *Times Literary Supplement* in 1931.

The only documented evidence that Bagenal and Terry ever met exists in letters – notably one from Bagenal to Sabine, recommending Terry and describing him in terms of his professional achievements and standing in Westminster, but not mentioning him by name[12] – and in oblique references in their published articles. Cross-referential aspects of their respective research interests can be seen particularly in references by Bagenal to ongoing work in reviving Catholic church music in a city centre cathedral – for which Terry and Westminster were noted – and by Terry in re-appraising his thoughts on music of the era, when considered in the light of acoustics and architecture.

One comment that Bagenal attributed to Terry, and to which he frequently alluded in his writing over the first half of the twentieth century, was in reference to a piece of music written by Robert Fayrfax that seemed to take advantage of its intended context to the extent that 'a fourth voice was provided by the church', the church in question being St Albans Cathedral.[13]

Fayrfax had been organist at St Albans at the beginning of the sixteenth century. He was one of the composers whose music Terry had revived and was working with in Westminster. Terry had also been involved in the fourth centenary lecture and sung service commemorating both the composer and his work the *Missa Albanus*. St Albans was the cathedral for the diocese in which Bagenal lived. Terry's lecture is reported as having discussed the manner in which the work was balanced and adapted to the acoustic of the building.[14]

Fayrfax's music was representative of an intriguing era in musical composition. The English term 'acoustics' did not exist in the Fayrfax era, but the concept was one that was relevant to, and informed by, a number of interacting disciplines, architecture and music among them. Science, mathematics and empirical reasoning to varying degrees underpinned comprehension of the concept and its application. What has been documented of sixteenth-century music theory – particularly in early twentieth-century retrospectives on the subject – is suggestive of an intuitive or empirical understanding of the reverberant acoustic response and its effect on overtone structures, an effect made perceptible by the periodicity of pure chords in a sustained acoustic. In so doing, it indicates an engagement with the acoustic and architectural condition that preceded the recognition afforded by scientific analysis and quantification. In standard tuning of the era, notes of the scale were proportionally related to each other rather than equally divided into the octave in the manner in which the scale is divided now. The tonic triad chord was referred to as a sestina, in reference to a conception that six notes were heard when emitted in a sustained acoustic. Certainly the harmonic structure of proportionally tuned notes would correspond with this theory, in that the first four harmonics of a given note constitute its major triad. Thus, in a proportionally tuned tonic triad chord, when three notes are played simultaneously, each with their own set of harmonics, the overlap between notes would result in the reinforcement of the common harmonics, which could theoretically be further enhanced by a sympathetic acoustic with a lengthy reverberation, typical of a large internal space such as a cathedral.

The Fayrfax era was also notable as the point when music first became accepted as a doctoral discipline in its own right. By virtue of its new status within academia, the discipline of music was intellectually 'upgraded' so as to render it academically worthy. Worthiness in this instance was measured in terms of compositional complexity, and a demonstrable basis in scientific and mathematical concepts of the time. The idea was that acoustics straddled mathematics, science and music. The result of that style of composition was an integration of art and science, articulated in the construction of a unique style of 'academic' music that embodied complex mathematics, academic theory, logic, 'the causes, properties and natures of sounds by themselves and compared with others', all firmly structured on a knowledge of current scientific principles.[15] Fayrfax – the subject of Bagenal and Terry's interest – held two of the earliest doctorates awarded for music of this type in England, one from Cambridge in 1504, and a second in 1511 – the first issued by that university – from Oxford (Carpenter 1958: 161). Investigation into music of the Fayrfax era has followed a somewhat fractured course of interrogation and recognition. Following the Reformation, Latin church music of the era was suppressed, and while it would be incorrect to state that intellectual and stylistic developments were entirely interrupted, the new religious context did have an impact on the status and expectations of music within academia. For the brief window of time between music attaining doctoral status in the university and the changes wrought by the Reformation, the music of the Latin liturgy, combined with scientific nous, had been the basis for all doctoral compositions. The liturgy was considered to be the only vehicle of sufficient complexity and worth to showcase the level of achievement and knowledge required of a doctoral composition. After the Reformation, complexity and science were still expected to underlie composition at this level, but polyphony was becoming less and less tolerated within the established church and the stylistic basis on which the earlier music had been structured began to peter out. The revival of interest in the scientific basis of composition and the significance of its architectural context reappeared almost 400 years later.

In the twentieth century, two broadly defined periods of investigation and resurgence of interest can be identified. These periods, while not completely self-contained, form part of a broader matrix of interwoven research interests, stretching over decades. Work on the music of Fayrfax has not been confined to these brackets in time, but there are, however, two particularly pronounced periods of focused work situated in the opening decades and the closing decades of the twentieth century. Interstitial work, while less concentrated and with fewer people involved, has nevertheless been conclusive in opening up the direction of research and amassing information with which to approach that complex, relatively undocumented – and as such mysterious – era of composition.

The era of Bagenal and Terry in the early 1900s was characterised by huge changes in the overall intellectual, scientific and religious context. It heralded the first real renewal of interest in pre-Reformation music, and recognised the importance of architecture and acoustics in the development of an understanding of the music. Many musicologists who had encountered the work only 'on paper' had previously dismissed it as dull and contrived. It was considered in context, certainly, but context was limited to the historic and the religious, and prior to the advances and dissemination of the work of Terry and Bagenal, had not been generally considered to extend to the acoustic. Successive editions of a book by Terry – one in 1907 and the second in 1931 – amply map this changing mindset, which was the result of having heard the work of Fayrfax in an appropriate architectural and acoustic context.[16]

Terry once referred to a colleague's reading and working of early music scores as being 'more than a matter of ink and paper' (Gray 1934: 272).[17] The reference was to a manner of interpretation that brought the art to life; that somehow expressed those elements of music scoring that are at best tacit, and more often unobserved (if not unobservable) in paper form alone. Terry's own work on early music was powerful and unique precisely because it was predicated on performance in context. Throughout his writings and criticisms, it becomes abundantly clear how much more he felt was communicated by each piece of music he rediscovered and/or revived when performed in context. In architectural terms, Terry's scoring may have been more comparable to a sketch than a presentation drawing, and this was the cause of no small amount of strife when it came to issues of publication and editing.[18] As such, there is an element of expression on the handwritten page that is usually lacking in the refined and published version. The sketched score retains an enticing sense of fluidity and openness, qualities that were mirrored by the music in question, which, stylistically, did not lend itself readily to standard forms of contemporary notation. In essence, for Terry, a piece of music could be considered to be more 'truthful' in its incompleteness; as to his mind, while it remained unperformed, the music was incomplete. To be understood as it was intended, it had to be read in context, and to be read in context it had to be brought to life and given dimensions through appreciation and audition in the correct acoustic context (Day 1994: 301).

> [W]e should not listen to 16th century music with the ears of the 20th . . . we should not apply to 16th century writers 'rules' which only began to be formulated in the 18th; and . . . we should realise that in music – as in literature – a grammar must be based upon the literature and not vice versa.[19]
>
> (Collins 1913: 81)

Bagenal's innate poeticism also allowed his research on the comparatively problematic area of church and cathedral acoustics to accommodate nuance, and to recognise alternate cross-categorical purposes of the spaces under analysis. His was a layered perspective, where art combined with science to result in a truer analysis/portrayal. Throughout his work, it can be seen that spaces were considered simultaneously as generalised entities, as independent subdivisions and as composites of interacting subspaces, an approach that was ahead of his time and that piqued the interest of both musicians and architects. Subsequent to the publication of *Planning for Good Acoustics*, an article in *Music and Letters* once again singled out both Bagenal's work on architectural acoustics and the Fayrfax legend, with recognition given to the 'invisible factor' – the mediating effect of building on music.

The science of architectural acoustics moved on rapidly in the early twentieth century, and it has not ceased to do so. The second resurgence of interest in music of the Fayrfax era – at the latter end of the twentieth century – has shone more light on its inherent scientific and mathematical principles, and has seen some excellent work in piecing together technical, structural and historical aspects of the music. As work on the musical analysis has become more and more precise, benefiting from advances in technology and in mathematics, as well as in the perspective of further historical research, capacity for acoustic analysis has both broadened in scope and become more refined in application. Since the 1960s, mathematical assessment of space – or at least mathematical methods of quantifying spatial perception – has become increasingly relevant to acoustic, if not musicological, analysis as the range of measurable parameters in architectural acoustics expands in line with methods of recording and recreating acoustic spaces. Measurement techniques, equipment and technology are becoming increasingly accurate, allowing investigation to sift through the minutiae of acoustic behaviours across a broad spectrum.

Conclusion

The debate on the correct pronunciation of the term 'acoustics' expressed in Fowler's was reiterated in the 1920s in the discussions that followed a very well-received presentation on the topic by Hope Bagenal to the RIBA. The lessons of Bagenal and Sabine were rapidly assimilated into the architectural lexicon, and by 1937 an architect had written defensively to *The Gramophone* complaining about a popular assumption that acoustical issues were, 'matters about which an architect has very little practical knowledge'. The letter writer further stated that

> The Science of Acoustics as evolved by Sabine, Hope Bagenal and others now reduced the correction of the most complicated of acoustical defects to a mere matter of applying a formula and absorbents to a building, but also that all qualified architects now have at least a working knowledge of the principles involved and the ability to apply them.
>
> (Falconar Fry 1937: 43)

While this declaration may have been somewhat optimistic, it nevertheless is indicative of a professional mindset that had rapidly changed from diffidence to acceptance and comprehension in embracing the science of architectural acoustics. Under the guidance of Hope Bagenal, and as the result of his comprehension and interest in multiple fields, acoustics in England was brought forward from its rather disparaged beginnings to reach a much wider audience and far greater level of acceptance across disciplines. The decade that saw the word 'acoustics' finally become an accepted part of the everyday vocabulary, also saw the introduction of the terms 'Hertz' (denoting a unit of measurement) and 'decibel', while in musical circles, the term 'Tudor music' was coined to define the particular style of music of the Fayrfax era that emerged from the 'long sixteenth century'.[20] Terminology, in tandem with knowledge and cross-disciplinary collaboration, was expanding to express developments, investigation and rediscovery in science, architecture and music.

This same era, the early twentieth century, which had seen the revival of a science-based style of music and the beginnings of the science of specifically architectural acoustics by virtue of these interactions, also bore witness to increasing recognition of the importance of appropriate architectural (and hence acoustic context) in moving towards an understanding of music of that era, with identifiably separate disciplines becoming intertwined in that new mindset. As such, it constitutes the ideal intellectual context from which to begin quantitative consideration of the interaction of sound with space, inspired as it was initially by an appreciation of the multiple dimensions arising from that interface and the idea of a diaphanous music made audible through architecture.

Acknowledgements

The author wishes to gratefully acknowledge a bursary from SMI (Society of Musicology in Ireland), which enabled the archival research.

Hope Bagenal and Richard Terry were pioneers of thought. Although no longer with us, they still maintain a vibrant presence through their writings and the intellectual legacy they have left behind, as well as in the memories of a number of people close to them. To this end, the author is eternally grateful to Patience, Rachel and Beauchamp Bagenal, and to Miriam Powell and Aoife Daly from Westminster Cathedral, for taking the time to share anecdotes, memories, papers, photographs and letters, and in the process making two very great men very much alive for me, and, I hope, for you also.

Notes

1. This is the first documented use referenced in the *Oxford English Dictionary*.
2. The term in its current adjectival (as opposed to nounal) form, particularly when applied to music-making, has retained a greater sense of the earlier mechanical connotations that defined the noun.
3. This is the first documented use referenced in the *Oxford English Dictionary*.
4. The paper, which is unpublished, was entitled 'Acoustics Relative to Architecture'. For personal recollections on Bagenal's presentation to the Royal Institute of the Architects of Ireland (RIAI), see

Bagenal (1984) – a lecture given by John Bagenal in honour of his father Hope as part of a symposium on his life and work. The symposium was held in 1984 in the *Art Workers' Guild*. A printed copy of the lecture is in the RIBA archives. Further notes by John Bagenal are held in the Acoustic files in the Bagenal archive in Hertford County Hall.

5. General acoustic counsel was largely based on ideas of 'harmonious proportion' and even number symbolism, rather than quantifiable science. This is discussed in more detail by Paul Sabine in an article he wrote commemorating his cousin Wallace Clement Sabine. The article is entitled 'The Beginning of Architectural Acoustics' and was published in 1936 in the *Journal of the Acoustical Society of America*.

6. Bagenal's colleague and co-researcher Wood first encountered Sabine in 1916, some two years after Bagenal himself had, as evidenced in the published discussion following a presentation by Bagenal to the RIBA on acoustics (*RIBA Journal* vol. 32, 1924).

7. The article on acoustics written by Sabine appears in vol. 1 (42–8).

8. Sabine was constantly on the lookout for suitable rooms to analyse. The *Brickbuilder* article included an invitation to architects to keep him apprised of suitable rooms – usually of a particular and unembellished materiality. His initial studies on concrete had taken years, and on foot of the results he had derived, he was able to extend materials investigation from concrete to glass in the context of new greenhouses in the Harvard Botanical Gardens. These greenhouses, for a short time, provided the ideal location for analysing the acoustic properties of glass, until the introduction of plants altered the acoustics and interrupted his experiment. See Sabine (1922) for Sabine's own account of this. For an excellent and in-depth account of Sabine and his work on acoustics, see Thompson (2002).

9. Republication in additional journals was not unusual for Bagenal. As his work successfully spanned disciplines, a number of his papers and findings were published in both architecture and music journals.

10. This exhortation to his students at the Royal College of Music came from Charles Villiers Stanford. It is sometimes quoted as 'polyphony for a penny' rather than 'Palestrina for tuppence'. The instruction is referenced in Dibble (2002). It is also mentioned in Hilda Andrew's biography of Terry (Andrews 1948).

11. Richard Terry writing for the *Cathedral Chronicle* in February 1918, cited in 'Westminster Retrospect: a memoir of Sir Richard Terry' (Andrews 1948).

12. This letter was retained among Sabine's papers in the USA and text from it can be seen in Orcutt (1933); Sabine's response to Bagenal is in the UK.

13. The Fayrfax legend was frequently alluded to by Bagenal in his writing over the first half of the twentieth century, but only once was it attributed to Terry. Reference by Bagenal to the legend was made in at least four separate publications in the 1920s, 1930s and 1950s.

14. Review of the lecture published in *The Times*, 29 October 1929 — Westminster Cathedral Archives.

15. Requirements as written by Thomas Morley (1597) in *A Plaine and Easie Introduction to Practicall Musicke*, cited in Bray (1995a). For an excellent review of music and music theory of the era see also Bray (1995b).

16. Terry's 1907 book *Catholic Church Music* was republished in 1931 as *The Music of the Roman Rite: a manual for choirmasters in English-speaking countries*, with revised reference to Fayrfax and the suitability of context.

17. The comment formed part of a 1934 tribute by Terry to Philip Heseltine, a composer and theorist/journalist of music. The quotation is to be found in a contribution by Terry to a book written in memory of Heseltine by Cecil Gray (Gray 1934).

18. Turbet (1995) references a number of letters attesting to stormy relations between Terry and colleagues who were working on the publication of a series of music entitled 'Tudor Church Music' for the Carnegie Trust.

19. Comment by Terry which formed part of the discussion following a presentation by H.B. Collins to the Royal Musicological Association in 1913.

20. The long sixteenth century is deemed to encompass the timeframe from approximately 1485–1625. See Wulstan (1985).

Architectural scale
Psychoanalysis and Adrian Stokes

Janet Sayers

Much has been written about the influence of the human body on architectural scale. Much less has been written about the effect of architecture in giving form to the ego. An exception is the London-born writer, Adrian Stokes (1902–72). In explaining his achievement in this respect, I begin with Freudian accounts of the ego before turning to Stokes's rejection of massive and phallic scale in favour of architecture containing and unifying related forms to create an integrated image of the ego. I then end with the ramifications of this in Stokes's account of modern art, which in turn arguably influenced a revolution in psychoanalysis that continues today.

Freudian accounts of the ego

Freud had difficulty accounting for the ego. A 'unity comparable to the ego cannot exist in the individual from the start; the ego has to be developed', he argued. 'The auto-erotic instincts, however, are there from the very first; so there must be something added to auto-eroticism – a new psychical action – in order to bring about narcissism' (Freud 1914: 77).

What is added? How do the auto-erotic, part-object, oral, anal and genital instincts become integrated into the ego? Freud (1917) found a partial answer to this in theorising melancholia as the effect of melancholics identifying with those they love, hate and have lost as loved and hated figures in the ego. 'It may be that this identification is the sole condition under which the id can give up its objects', he speculated. 'If this is the case then', he reasoned, the ego might begin in identification with 'abandoned object-cathexes' (Freud 1923: 29).

Freud's follower, Melanie Klein, in turn, understood her child patients' drawings as indicating that the ego is initially constituted by part-object representations of the mother with the father inside her. As evidence, she cited drawings by a nine-year-old patient, Werner, in which he depicted a motor-cycle with 'an enormous motor, clearly drawn as a penis' on which sat 'a woman who sets the motor-cycle in motion'. He then drew 'a giant with huge eyes and a head containing aerials and wireless sets' to which he added a drawing of a giant climbing up the Eiffel Tower connected with a skyscraper. Klein interpreted these drawings as signifying Werner's expression of 'admiration for his father' through 'admiration for his mother' (Klein 1925: 119, 120).

She recounted in similar terms map-drawings by a ten-year-old patient, Richard. She interpreted them as depicting Richard's mother's body as attacked and pierced by the penis of his 'father, brother and himself' (Klein 1945: 376). '[T]hrough [Klein] we have the cartography, drawn by the children's own hands, of the mother's internal empire', approved the psychoanalyst Jacques Lacan, 'the historical atlas of the intestinal divisions in which the *imagos* of the father and brothers (real or virtual), in which the voracious aggression of the subject himself, dispute their deleterious dominance over her sacral regions'. These drawings demonstrate the 'fragmenting effect' on the ego of the child's first identification with its mother, he claimed (Lacan 1948: 20–1).

How, though, does development proceed from fragmentation to integration? Influenced by his psychoanalytic work with a patient who alienated aspects of herself in paranoid identification with an actress whom she attacked, Lacan (1949) argued that the image of the ego as a whole originates in the infant alienating itself in identification with its reflected mirror image. Out of the infant's initial identification with the mother as a 'body in bits and pieces' emerges the ego through identification with 'the stability of the standing posture, the prestige of stature, the impressiveness of statues', he argued (Lacan 1953: 15). Reiterating the point, he insisted that the ego develops through identification, from infancy onwards, with whatever seems to signify the phallus, as this is 'the most tangible element in the real of sexual copulation' (Lacan 1958: 287). This entails that, contrary to accounts by Freud and Klein of the ego as a self-generating effect of the psyche or libido, our self-knowledge comes from what we see and find in the world around us.

Massive scale

From an early age, Stokes was very much aware of the impact on his self-knowledge (or ego) of massive scale in the world around him. As a schoolboy, he memorised lines from Conrad's novel *Heart of Darkness*:

> Trees, trees, millions of trees, massive, immense, running up high; and at their foot, hugging the bank against the stream, crept the little begrimed steamboat, like a sluggish beetle crawling on the floor of a lofty portico. It made you feel very small.
>
> (Conrad 1899: 41)

A lofty portico fronted Stokes's childhood home, 18 Radnor Place, London. It was similar in scale and character to 'classical houses of brick with stucco ground floors' in nearby Sussex Gardens, providing 'a larger gentleman's version of the simpler buildings of Star Street', also close to Radnor Place (Kite 2009a: 16).

'As for the Edwardian buildings in my childhood, I can truly say I experienced from them the shamelessness of pretence', Stokes recalled towards the end of his life (Stokes 1972: 147). 'Lingering yesterday in all the part / Where I was born today / I saw twin porticoes as upright pain', he wrote. '[M]ade the neighbourhood so large / It seemed no room could hold this charge / Of hope and dynamite to undermine / A terminal of staid smooth shafts / Enclave with no shouldered home' (Stokes 1981: 36).

He deplored the large and massive scale of buildings in Oxford, where he studied philosophy after the First World War. 'Oxford is so massive, / So dismally imposing. / The giant grey blocks of clerical stone / Frown down and breathe tradition', he recalled. 'St. Mary's spire is massive, immense, / So dismally imposing, / Short, stumpy, lacking sympathy' (Stokes 1929a: 173). This was published while he was suffering a nervous breakdown, for which he began psychoanalytic treatment with Melanie Klein.

Soon she recounted his case as that of an anonymous patient, Mr B. She interpreted his breakdown as due to 'his unconscious idea that the woman was so full of the father's penises and dangerous excrements equated to the penis, that they had burst her open' (Klein 1932: 265). Stokes in turn adopted this interpretation in recounting his childhood memories of massive buildings and monuments near his childhood home. He recalled his loathing of 'the giant Achilles statue at Hyde Park Corner' and 'the Watts equestrian statue in the middle of the Long Walk' as 'stern yet impotent . . . figures of a father . . . who both attacked and had been attacked'. He also recalled the Albert Memorial. 'Here was a great fuss about solid matter; here was a thing of arrest which, unlike the prohibiting railings, protested as well as forbade', he wrote (Stokes 1947: 148).

'The best epitome of massive, meticulous incoherence provided by the park, was the Magazine at the end of the Serpentine Bridge. Explosive powder stood stored in this building of grey brick', he added. 'Potential murder and death were guarded with careful pageantry.' Together with other buildings and monuments in and near Hyde Park, he remembered this arsenal as signifying paternal and part-object phallic attack on the park as 'a destroyed and contaminated mother' (Stokes 1947: 149,158). He deplored their impact on his ego. 'What I saw outside confirmed with hideous amplification the self-distrust, the shame and the division that lay inside beneath the threshold', he recalled (Stokes 1951: 228).

To this he added, some years later, disapproval of the scale of the gasometer near London's Oval cricket ground. '[T]his squat, erectile cylinder could be destructive [in evoking] images of the child's impotence in conjunction with monstrous phallic attacks on the mother by a monster father', he claimed. 'A bad mother as well, possessing a bad phallus, it does not attempt to pierce and mingle with the vaporous sky but takes on bullying duties', he added, 'namely to outrage the houses of the poor (with small apertures) that miserably cluster near the naked plant'. He psychoanalysed these and other examples of massive architectural scale as part-object, phallic, and 'manic' counter to weakness, against which he urged architects to be 'convinced' of the whole-object 'integrative purpose of art' (Stokes 1965: 280, 282, 283).

Janet Sayers

Mass-effect

'In contrast to his native town, which he thought of as a dark, lifeless and ruined place', Klein had written of Stokes as Mr B, 'he pictured an imaginary city full of life, light and beauty, and sometimes found his vision realized, though only for a short time, in the cities he visited in other countries'. She attributed his image of his native London as 'dark, lifeless and ruined' to dark fantasies of his father's penis wreaking mayhem in his mother's body, and to fantasies stemming from the ferment of his divided identification and desire for men like his older brothers, one of whom he idolised, the other of whom he hated, dominated over and tormented. As for finding 'light and beauty' in cities in other countries, he found this particularly in buildings, which he later described in terms of their integrating mass-effect on the ego (Klein 1932: 273).

'Marble, when in such beautiful proportions, has the attractions of a little model or a delicate doll's house – definite, complete and suggestive only of itself', he wrote admiringly in recalling his post-Oxford visit to see the Taj Mahal in India. He recalled too seeing Benares from a boat on the Ganges – 'a mass of colours and cracked storeys forming the wonderful sweep of the river crowned by a Venetian sky', 'the mosque of Auranzebe with its high minarets', and 'half-hidden, half-forgotten, temples and palaces merging into open country' (Stokes 1925: 160, 171).

'By doorway, in relief, on window and chimney-piece, Francesco di Giorgio, Agostino di Duccio, Luciano Laurana emblazoned the arms of Europe', he wrote of buildings he later saw in cities near the eastern seaboard of Italy (Stokes 1926: 45). 'The universality of arabesque decoration in the Renaissance, beside frequency of domed buildings, demonstrate how deeply Mahommedan variant of Byzantine culture had penetrated beneath the skin of the West', he also wrote in praising the influence of Byzantine Ravenna on architecture in Rimini (Stokes 1929b: 44).

The German scholar Heinrich Wölfflin had praised Renaissance buildings in Italy presenting 'extremely clear solids' with 'definite proportions of planes and solids', revealing an entire 'self-contained life' (Kite 2009a: 100, 101). Perhaps this influenced Stokes. Certainly, he applauded in terms similar to those adopted by Wölfflin the courtyard designed by Luciano Laurana and built in the early Renaissance for the ducal palace in Urbino. 'The stone, then, lies on the brick in low relief, yet stands out simple, distinct, a white magic, *nitidezza* [clearness]', he wrote in emphasising the uniqueness of each pilaster flowering from the brick, the whole containing and unifying 'Ones each as single as the Whole' (Stokes 1932: 133, 134 – italics in original).

'An effect of mass is one connected with solidity or density of three-dimensional objects', he argued. '[S]olids afford an effect of mass only when they allow the *immediate*, the instantaneous synthesis that the eye alone of the senses can perform', he continued. This mass-effect is particularly well achieved by an undecorated wall with variations of colour and tone, which, he maintained, 'the eye with one flash discovers coherent, so that perceptions of succession belonging to any estimate of length or height or density, retire in favour of a feeling'; he went on, 'that here you witness a concatenation, a simultaneity, that the object is *exposed* to you, all of it all at once' (Stokes 1932: 134 – italics in original).

Stokes applauded in these terms the facade and encasement designed by Leon Battista Alberti for the transformation, in 1450, of a Romanesque church in Rimini into an early Renaissance temple, the Tempio Malatestiano. 'It is true that the massive centrality of the [facade's] door is emphasized', he acknowledged. 'Yet the ratio between the shapes, between the oblong imposts, the depth of the stylobate ledge, the blankness of the blind arcades, and the triangular depth of the pediment, overcome the massive centrality in favour of a general steadfastness' (Stokes 1934: 264).

He praised too the steadying effect of the transformation of inner ferment into outer form achieved in paintings by Alberti's near contemporary, Piero della Francesca. Examples included Piero's oil painting, 'The Nativity', in London's National Gallery, in which, Stokes noted, 'light-grey bricks of the manger's open wall' and 'the silver greys of the landscape and of the township' are built with 'shapes and declivities that together with the angels achieve synthesis in the Virgin's grey-blue robe' (Stokes 1937a: 80). 'Connexion is always architectural in the sense of a division of an order', he added in summarising the effect of Piero's fresco paintings in Arezzo showing 'the darkness of an aperture circled with stone and the dark centres of eyes flanked with their whites' and 'an emperor's conical hat surrounded by heads of coiled, pleated hair against a background of arches and circular disks'. Like the best early Renaissance buildings, Piero's paintings show, Stokes maintained, 'the mind becalmed, exemplified in the guise of the separateness of ordered outer things' (Stokes 1949: 198).

By the time this was published, Klein had theorised the ego as constituted by 'paranoid-schizoid' part-object representations of the mother and others, and by their 'depressive position' representation as loved, hatefully attacked, repaired and whole (Klein 1946: 16). To this, Stokes added Klein's argument that 'depressive anxiety, guilt and the reparative tendency are only experienced when feelings of love for the object predominate over destructive impulses' (Klein 1948: 36). He went on to praise buildings in Italian cities in these terms. 'We are grateful to stone buildings for their stubborn material, hacked and hewed but put together carefully, restored in better shape than those pieces that the infant imagined he had chewed or scattered', he wrote. He praised buildings that, through their form, convey 'accentuated otherness' and 'self-subsistence' rather than 'juxta-positions through which we are made vividly conscious of tensions of the mind'. He praised architecture that 'resuscitates an early hunger or greed in the disposition of morsels that are smooth with morsels that are rough', and which, with its openings, suggests infantile fantasies of tearing the mother's body with 'revengeful teeth' and its outcome – 'fierce yet smoothed' (Stokes 1951: 241, 242, 243).

'Such is the return of the mourned mother in all her calm and beauty and magnificence. She was mourned owing to the strength of greed, owing to the wealth of attacks that have been made on her attributes', he argued. 'And so, we welcome the appearance or re-appearance of the whole object which by contradistinction has helped to unify the ego; the joining, under one head, of love and of apparent neglect' (Stokes 1951: 243). 'One of the pleasures of reading Mr. Stokes's writings on art has always been in the discovery of a poet's sensitivity to the textures and – one might almost say – the "soul" of the various building stones of Italy', admired Michael Swan in *The Spectator*, also noting Stokes's psychoanalytic development of the architectural historian

Geoffrey Scott's dictum: 'we both transcribe ourselves into terms of architecture and architecture into terms of ourselves' (Swan 1951: 392).

'We can always discover from aesthetic experience the sense of homogeneity or fusion combined, in differing proportions, with the sense of object-otherness', Stokes told a meeting of the Imago Group of artists and psychoanalysts, which he helped found in 1954 (Stokes 1955a: 110). 'Art, if only by implication, bears witness to the world of depression or chaos overcome', he added, perhaps mindful of Klein's diagnosis of his daughter as suffering with the chaos of paranoid-schizoid disintegration (Stokes 1955b: 413).

Increasingly, in subsequent months, he emphasised the integrating influence of architecture, scaled to the human body, in providing an integrated image of the ego or mind. 'Drawings of Renaissance architects reveal preoccupation with the attempt to relate architectural proportions with those of the human figure', he noted in a lecture at London's Institute of Contemporary Arts in February 1956. 'In other words, all graphic art in some sense reconstructs for us a very primitive but forgotten image of the body' (Stokes 1956a: 21). '[I]n the best periods of the Renaissance, building was deeply felt as the giant of the body', he insisted (Stokes 1956b: 278–9). 'Freud said the motto of analysis was: where the id was ego shall be. I think it will do as well for art, i.e. the projection of a stable body-image, attacked as it is on every side', he told the art critic, Herbert Read (Stokes 1956c: n.p.).

'[A]n imago of ego-integration', he now argued, 'comes to us from the external world in the terms of a whole and independent and corporeal-seeing structure'. It answers 'anxiety concerning ego-integration' by conveying 'balance, pattern, movement, rhythm, surface quality (that is, texture), volume, proportion of parts to the whole'. As 'a self-contained object', art 'crystallizes experience' through its 'otherness' and simultaneous oneness with the self in 'realizing the structure, the stability, of the ego-figure in the very terms of object-otherness' (Stokes 1958: 98, 99, 109, 114).

Stokes followed this by illustrating the integrating mass-effect of architecture symbolising the body in giving form to the ego in a talk about Romanesque churches in France. 'I shall be remarking the most generalized imagery that, in my view, a due proportion of masses, between textures, of light and shade, of mass and space, void and aperture, serves to express', he told the Imago Group. 'In the fusion of stone shapes, then we may apprehend the symbol of a whole body: a due proportion of darkness, light, rectangularity, roundness, roughness, smoothness, wall, aperture, may provide both solace and reassurance', he continued, referring to a photo of Saint-Trinit in the Vaucluse. 'A further connexion with ourselves and with others evolves from the interrelation of planes, volumes, textures, in that they serve the corporeal image – it can only be a corporeal image – of mental or emotional stability', he emphasised (Stokes 1961a: 196, 197).

Modern art and psychoanalysis

Stokes's emphasis on the mass-effect of architecture in providing a stable and integrated image of the body, and thus of the ego, had its ramifications in his account of modern art, which in turn arguably influenced a revolution in psychoanalysis. After the end of his six years' psychoanalytic treatment by Melanie Klein in 1935, and after applauding the integrating mass-effect of Luciano Laurana's courtyard in Urbino, he applauded in similar terms abstract modern art paintings by his close friend, Ben Nicholson.

> I have always been able to discover in [Nicholson's] non-representational work, and in very few other works of this kind, the slow elucidation and isolation of factors that are constant in all that is pleasurable in the process of visual perception . . . I mean exercise, physical exercise of those synthetic powers which the eye as a visual organ has developed in association with the brain [whereby] basic fantasies of inner disorder find their calm and come to be identified with an objective harmony.
>
> (Stokes 1937b: 315–16)

He likewise praised Picasso's painting 'Woman with a Mandoline'. 'In terms of two forms "going into" a third, of one texture as the sum of another of larger area and so on, there is perhaps expressed the wished-for stabilizing', he argued, 'not so much of our personalities as of its qualification by those miscellaneous mixed-up archetypal figures within us, absorbed in childhood, that are by no means at peace among themselves' (Stokes 1937a: 33–4).

Braque, as well as Picasso, he noted many years later, fragmented and rebuilt the material of their paintings to crystallise experience symbolically as a unified 'ego-figure' (Stokes 1958: 114). 'The thread of life persists, in the case of early Cubist paintings a glass, a pipe, a newspaper, a guitar whose humming now spreads beyond once-sounding walls that have become clean and tactile remains', he added. 'Later work by Picasso is more disturbing, since he has broken off and re-combined parts of the body, often adding more than one view of these part-objects', he continued, 'the sum of misplaced sections does not suggest the parts of a machine: on the contrary, in the translated bodies, as in the rent room, of Guernica, there exist both horror and pathos as well as aesthetic calm' (Stokes 1961b: 155).

The following year, perhaps influenced by Stokes, a fellow-member of the Imago Group, the psychoanalyst Wilfred Bion, inaugurated today's continuing revolution in psychoanalysis with his emphasis on psychoanalysts containing and transforming their patients' otherwise fragmented and meaningless sense-data into meaningful form. He likened this to the mother accepting, containing and transforming her baby's otherwise frightening fragmented experience of itself into 'a form that it can tolerate' (Bion 1962: 115).

'[A]rt devotes itself entirely to sense-data, to every significance attaching to them, in order to focus steadily on integration of the inner world as an outer image', Stokes had previously argued, in a paper subsequently published together with the response of Bion's psychoanalyst colleague, Donald Meltzer (Stokes 1963: 209). The best art, like the best talking cure interpretation, enables us to experience both aggressive and furious fragmentation, and the integration of the resulting fragments through an 'orderly process of their reconciliation', Stokes later added (Stokes 1965: 294).

'Form, then, ultimately constructs an image or figure of which, in art, the expression of particular feeling avails itself', he told an audience at the Slade. Again he gave the example of Luciano Laurana's courtyard in Urbino. 'Each plain yet costly member of this building has the value of a limb: in the co-ordination of the contrasting materials there is equal care for each: together they make stillness that, as it were, breathes', he now said of this building and its integrated image of the body, and thus of the ego or mind (Stokes 1967: 332, 334).

To this, Stokes added the 'image in form' evoked by a modern art construction by Jesús Rafael Soto combining square plaques projected against a background of black and white lines. He also added the 'image in form' evoked by Picasso's painting, 'Three Dancers', acquired like the Soto construction by the Tate while Stokes was one of its Trustees. '[E]very line and tone and division helps in the setting up of various relationships across and down the face of the canvas', he said of the Picasso painting. Like the best architecture, and like other examples of modern art, it conveys 'an emotive or poetic whole' through 'a rich language of form' (Stokes 1967: 331, 334).

Applauding Stokes's emphasis on the mass-effect of architecture and modern art in giving integrated, embodied form to the ego, another member of the Imago Group, the artist and art education lecturer Anton Ehrenzweig, allied Stokes's achievement with the then-beginning revolution in psychoanalysis towards today's greater recognition of the role of psychoanalysts in integrating their patients' otherwise distressingly fragmented experience into integrated form. Just as Stokes described modern art, like the best architecture, uniting fragments as a whole, so too, wrote Ehrenzweig (1967), psychoanalysts had begun to recognise the importance of their function in uniting fragments as a whole in the ego.

'Ceaseless seas of experience construct the coral mind', Stokes had long before written (Stokes 1951: 234). 'A great library is like a coral reef whose exquisite structure as it grows proliferates a living network of connectedness, and its ramification is all of a piece, like knowledge itself', observed Colin St John Wilson, the architect of London's British Library, in adopting Stokes's ideas about the scaled integration of parts as a whole in architecture and in the ego (McCarthy 2008: 12).

Beginning with the rather different accounts of the ego developed by psychoanalysts from Freud to Lacan, I have sought to show how Stokes arrived at his architecturally based account of the ego by rejecting massive scale in favour of the mass-effect of architecture in giving integrated bodily form to the ego. This, in turn, I argue, determined Stokes's account of modern art and his influence in shaping psychoanalysis today.

Acknowledgement

My thanks to Adrian Stokes's literary executors, Ian Angus and Telfer Stokes, for copyright permission to include previously unpublished material by Stokes in this chapter.

Sublime indifference

Helen Mallinson

> We were on the deck at the time, and the headman of my wood-cutters lounging near by turned upon him his heavy and glittering eyes. I looked around, and I don't know why, but I assure you that never, never before did this land, this river, this jungle, the very arch of the blazing sky appear to me so hopeless and so dark, so impenetrable to human thought, so pitiless to human weakness.
>
> (Joseph Conrad, *Heart of Darkness* 1899)

Scale is the last redoubt of humanism; the implicit mean. But is scale something we invent, a nominal device to measure with, or something we discover, like nature's secret signature? This chapter explores the ontological dimensions of scale in a landscape governed by emotions, not geometry.

The terrible truth in Conrad's *Heart of Darkness* is 'The Horror! The Horror!' But, in the dying words of Kurtz, through whom Conrad portrays the human heart as a kernel hollow, empty and dark as the universe, expression nevertheless resounds. In Camus's *The Outsider* (1942), the sun blazing down on Meursault is no less unremitting. In *Heart of Darkness*, the native woodcutters are cannibals: in *The Outsider*, the apparently civilised Meursault cannot help but commit murder. The existentialist challenge set by Conrad and Camus is that we should face up to the fact that nature has no heart, no sentiment, no inner meaning. So is human nature any different? The justice system that Meursault's crime invokes is so contrived that Meursault cannot not help but become an outsider. In *Heart of Darkness*, the tide that sweeps its flotsam of colonisers, missionaries, adventurers, mercenaries and traders into Africa, and Kurtz into the Congo, is civilisation itself. In both stories, 'light', whether sought in nature or human nature, blazes dark.

If neither Conrad nor Camus provides ontological succour, at least of the enlightened variety, they nevertheless see existence itself as real *being*, even if the meaning of *being* escapes jurisdiction. One might imagine that scale does not belong in this unbound world. However, there is a twofold reason for introducing their works; on the one hand, our writers remove the handrails and invite us to consider how truly we experience *being*, and, on the other, through the act of removal they draw attention to our topology of restraints and the precision embodied in their preventative measures. Marlow, Conrad's narrator, and even the flesh-eating woodcutters, exercise restraint: Kurtz does not. He tips into the abyss, and not by accident. Meursault is doomed because he is bound to a truth 'born of living and feeling'. Meursault refuses to lie, to conform to expectations, to exaggerate or pretend what he actually feels: emotional honesty overrides even self-preservation. The boundary exercise that Conrad and Camus instate is centred on personal fidelity; authentic feeling is the only guide. So, one way of thinking about scale in a landscape governed by emotions is as something like handrails, close up, as something like boundaries in the middle distance and as something like the horizon at the outer limits of our view.

Jungle geometry

> So, my kind of hero for this in the natural world are these tropical frogs. I got interested in them because they're the most extreme example of a surface where the texture and the – let's call it the decoration . . . are all intricately connected to one another. So a change in the form indicates a change in the colour pattern . . . So, when doing a centre for the national parks in Costa Rica, we tried to use that idea of a gradient colour and a change in texture as the structure moves across the surface of the building.
>
> (Lynn 2005)

The idea for this chapter was provoked by Greg Lynn's 'Ark of the World', his project for an eco-centre set in the tropical rainforest of Costa Rica. The project eschews conventional architectural form and materials in favour of something that looks frankly biological, even fleshy. The forms and colours of the building mould seamlessly into one another like a clump of deadly rhizomes. The visual scale of the building is psychotropic: it looks pungent. It would be a mistake, however, to assume that Lynn has no interest in traditional architectural scale. Rather the opposite. He presents his work as heir to a tradition that equates beauty with geometry with nature. What has evolved over the centuries, Lynn claims, is the mathematics: the right kind of mathematics gives us direct access to both nature and beauty and their unproblematic translation into architecture.

> So, for roughly 300 years, the hot debate in architecture was whether the number five or the number seven was the better proportion to think about architecture, because the nose was one-fifth of your head, or because your head was one-seventh of your body. And the reason that was the model of beauty and of nature was because the decimal point had not been invented yet . . . and everybody had to dimension a building in terms of fractions . . . finer and finer and finer.
>
> In the 15th century, the decimal point was invented; architects stopped using fractions, and they had a new model of nature. So, what's going on today is that there's a model of natural form which is calculus-based

> and which is using digital tools, and that has a lot of implications to the way we think about beauty and form, and it has a lot of implications in the way we think about nature.
>
> (Lynn 2005)

Lynn's work suggests that the existential prospect is not without its own brand of hubris: the blank unbound has its attractions. One of Lynn's current collaborative projects is called 'New City'.[1] It is billed as a 'living virtual world', and a trailer was produced for the 2008 MoMA exhibition, 'Design and the Elastic Mind'. The theme and title of the exhibition addressed the ability of the mind to constantly switch scales, from nano to cosmo, from real to virtual, and back again in an instant, and presented the latest developments in design and science. The 'New City' project set out to create a real virtual environment, by which Lynn meant an architecturally scaled, high-definition, cinema-quality submersive world as distinct from the low-quality, cartoon-like versions currently available on the web. Lynn began the project by posing the question 'Is a sphere the optimal shape for our world? If physical laws were no longer a concern, how would we mold the Earth to better suit our global economy?' (Lynn 2011). Thus the geometric model for 'New City' is not the spherical Google globe with its primitive zoom control, but a series of interlocking, elastic torus rings designed to meld images from real time and data projections, their witting and unwitting congress.

The 'New City' project works on the assumption that there is an actual world upon which to model the virtual. Lynn's blank unbound is not in fact the actual world, at least not in the first instance, but the ability to represent or model the actual world – even in its entirety; such is his excitement. In Lynn's mind, architecture completes the torus ring, because you can build in the real world what can be imagined in the model. In this scenario, the role played by the calculus of modelling is an interesting one. On the one hand, the mathematics is understood as real, as transparent to nature's secret design code; on the other hand, the mathematics is sold as imaginary, as transparent to the desires of the designer/consumer. We thus have truth to nature and an unlimited horizon. Scale in this instance is elastic. The 'New City' project takes it for granted that mind and body work together in assembling the perception of 'environment' in any number and configuration of navigable space. Indeed, our ability to shrink and grow in tune with our perceptual environment makes Alice's efforts in *Alice in Wonderland* look positively somnambulant. But if feeling in the physical sense of being able to scale up or down is elastic, then what about feeling in the emotional sense? How do we take our bearings in this jungle?

Biology versus culture

> The past relegation of emotions to the sidelines of culture is an artefact of the view that they occupy the more natural and biological provinces of human experience, and hence are seen as relatively uniform, uninteresting, and inaccessible to the methods of cultural analysis.
>
> (Lutz and White 1986: 405)

For much of the twentieth century, the culture industries were indifferent to the emotions as a subject of study. Lutz and White were among the first to comment on the change in emotional climate that started in the 1970s when anthropologists noted how specific cultures seemed to influence the particular expression and social dynamics of emotions. Were emotions universal or culturally specific? Were the emotions a pan-human, inner potential that was moulded by the outer forces of social life or did social life engender emotional life?

Insofar as the subject of the emotions is treated in architectural terms, it generally assumes a psychobiological frame that can be accounted through behavioural science. A simple example is the application of colour theory to therapeutic environments in the bid to make patients feel more cheerful or children calm down. Alternatively, we might look at aesthetic theory. Curiously enough, both disciplines struggle at the social scale when they make the assumption that there is an emotional unit called the subjective individual. The behavioural scientists scale up using statistical averages, whereas in aesthetics the equivalent gesture is in the ratings. But, to track back for a moment, what are the phenomena called the emotions in any case, and, critically, how do they scale?

Historically speaking, the science of the emotions took a decisive step with Darwin when he applied his evolutionary theory not just to the development of living forms but also to their behaviour. Darwin published *The Expression of the Emotions in Man and Animals* in 1872. In it, he argued that there was a biological link between emotional states, human expressions and movements of the body that ultimately derived from purposeful animal actions, like responses to pleasure or pain; human emotions were just more developed. William James published his seminal article, 'What is an Emotion?' in a philosophy journal called *Mind* in 1884. What focused the debate from James onwards was the problem of how to explain the stimulus-to-feeling sequence that defined how an emotion evolved within a subject. The question was whether the bit called 'emotion' was based in the physical or the cognitive, given that it included physiological changes, like heartbeat, as well as the consciousness of a feeling, like anger. James argued from animal physiology, that in effect we are sad because we cry, that the body is the first to respond and that our emotions are our conscious interpretations of shifts in our physiology.

Jean-Paul Sartre argued the opposite in his *Sketch for a Theory of the Emotions*, published in 1939, claiming the cognitive case, because emotions amount to intentional and strategic ways of coping with difficult situations:

> We can now conceive what an emotion is. It is a transformation of the world. When the paths before us become too difficult, or when we cannot see our way, we can no longer put up with such an exacting and difficult world. All ways are barred and nevertheless we must act. So then we try to change the world; that is, to live it as though the relations between things and their potentialities were not governed by deterministic processes, but by magic.
>
> (Sartre 2010: 40–1)

Today, although it is still assumed that the emotions have a psychobiological framework, their involvement in social and cultural relations has provoked new areas of study. After the 1970s anthropologists went on to argue that the notion of emotions representing an inner potential moulded by social life reproduced a false dichotomy between 'nature' as a universal inner reality versus 'culture' as a particular public outcome (Milton and Svasek 2005: 8). Now a range of social-constructivist philosophers, moral philosophers and social historians all draw attention to the constitutive role played by the language, moral norms and institutions of different cultures in creating emotions: emotions are more like crimes than sneezes (Dixon 2003: 247). There is also a new interest in Aristotle's *Rhetoric* and the argument that the emotions are fundamentally 'psychosocial' – that all expressions of feeling are obviously and irreducibly social rather than private (see Gross 2006) – a subject to which we will return.

Feeling ugly

> It's always interesting to watch a psychotropic house try to adjust itself to strangers, particularly those at all guarded or suspicious. The responses vary, a blend of past reactions to negative emotions, the hostility of the previous tenants, a traumatic encounter with a bailiff or burglar (though both usually stay well away from PT houses; the dangers of an inverting balcony or the sudden deflatus of a corridor are too great). The initial reaction can be a surer indication of a house's true condition then any amount of sales talk about horsepower and moduli of elasticity.
>
> (Ballard 2001: 187)

In his story 'The Thousand Dreams of Stellavista' written in 1962, J.G. Ballard imagines a house of the future tailored to embody and respond to the particular emotions of its inhabitants. At one level, the house is just a piece of technologically advanced real estate; at another it is the emotions of the house that endure and give form not just to the physical landscape of the house but also to the moods and events that take place within it. The house takes on a borrowed life and finds it hard to kick deeply engrained emotional habits, at least when it is switched on.

Ballard's vision of a psychotropic house is not yet on the market but there is plenty of evidence to suggest that we are attracted to designs that engage our emotional response. Savvy designers like Hartmut Esslinger, who founded Frog Designs, market themselves on this very premise. This successful global company designed Apple Mac's revolutionary user-friendly styling and more generally helped to popularise curvy, biomorphic product design.[2] Esslinger's take on the frog – a classic green frog in his case – is the idea of metamorphosis and the fairytale frog that changes into a prince. His strapline is 'form follows emotion'. It might be commented that Esslinger makes a successful commercial enterprise out of Sartre's insight: design can deliver emotional magic.

The point behind summoning Ballard's psychotropic house is not to suggest that it should remain in the realm of science fiction because crossing that boundary has already become an investment opportunity. Ballard himself has contributed to Lynn's recent publication *Form* and is billed as a 'futurist'. The point is to examine how aesthetic theory might deal with emotional scale. For example, if built, how would the psychotropic house materialise what Ruskin famously called the 'pathetic fallacy'?

When he coined the term, Ruskin was referring to the task facing modern writers in his book *Modern Painters* (1856).[3] He was preoccupied with truth and recognised two sorts: the truth of plain facts and the truth of real feeling. To begin with, Ruskin described the pathetic fallacy as the reification or personification of the natural or inanimate world, the false ascription of emotions to, say, leaves, clouds or waves, as if they were alive and sentient beings when clearly they were not. He went on to elaborate in far greater detail the second and more difficult version of the pathetic fallacy. This had to do with the quality of the poet and his or her ability to convey real emotions without getting carried away. Good poets did not make the mistake of flooding the natural or inanimate world in their emotions in order to convey their sorrow, anger, astonishment, or love. Ruskin instructed the ambitious writer to keep the eyes fixed 'on the *pure fact*, out of which if any feeling comes to him or his reader, he knows it must be a true one'. There had to be some kind of correlation between subject and object – like the perfect accord between the emotion Conrad ascribes to Marlow and the stark facts of his surroundings. The weak writer, in contrast, happily ascribed fallacious emotions to inappropriate objects.

When discussing the pathetic fallacy, Ruskin observed with some irritation that there were new-fangled categories that had to be dealt with – the categories of subjective and objective. These did not exist until the early nineteenth century (Daston 2005: 25). Some responsibility for their invention can be ascribed to Kant through his founding of modern aesthetics in *Critique of Judgement* (1969; first published 1790). This new discipline heralded a revolution in which Kant undertook an even more important emotional boundary-setting exercise than Ruskin. After Kant, the determination of aesthetics would depend not on the properties of the dumb object but the experience of the viewer. What prompted this revolution was the inclusion of the sublime, a category quite different to that of traditional beauty. It had been under development by a number of authors during the eighteenth century, partially in response to the new Newtonian cosmology of infinity. The aesthetics of the sublime began in the attempt to capture an overwhelming experience of immensity, an experience that could not be grasped by the immediate senses or even through calculation. Paintings of mountains, abysses, volcanoes, for example, could evoke the sublime feelings of awe, terror or astonishment. But, what made this emotional experience aesthetic was the sharp division Kant drew between cognition and appetite. Emotions in the aesthetic register depended for their satisfaction on representation: one should be able to feel the emotion of awe or terror, but without being indisposed in actuality.

Ballard's psychotropic house clearly crosses that boundary, even to the point of endangering its occupants. Is the psychotropic house a type of pathetic fallacy, or a mechanical object come to life and mind? It seems as if the animating world soul, having been banished by science through the front door, has returned via the service entrance – but unencumbered by any moral baggage.

The whole soul

Newtonian cosmology may have evoked a feeling for the sublime, but it also worked very well without the 'God hypothesis' – as Pierre-Simon Laplace put it.[4] The chilling consequence of Newtonian physics was a mechanically sufficient universe, one quite indifferent to the fate of man and men. It was against this indifferent universe that the characters in Conrad's and Camus's novels struggled to retain the integrity of their emotions or what might be read as the last redoubt of the individual soul. Neither author could justify recourse to an idea of soul at a larger scale, whether manifest through God or nature, reason or civilisation. Nor could Ruskin, nor even Kant, despite the fact that they still saw everywhere the hand of a designer deity. This was not the case when God and nature took more of an interest in the consequence of man and played an active role in his animation. What disappeared along with God from the Newtonian cosmos was the once-ubiquitous agency called 'soul'.

Entrenched in the concept of soul was the concept of the good. While soul still existed, the realm of the emotions had a place vis-à-vis the soul because the emotions were thought of as the outward manifestations of the soul's inner workings. They were better known as the passions. The passions marked the territory between the bodily appetites and the reasoning mind, and were susceptible to the influence of both (see Hampton 2004: 273). Their orientation was vertical and their composition hierarchical, with the good emotions at the top and the bad emotions at the bottom. The emotions were far from being morally indifferent. They provided the motive force that engaged the will and the pulse by which the soul's upward or downward trajectory could be assessed (Dixon 2003: 18–23). When the soul disappeared as the integrative agency, a process that started with the scientific revolution in the seventeenth century (specifically, with René Descartes), the status, origin and purpose of the emotions began to change (Lagerlund and Yrjönsuuri 2002: 28).

The moral reading of the emotions in relation to soul is obviously Christian, but the association was first formalised by the classical philosophers.[5] In *The Republic*, Plato developed the model of the tripartite soul along with the first systematic account of emotional phenomena. He demonstrated that the notion of the good in the form of justice applied equally to the individual and the city-state. The structure of both – their tripartite organisation, the relation between the whole and the parts, their optimum dynamic – was perfectly analogous. His ideal city had three classes of citizens capable of acting for the common good: the leaders or guardians who were rational and wise, the soldiers who defended the city and were obedient and courageous, and the ordinary citizens who were able to moderate their desires. Plato conceived the individual soul in parallel terms. The three constituent parts had to act in concert and as a whole in order to act for the best. Plato described the three parts of the individual soul as the *rational soul* (which understood what was real rather than apparent), the *spirited soul* or volition (which was the active part able to carry out what the rational soul thought best) and the *appetitive soul* (the emotions and desires that want and feel, and the part that had to be kept under strict control).

Aristotle took his idea of tripartite composition from Plato, but he made a different interpretation of the emotions, in line with his different construction of the soul. In Plato's view, emotional reactions were not to be trusted because they did not evaluate what was truly real and thus could lead to false judgements. Moreover, the emotions tethered the soul to material things that might disturb the higher activities of the rational soul. Plato imagined the emotions as by nature wild. Aristotle did not share Plato's detached attitude to life, nor the view that nature was intrinsically wild rather than ordered. Aristotle's comprehensive treatise on the soul, *De anima*, explained what imbued animate nature with order. *De anima* can be translated as 'on life', and it covered plants and animals as well as humans. Aristotle framed a unified system in which the whole range of vital functions, from metabolism to reasoning, was treated as functions performed by natural organisms depending on their sophistication and complexity. His tripartite organisation of soul was both similar and different to that of Plato. The lowest level of soul was shared by all living things, and accounted for the activities of growth, nutrition and reproduction. The next level was shared by animals and people, and accounted for self-generated movement and the senses. The highest level was specific to humans, and accounted for thought and reason. Each level could be further subdivided and furnish taxonomies of phenomena that linked the lowest forms of life to the highest.

Aristotle shared Plato's interest in 'the good' as a goal for both individual and civic conduct, but he emphasised the knowledge born of experience and practice rather than the pursuit of idealised virtues. Aristotle thus made room for the emotions as a necessary part of the interaction that made up an individual and a social life. Part of this practice, like all knowledge-based skills, involved learning and moderating appropriate emotional responses in line with particular circumstances. Aristotle's most detailed analysis of the emotions was presented in *Rhetoric*. He distinguished between four basic components – cognition, psychic effect, bodily effect and behavioral impulse – and was particularly interested in feelings, the pleasant or unpleasant modes of being aware of oneself in various situations – an aspect favoured by modern interpreters.[6] Aristotle's interest, however, was more extensive. *Rhetoric* was Aristotle's philosophical treatise on the art of persuasion, and aimed at politicians and poets, or all those who sought to sway their public. He framed the use of rhetoric as part of an ethical system of practical debate. Plato's stance on the topic had been more ambiguous. Although he began by condemning the arts of 'flattery' as ignoble and designed to deceive, he also offered a more moderate view by acknowledging that the soul itself was susceptible to right discourse. Aristotle's *Rhetoric* proceeded on this basis. It helped to underpin the ideology of the city-state and the idea of Greek democracy.

Figuring the emotions

> They praise Euphranor because in his portrait of Alexander Paris he did the face and expression in such a way that you could recognise in him simultaneously as the judge of the goddesses, the lover of Helen and the slayer

of Achilles. The painter Daemon's remarkable merit is that you could easily see in his painting the wrathful, unjust and inconstant, as well as the exorable and clement, the merciful, the proud, the humble and the fierce.[7]

(Alberti 2004: 77)

In *On Painting*, Alberti set out principles of geometrical composition that ultimately referred back to Plato's notion of the ideal realm and the rational part of the soul. However, Alberti went on to explain how painting a *historia* could act in the same way as writing poetry, by which he meant the rhetorical tradition canonised by Aristotle. The painter could move his audience to laughter or tears when the painted figures represented their emotions clearly. The key to painterly success lay in the movements of the body; these the painter had to study with care because, as Alberti pointed out, 'it is extremely difficult to vary the movements of the body in accordance with the almost infinite movements of the heart' (Alberti 2004: 77). Representing mixed emotions, like the accomplished ancients Euphranor or Daemon, was the most difficult art of all.

In *On the Art of Building in Ten Books*, Alberti again began with geometric lineaments before turning to the content of architecture and its purpose, beginning with 'public works'. The equivalent scale in building to the history painting was that of the city and its citizens (Alberti 1988: 95). Alberti noted what the ancients had to say about the different levels and types of citizenship, and how cities should be characterised. He observed that buildings were built to occasion pleasure as well as to serve practical requirements; they were also very varied. The innumerable movements of the heart had their parallel in its innumerable desires. Finding the right balance of architectural expression was a civic task. Alberti stuck firmly to the principles set out by the tripartite organisation of the soul.

Things indifferent

If Kantian aesthetic pleasure overlaps with the realm traditionally occupied by the emotions, but without any of their moral baggage, there is a Stoic precedent for this in what the Stoics called the 'indifferents'. These are objects that are indifferent in themselves rather than requiring that one is indifferent to them. *Adiaphora*, or things outside the application of moral law, do not promote or obstruct moral ends in themselves (Graver 2009: 49). Kant's use of indifference, however, was more extensive than that of the Stoic philosophers. Like Platonist and Aristotelian philosophy, Stoic philosophy upheld the idea of an intelligent universe and the pervasive notion of soul. The Stoics, however, were unambiguous monists: their notion of soul, or *pneuma*, was entirely immanent and material as well as rational and continuous. They held a complex view of the emotions in that they aspired to eradicating their emotional reactions – *apatheia* – under the rule of reason. But, in their view, reason was in itself a pervasive, good and immanent material force: one just needed to realise it. Leibniz reworked the Stoic idea of an intelligent nature, but Kant, who became a disciple of Newtonian cosmology, held no such confidence. Kant saw the hand of God the designer but did not think that nature possessed an inner natural harmony or that the emotions represented any such order in themselves. For Kant, nature and the emotions were morally indifferent (Schneewind 1996: 295). He thus chose to root his important theory of freedom and moral law in man's transcendental nature.

The Kantian justification of the aesthetic realm lay in its dedication to a freedom enacted by freeing aesthetic pleasure from ruling interests, even the good. Since Kant, the sublime has grown to become an accommodatingly diverse category as well as being godmother to the ugly and ordinary. It represents a genre of experience that suggests ontological status while being under no compunction to be 'good'. Kant both institutionalised ontological indifference and used indifference in the form of the disinterested gaze to realise his new aesthetic philosophy. One of the most influential modern commentators on Kant, Jean-François Lyotard in his *Lessons on the Analytic of the Sublime* (1994), claims that though the idea of the good became far more abstract under Kant, it did not disappear. The aesthetic realm that Kant founded not only underpins the freedom of modern art, its notion of ulterior freedom now acts as an open model for human understanding.

So what role should the emotions play in figuring this more open landscape? Should scale in architecture, for instance, be treated as a matter of sublime indifference in order to preserve a wider horizon of freedom, or should scale be used more like music in its emotive intent and cultural expression – but submit to Ruskinian rules? One might ask whether indifference is an emotion in itself or an absence of emotion; whether the absence of emotion represents a lack, or, alternatively, an achievement (bearing in mind that Stoic philosophy recommended emotion's extirpation). The question is of particular interest when it broaches the public realm. Which is why Aristotle's *Rhetoric* is back in the frame.

Notes

1. The collaborators for 'New City' at the MoMA exhibition were Peter Frankfurt, Greg Lynn, Alex McDowell and Imaginary Forces. Available at www.imaginaryforces.com/featured/3/435 (accessed 11 April 2011).
2. Founded in 1969, Frog is a creative global network designing products, corporate identities and new media for a vast range of international clients including Disney, Levi's, Lufthansa and the San Francisco Museum of Modern Art.
3. See John Ruskin, 'Of the Pathetic Fallacy', *Modern Painters*, vol. iii, pt. 4. Available at www.ourcivilisation.com/smartboard/shop/ruskinj/ (accessed 11 April 2011).
4. In 1799 Laplace published his post-Newtonian *Treatise on Celestial Mechanics*. When Napoleon Bonaparte asked him why he made no mention of God in his theory – unlike Newton – Laplace famously answered 'Sire, I have no need of that hypothesis'.
5. The following summary of the Platonic–Aristotelian soul is from Knuuttila (2004: 5–46).
6. See Knuuttila's comments on Heidegger and moods (2004: 41).
7. Alberti (2004) was quoting a passage from Pliny.

Measuring up
Measurement pieces and the redefinition of scale in conceptual art

Elise Noyez

You line up against the wall. Someone puts his hand on top of your head and marks its position with a short, horizontal line. You step away and look at the wall. This is how tall you are.

In Roman Ondák's 'Measuring the Universe', first performed in 2007 at the Munich Pinakothek der Moderne, visitors relive a common scene from childhood. Substituting for the parent, museum attendants ask visitors whether they want to be measured and mark their height with black felt-tipped pen on the exhibition room's wall, annotated with their name and the date of their visit. As in the common household tradition, the marks indicate a passing of time. Not as a document of a child's growth, however, but as a reminder of the succession of visitors. Over the course of an exhibition, 'Measuring the Universe' grows from a single black mark on the wall into a hazy wall drawing that eventually encircles the space. As more and more people are measured, the marks accumulate, and a dense, almost entirely black area appears – a dark horizon that indicates the average height of the exhibition's visitors. While Ondák argues that 'the performance has the same status with one mark on the wall as with thousands of them' (Ondák 2009: 78), the relation between the black horizon and the space points to a specific proportion between body and space. So, if the title of the work refers to 'humankind's age-old desire to gauge the scale of the world' (MoMA 2009), as the curators of MoMA's 'Performance Exhibition Series' claim, how exactly does measuring the body function in determining that sense of scale?

Measurement as artistic strategy

Before Ondák was even born, the act of measurement had already been referred to or implemented by a number of artists. In 1963, for example, Robert Morris presented a work entitled 'Three Rulers', an oblique reference to a much older work: Marcel Duchamp's 'Three Standard Stoppages' (1913–14). Most examples, however, date from around the time of Ondák's birth in 1966. Most importantly, it is then that two dedicated artists started to build an entire oeuvre around the premise of measurement. By placing Ondák's 'Measuring the Universe' in relation to the works of these two artists, this chapter considers the different ways in which measurement is employed as an artistic strategy and the implications thereof on defining a notion of scale.

Sometime during the late 1960s or early 1970s, the illusive Dutch artist Stanley Brouwn took on the task of meticulously measuring and recording distances and dimensions. In order to do so, however, he did not count on the metric system alone. Rather, one of the first things he did was to formulate a personal system of measurement, based entirely on the dimensions of his own body. Thus, Brouwn's earliest measurement pieces revolve primarily around the definition of a list of standard measures: the sb (or Stanley Brouwn) -foot, -ell, and -step. Most often, the standards were defined in relation to the metric system and transferred onto paper in a variety of ways. '1 Step' (1973), for example, is a filing cabinet holding 847 index cards in which each card represents 1 mm. As the title suggests, the total of 847 cards refers to the length of 1 sb-step. Another filing cabinet holds 1,000 of the same cards (1 m) and includes a bookmark to indicate the length of 1 sb-step. The same confrontation between a sb-step and a metre appears in the artist's book from 1976, entitled *Distance = Length*. Each page of the book is marked with a series of 10 cm lines, but whereas a left-hand page shows ten lines (1 m), the facing right-hand page only shows seven full lines and part of an eighth line (1 sb-step).[1] In later works, which he called 'portraits', Brouwn also measured other people – representing them in the form of a single aluminium bar and a note indicating their height.

It was around the same time, in the late 1960s, that the American artist Mel Bochner became interested in measurements. Rather than measure his body, however, Bochner took a ruler around his studio and measured more or less everything he could find, from cans of spray adhesive to the distance between the light switch and a shelf (Field 1995a: 34). Later, he started to tack cardboard pieces to the walls to measure the space between them, or he simply measured the width of a piece of cardboard and inscribed it directly onto the panel itself. His 1969 '8" Measurement', a sheet of graph paper with the simple notation of its width, is just one of the many examples of Bochner's self-referential measurement pieces.

Because both Mel Bochner and Stanley Brouwn are usually considered conceptual artists, and Roman Ondák is referred to as a *neo*-conceptual artist, it seems obvious to consider their respective interests in measurement from that vantage point. Given its seeming simplicity and the systematic way in which it can be applied, 'measuring things' must have appeared to the conceptual artist as a perfect way to make art. Just like counting, stacking and ordering, the systematic act of measuring implies but a simple premise that can easily be repeated: to compare an object's (or person's) dimensions to a standard measure such as the inch or the centimetre. By simply applying that premise, one can easily circumvent the need for personal, aesthetic and stylistic decisions, and produce an artwork that is instead based solely on a predetermined description and its systematic execution. As Sol LeWitt so elegantly put it in his 1967 'Paragraphs on Conceptual Art': 'The idea becomes a machine that makes the art' (LeWitt 1999: 12).

If we are to believe popular narratives of conceptual art, artists even aimed for an art in which the idea that initially led to the production of an artwork would simply replace it, altogether substituting 'the object of spatial and perceptual experience by linguistic definition alone (the work as analytic proposition)' (Buchloh 1999: 515). Accordingly, measurement pieces such as those by Brouwn, Bochner and even Ondák seem to replace the objects of spatial and perceptual experience by their straightforward geometric definition – geometry being, just like language, a sign-system and model of thought. We get measurements instead of objects; instead of people, even. Indeed, with their simple notations in black felt-tipped pen, their artist's books and their filing cabinets, the works under discussion are easily associated with what Buchloh called the 'aesthetic of administration'.[2]

Body and scale

> The human body enters into the total continuum of sizes and establishes itself as a constant on that scale.
>
> (Morris 1995: 11)

In a work from 1968, Mel Bochner obliquely addresses issues of size and scale. 'Actual Size' consists of two photographs printed on a 1:1 scale. Each photograph depicts a part of the artist's body as it is lined up along a black line annotated '12"'. In both photographs, the background is a simple white wall; all we see is Bochner's head ('Actual Size (Face)') or arm ('Actual Size (Hand)') next to the line of black tape. The juxtaposition of body and measurement, as well as Bochner's insistence on printing the photographs in 'actual size', raises the question as to how we determine an object's size when it is depicted in a medium that is essentially scaleless; for photographs are not usually printed in actual size, nor are we used to them featuring measurements. We might have seen rulers appear in detailed photographs of crime scenes or archaeological finds, but most of the time, there is no absolute way of telling how big a depicted object is in reality.

So how do we know the size of an object in a photograph (Field 1995a: 34); or in a painting, drawing or sculpture for that matter, as the issue is hardly exclusive to photography? When it comes to representation, most artworks have a very specific illusionistic scale, inherent to the work itself. We do not take pictures literally; we size up the depicted elements in relation to each other rather than in absolute terms. Yet, in order to get a sense of scale, we depend on a certain frame of reference. The depiction of bodies, among other things, constitutes such a frame of reference. A background, too, can provide a frame of reference, but there's nothing we know quite as well as (the size of) the human body. Claes Oldenburg, for example, made excellent use of this quality in his sketches of proposed colossal monuments. By adding tiny marks suggestive of human bodies or traces of a cityscape to his drawings, Oldenburg catapulted everyday objects such as popsicles ('Proposed Colossal Monument for Park Avenue: Good Humor Bar', 1965) and vacuum cleaners ('Proposed Colossal Monument for the Battery, NYC: Vacuum Cleaner', 1965) from the modest realm of their everyday use into that of giant buildings (Davidts 2008). When determining the illusionistic scale of a picture, bodies thus serve as excellent references of size.

'Actual Size', however, is about more than just illusionistic or imaginary scale. Here, the photographs are 'life size', creating a conflation between their illusionistic scale and the actual scale of the situation in which they are presented. Rather than being a point of reference between the realm of the photograph and that of the viewer, the depicted body becomes a point of confrontation, of collision, 'returning the photograph to a literal relationship with the world' (Field 1995a: 34). As such, 'Actual Size' does not obviate the issue of scale, as Richard S. Field suggests, but rather pulls it in a different direction – that of minimal art's (or, better yet, Robert Morris's) phenomenological notion of scale. Because minimal art renounced representation, there was no place for an imaginary scale. Instead of looking for relations *within* a work, minimal art called attention to the relations *between* a work and its surroundings. 'Sculpture no longer stands apart, on a pedestal or as pure art', Hal Foster observed in his seminal essay 'The Crux of Minimalism', 'but is repositioned among objects and redefined in terms of place' (Foster 1996: 38). Scale, then, revolves around a physical and phenomenological confrontation between a spectator and a work of art within a certain space. But Morris did not want just any relationship between these different aspects; he pleaded for a very specific one. Minimal art had what appears to be a very clear project: to make the viewer aware of how his or her own presence and position within a certain situation influenced perception. In order to do so, however, viewers could not be distracted by formal details or skewed relations between an object and its surroundings. In order to reveal the disjunctions in the perceptual process, artists thus opted for 'extraordinarily clear elementary polyhedrons, executed in specific materials at a precise scale in relation to the human body' (Mitchell 1995: 254). Scale, in other words, becomes a very specific dimensional rapport between the artwork, the spectator and the space in which they are confronted.

The question in this chapter, however, is what kind of relation between artwork, spectator and space is pronounced when the artwork seems to exist only as a simple notation of measurement. And what if, as Stanley Brouwn's insistence on the term 'portrait' implies, the body can equally be reduced to a mere dimension? What does this imply for a definition of scale in conceptual art?

Measuring bodies, measuring spaces

In a series of works started in the late 1980s, Stanley Brouwn used aluminium bars and wooden cubes based on his own bodily dimensions to measure (exhibition) spaces. The resulting works describe spaces in terms of a very basic equation, measuring x by y by z sb-feet, for example. Sometimes, the dimensions are inscribed on a plaque hung in the space itself, but in most cases they are simply printed in artist's books and referred to as 'portraits' of spaces. In pronouncing the specific dimensional rapport between an object, a body and a space, these works are directly related to minimal art's notion of scale. Moreover, by defining that rapport in terms of the body, they underscore and even literalise the body's role as a reference of size. Only, instead of doing so through the spectator's own, messy experience of such a relation, it is immediately reduced or 'purified' to a literal recording of it. Following a reductivist notion of conceptual art in which ideas can replace reality: if scale is a dimensional relation to begin with, why not pronounce it as a simple geometric equation, a basic proportion?

By literalising the body's role as a reference of size, however, Brouwn also seems to undermine that role. For, while everything is considered in terms of the artist's bodily dimensions, the actual body is inexorably absent. Throughout his career, Brouwn has made it a point to remain anonymous and to leave both himself and his body out of the picture. By presenting nothing but descriptive titles or collections of lines, the notion of a body as a reference of size is extracted from the realms of vision and experience, and reduced to a purely abstract, notational level. In the end, the body has become pure dimension, pure idea, much in the same way as the empirical system has lost all reference to our actual bodies and become mere convention. Although Brouwn's system of measurements may have been based on the dimensions of an actual body, to the viewer it is nothing but an abstract convention – a reference of measurement that is, quite literally, *disembodied*.

The notion of a disembodied measurement, however, is problematic. In the late 1960s, Mel Bochner had measured a distance of 25 inches between two pieces of paper, which he had subsequently removed – not unlike Brouwn, who 'removed' the actual reference of his measurements, namely his body. What remained was an isolated notation of 25 inches on the wall, nothing but a line and some numbers. According to the curator Brenda Richardson, the isolated measurement raised a large number of questions regarding the qualities of measurement. 'What is inside and what is outside a given measure of length or width or height? By what criterion can any unit of measurement be determined? How verifiable is a measurement?' (Bochner 2008c: 98). Bochner addressed these questions in a range of experiments. In a cardboard installation entitled 'Measurement: 36" + 36"' (1969), for example, he dealt with issues of visibility and accumulation by defining 36 inches as the width of one cardboard piece as well as that of all the visible parts of six other pieces put together. In a slightly more poetic work, 'Measurement: Plant' (1969), he measured not the plant itself but rather the projection of its shadow on the wall and the change therein. The work points to a problematic aspect of the act of measuring, namely that three-dimensional objects don't always allow for easy measurement. In order to measure something, one often depends on a one- or two-dimensional projection of the object. In other words, one often measures but a projection and not the object itself, suggesting that the act of measurement is hardly as straightforward as it may appear in popular narratives of conceptual art.

Bochner's oft-cited conclusion to all these experiments states that

> measurement reveals an essential nothing-ness. The yardstick does not say that the thing we are measuring is one yard long. Something must be added to the yardstick in order that it assert anything about the length of an object. This something is a purely mental act . . . an 'assumption'. If we subtract this assumption (avoiding any connotations of irony), what is left?
>
> (Bochner 2008c: 98)

In a 2005 essay entitled 'From Box to Street and Back Again', art historian Mark Godfrey calls upon this citation in a discussion of 'Actual Size'. He notes that

> if the photographs unusually doubled the scale of the situation, the measurement itself remained quite abstract. They did not show you how tall Bochner stood, but simply the length of his appendages. Remove the body, and the annotation would tell you nothing – for what is 12 inches alone on a wall?
> (Godfrey 2005: 33)

In reality, the 12-inch measurements did not even tell you the length of Bochner's appendages, as they acted as general references of size rather than specific measurements, but the point is that the measurement alone is essentially meaningless. It is the depiction of Bochner's body that provides us with a sense of scale, not the 12-inch measurement. Likewise, the abstracted dimensions of Brouwn's body can assert little about scale. They may tell you how many times Stanley Brouwn's foot fits into the height of a room, but they do not show 'how tall the artist stood'. Just like the terms of the empirical system – once based on bodily dimensions – they have lost all relation to actuality. They have become mere convention, or, in the words of Mel Bochner, 'signifiers with nothing to signify' (Godfrey 2005: 33), implying that the scalar equation too has collapsed and become meaningless.

This is exactly what differentiates 'Measuring the Universe' from Stanley Brouwn's works. For, while both Brouwn and Ondák refer to a certain proportion between a body and a space without that body being present, Ondák does show how tall someone stood. The terms of 'Measuring the Universe' are, in fact, quite different from those of Brouwn's spatial portraits, and so are the relations between object, body and space pronounced by the work. 'Measuring the Universe' unfolds only as a confrontation between a spectator and a specific space – the spectator's actual presence in that space, even if only for a little while, is essential. Ondák does not present the viewer with an established, though meaningless, 'fact' – 'that space measures x by y by z sb-feet' – but rather calls upon him to ascertain for himself how the height of the space relates to that of his own body.

A crucial aspect here is that Ondák never goes on to actually *measure* people. Unlike parents marking their children's height, no one ever puts a ruler to the marks made by the museum attendants. In 'Measuring the Universe', there are no numerical indications of people's heights whatsoever. Thus, contrary to Stanley Brouwn, Ondák does not reduce bodily dimensions to an abstract system of meaning that, in its turn, can be applied to a number of situations. Rather, he limits himself to projecting people's heights onto the wall, thus leaving the work grounded in the actual situation at hand. While the material component of 'Measuring the Universe' consists, just as in Brouwn's works, of little more than linguistic and numerical signs, these markings are far from absolute. Following the traditions of minimal art, their meaning is wholly dependent upon their position on the wall and in space. Here, there is no measurement to 'pick up' and apply to other things; there is only a mark on the wall that indicates the height of a body that was once there. As such, the work retains a close relation to minimal art's notion of scale and the role of the body as a reference of size. By confronting the spectator with a projection of other bodies onto space, he becomes aware of the relation of his own height to that of not only the space, but of other people as well. Unlike the projection of the length of one's stride onto the height of the room, which bears no relation to how one actually experiences that height, the marks in 'Measuring the Universe' are inherently related to how we ourselves are positioned in space. The spectator can thus relate to the markings on the wall in an actual, experiential sense rather than as abstracted measurements. Ondák does not attempt to capture or indicate the size of the body in a seemingly absolute and widely applicable abstract system, nor does he present the notion of scale as a simple equation between two dimensions; he aims to show the (past) presence of specific bodies in relation to a specific space.

Ondák's projection of people's lengths onto the wall might imply some level of abstraction; his insistence on a spectator's actual presence within the space keeps the work grounded in experience. One could say his work exists in the space of events, whereas Brouwn's exists primarily in the abstract space of statements. The terms 'space of statements' and 'space of events' are derived from a 1995 installation of Mel Bochner's 'Measurement: Room' (1969), which received the subtitle '(From the Space of Statements to the Space of Events)', and refer to categories of thought on the one hand and 'raw' material on the other. Instead of accepting the mental and the experiential as two distinct categories, Mel Bochner dedicated a large part of his career to examining the friction between abstract systems of knowledge and our experience of the world. Therefore, the artist has always insisted on coupling abstract measurements with the specific experience of the situation at hand – a coupling that, in light of this chapter, is most interestingly realised in 'Measurement: Room'.

Contrary to the works of Ondák and Brouwn, 'Measurement: Room' does not measure the body. Instead, it measures the specific architectural elements of an exhibition room and inscribes their dimensions directly onto the surface of its walls, right next to the element under consideration, resulting in what looks like a three-dimensional blueprint of the space. The abstracted space, in the form of its measurements, is thus inscribed directly onto the actual space. Yet, as Yves-Alain Bois has pointed out, the abstracted and the actual space do not coincide. 'The small intervals between the actual architectural elements (arris and apertures) and the taped mensuration were not insignificant. On the contrary, they reinforced the impression that the room had been duplicated' (Bois 1995: 168). Or, in the words of Bochner himself, '[t]he measurement projects a mental construct of the space onto the space itself' (Bois 1995: 168).

Despite the fact that 'Measurement: Room' entails the measuring of a space instead of that of a body, the work does propose a specific relation between measurement, body and space, if only because, just like in Ondák's 'Measuring the Universe', one has to actually enter the space to 'see' the work. More interestingly, though, it is exactly the fact that it is *not* a body that is being measured that makes the work such a valuable case study. In order to ascertain the work's and the measurements' relation to the body, consider the invitation card to Bochner's 1969 solo show at the Konrad Fischer Gallery in Dusseldorf.

Figure 1
Invitation card to the Mel Bochner exhibition 'Measured Room Series: 48″ Longitudinal Projection' at Konrad Fischer Gallery, Dusseldorf, 1969.

The photograph shows the artist inside his initial 'Measurement: Room' at the Heiner Friedrich Gallery in Munich, leaning against the door frame that is so often pictured to illustrate the work. In relation to the body, the measurements of the room function in much the same way as the 12-inch measurements in 'Actual Size': they are references of size, 'standard' measures to which one can compare the body but not actually measure it. Unlike in the photographs of 'Actual Size', however, Bochner does not even try to 'line up' to these measurements anymore. Instead of the controlled, static pose of 'Actual Size', the artist is nonchalantly slouched against the door frame. This is not the passive object/body that serves as a mere reference of size, as in Brouwn's spatial portraits and, to a less abstracted degree, 'Actual Size'; it is a specific subject that occupies the space. Thus, what the opposition between Bochner's casual pose and the geometric rendering of space points to is not only that the body does not allow for easy measurement or that there exists no unilateral relation between the measurements of a body and those of a space, but primarily that one's height is not the only point of reference in a relation between body and space. It suggests that the question of scale revolves not just around 'how one measures up', but more elaborately around how one occupies, uses and experiences space.

Instead of merely presenting the space or its relation to a body in the most reductive and abstract of terms, Bochner deliberately posits the subjectivity of the viewer's experience as an essential counterpart to the supposed objectivity of geometry. He highlights the tension between our experience of the world and the terms in which we try to grasp it. This confrontation between a space of statements and a space of events illustrates that abstraction is a one-way street and that, while our experience may be influenced by dimensional notations, the latter can never replace that experience. No matter how accurate a geometric description, 'our only means of verification', as Bochner once explained in an interview with Lisa Haller, 'is our own experience' (Bochner 2008a: 108). While at significantly different levels of bodily and spatial engagement, the works discussed in this chapter eventually all underline the impossibility of reducing body and space to mere dimension, to pure references of size. For, while the measurement might be disembodied, the spectator never is, and the work never appears in a spatial vacuum.

Body and scale (reprise)

Each artwork asks a spectator to relate to it, and it is this relation that constitutes a work's scale, not the object–body–space relations within the work. Thus, if Ondák asserts that 'Measuring the Universe' has the same status with one as with a thousand marks, he does so because what matters is each spectator's personal experience of his relation to the space, not the average proportion of space to spectator. Likewise, the scale of Stanley Brouwn's works is not the proportional relation between the artist's body and the space 'portrayed', but rather that between the spectator and the 'portrait'. As 'spectators' of these abstracted measurements, our relation to the work is dependent on a specific frame of reference, just as in representation. Only, as we cannot grasp

Brouwn's works in their purely notational form, the work itself does not provide us with such a frame. The measurements themselves mean little to us, and we inevitably project them back onto our own situation, considering that, if Brouwn's feet are more or less the same size as ours, the space represented in his portrait must be slightly higher than the one we are in, for example. Maybe we even walk through the space, retracing Brouwn's steps, even though they were taken at an entirely different place. Our confrontation with even a simple dimensional notation, even if it refers to a wholly different situation, inevitably triggers a certain experiential relation to our own situation. Thus, the use of measurements does not reduce the matter of scale to a purely dimensional rapport, nor does it collapse the relation into abstract meaninglessness. Rather, the measurement pieces show that a scalar relation between body and space considers more than just one's height or size; it also considers how one uses, occupies and experiences space in terms of size, movement and time. If scale is considered as a relation between the spectator and a work of art, works of conceptual art underline the origin of such relations in subjective experience.

Notes

1. Contrary to the sb-foot and the sb-ell, measuring 27 cm and 47 cm respectively, the sb-step is not considered an absolute dimension. Rather, the length of Stanley Brouwn's stride was re-ascertained with every application of it, explaining the different definitions of an sb-step.
2. The term refers to how 'Conceptual art came to displace even that image of the mass-produced object and its aestheticized forms in Pop art, replacing an aesthetic of industrial production and consumption with an aesthetic of administrative and legal organization and institutional validation' (Buchloh 1999).

Scaling haptics – haptic scaling

Studying scale and scaling in the haptic design process of two architects who lost their sight

Peter-Willem Vermeersch and Ann Heylighen

In this chapter, we explore how two architects who lost their sight found ways of continuing their practice.[1] The first architect we study is Carlos Mourão Pereira, a Portuguese architect who lost his sight in 2006. However, he continues to run his small-scale office and even found his sight loss an opportunity to further his understandings of the multi-sensory nature of the built environment. In this context, he started designing a series of bathing facilities, and our study focuses on the design of one facility in particular: the Sea Bathing Facility in Lourinha on the Portuguese coast. These facilities are not yet built; for Pereira, they are in the first place a way to learn new design methods and explore his new understandings of space. The second architect, Christopher Downey, already had a more extensive career in architecture when he lost his sight. But, like Pereira, he chose to continue his design practice. He joined Smith Group, an architecture firm based in San Francisco, to assist them in the design of a new polytrauma and blind rehabilitation centre in Palo Alto. He is a design consultant for people with a visual impairment and assists in the communication with the client organisation, of which some people are blind as well.

Staging the question of scale and haptic perception

In both Pereira's and Downey's practices, as in any architectural practice, scaled representations play an important role in the design process. Scale in architecture considers the different relations between a building and its elements, its environment or context, the human body, and the design process. Furthermore, these static notions of *scale* can be extended with a more dynamic notion of *scaling* to describe how architects develop a design by moving cyclically between different scaled models.

For Ralf Weber and Silke Vosskoeter (2008), scale is defined as 'the perceived or apparent size of a building'. They analyse scale, then, in terms of human scale, outer scale and inner scale; in other words, how the building relates to the size of people, the context of the building and the building's individual architectural elements. This notion of scale only concerns the perception of an existing building. Phillipe Boudon (1971), on the other hand, defines scale as a relationship between the conceived architectural space and the perceived architectural space, linking the building to its conception; that is, the design process. Architectural space in this definition is 'a whole consisting of two spaces, real space and mental space' and scale is 'the rule of transition of one space into the other'. Albena Yaneva (2005) goes even a step further in relating the notion of scale to the design process. She argues that it is insufficient to understand scale as a static notion of a proportional relation between a model and the real building, referring back to Boudon. Instead, she advances the more dynamic notion of scaling as 'some frequently repeated moves, such as "scale up", "jump", "scale down". Their successive repetition and redundancy compose a rhythmic conduit through which the building develops'.

However, the notions of scale discussed so far are interpreted implicitly or explicitly in a mainly visual way. Overall, architecture is characterised by a bias towards the visual. This features in how the built environment is analysed in architecture (Pallasmaa 2005), but also in the way designers in general think and work (Cross 1982). Martha Dischinger (2006) finds evidence for this overemphasis on the visual (and also intellectual and conceptual) dimensions of architecture in the traditional tools to represent architecture using mostly visual media. Both Pereira and Downey thus had to reinterpret, or even reinvent, the tools and representations they were used to in their design practice to overcome the consequences of this visual bias in architecture and its design process. They rely more on their other senses when interacting with their tools and representations. For instance, Pereira experiments with sound, and even smell, for the (re)presentation of his sea-bathing facility, a basin that offers a multi-sensory experience of the sea in a safe and more controlled environment (Vermeersch and Heylighen 2011). But when it comes to their day-to-day design practice, both architects rely to a large extent on their haptic sense to interact with the numerous artefacts involved in designing.

We will refer to the design tools Pereira and Downey use as haptic. They are developed to provide design information through the skin and muscles of the hands. Jack Loomis and Susan Lederman (1986) define haptic perception as a combination of tactile perception and kinaesthetic perception. Tactile perception is mediated solely by variations in cutaneous stimulation, which provides information by means of receptors in the skin. The cutaneous sense can inform you, for example, of the temperature, roughness or texture of a certain material. Likewise, kinaesthetic perception is mediated by variations in kinaesthetic stimulation, which provides information about dynamic and static body posture by the relative positioning of head, torso and limbs. For instance, perception of the length of a rod held between thumb and index finger is informed by kinaesthesis. So when Pereira and Downey evaluate a model by taking it in their hands, or letting their hands move over its surfaces, they are informed of its shape, size, temperature and texture by the haptic sense through their fingertips, and the relative positions of their fingers, hands and arms.

How, then, are design artefacts used in a haptic way? And how does this relate to certain haptic qualities that Pereira and Downey want to investigate through these scaled representations?[2] One aspect that makes visual representation so powerful is optical consistency while scaling, so that different scales (for example, city and building, building and building detail) can be reshuffled and recombined (Latour 1990). However, when trying to find these qualities in haptic representations, this seems problematic at first sight, because of the proximal nature of the haptic sense. While scaling in visual terms maintains internal proportions – the elements of a pattern look smaller when taking a few steps back, but the pattern itself is not perceived differently – this is not so evident for a haptic pattern. Taking a few steps back is not possible when dealing with haptic perception. Scaling the texture of a surface will maintain internal proportions, but the haptic perception of that texture will alter much more distinctively than when perceiving that texture mainly visually.

Haptic design tools for a dynamic design process

When Christopher Downey joined the Smith Group, he had to find a way of designing that could fit in with the day-to-day practice of the architects working there. As they rely heavily on BIM (building information modelling) based on an integrated CAD model, Downey had to find a way to access the CAD drawings taken from this model and to formulate and communicate design ideas based on his interpretation. Therefore, he plots these drawings on an embossing printer (a type of matrix printer that prints Braille dots and patterns on a thick sheet of paper), which he can then read with his fingertips and hands. To design, he combines these drawings with Wikki Stix®, wax sticks he can cut, bend and stick to each other and to the paper (Figure 1). This allows him to test design ideas by shaping some sticks and temporarily fixing them to the original drawing. After reading the whole with his hands again, he can re-adjust the sticks and manipulate the sketch he has just made, analogous to sketching on tracing paper laid over a print-out or another drawing.

In Pereira's case, we observed a similar dynamic process of manipulating and (re-)interpreting a design situation, but in a way that is somewhat further removed from more day-to-day architectural design tools. Pereira too uses his hands to explore a model or a raised line drawing, and to manipulate that model or drawing, but his hands sometimes even become the model. In a conversation we observed, Pereira used his hands to explain a certain shape to one of his collaborators. His collaborator took that hand and started pointing on it to address specific points in the design, and even started gently manipulating the shape of Pereira's hands. This became a very fluent process of fixing and manipulating to further develop this shape. As Pereira explained, 'the hands can become anything', so they can change scale level almost instantly within a design conversation. Using their hands, Pereira and his collaborator can go back and forth between building part, building, site and so on.

Figure 1
Christopher Downey combining Braille plots with wax sticks to design.

Both Pereira and Downey are seeking in their more haptic design practice to incorporate artefacts that allow them to dynamically develop their design ideas in interaction with spatial representations and other collaborators. A design is not just an outcome of a process going on in the designer's mind, but grows in the interaction between the designer's thoughts, actions (like sketching) and the objects being created (like drawings). Donald Schön (1983) describes this process as a reflection-in-action, where '[the designer] shapes the situation, in accordance with this initial appreciation of it, the situation 'talks back', and he responds to the situation's back-talk'. Yaneva (2005) relates these interpretative actions of designers to not just one drawing, but to a particular rhythm of scaling up and scaling down, as moving between different scaled models of a design. In the example of Pereira, we observed this process of scaling as it occurred within a single flexible 'model' being the hands of Pereira and his collaborator. This way of designing is almost like a conversation in that it allows for a flexible interpretation and a quick change in configuration, but it has the advantage of a model as it constitutes a spatial representation. On the other hand, it is more fleeting in nature as there are no physical traces of this haptic communication.

Of course, Pereira also makes more lasting representations of his designs, and again we observed this concern with different scales of models that together form the sea-bathing facility. What the right scale is for one of these models depends on the aspect of the design that needs to be investigated, the haptic nature of handling the model and the model itself. For instance, Pereira makes a series of models of the sea-bathing facility that all concern certain aspects of the design, from the larger context of the site to a more detailed spatial configuration of the bath itself. These models are all at different scales, but of approximately the same size. Bryan Lawson (1994) has found a similar phenomenon in a more traditional visual design process. Several architects he interviewed liked to sketch on a sheet of A4 or A3 paper because this allows for a quick overview. The size of the models Pereira makes also allows for a quick 'overview', not in a visual sense, but haptically. The size of Pereira's models is thus partly characterised by how he can encompass these models by his hands allowing for an exploration of a specific detail without losing contact, literally, with the broader context of the whole model (Figure 2).

Next to these smaller models, Pereira makes (or asks a collaborator to make) larger models where his hands can go inside. These give him more information about

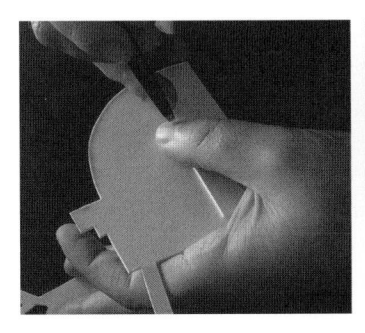

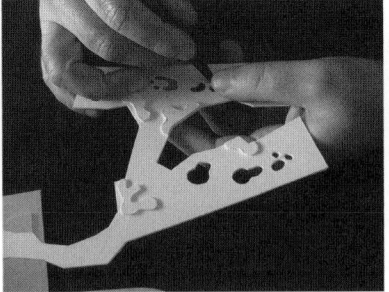

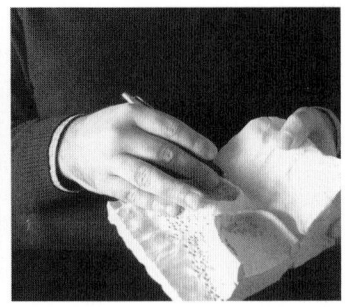

Figure 2
Carlos Pereira using multiple models at different scales encompassed by his hands.

the spatial qualities. We perceive spaces from within, so besides models he can encompass with his hands, Pereira also needs models he can enter with his hands to let his hands be encompassed by them. These models are of course larger than the former ones, but together they allow Pereira to go from a representation of the whole to a more detailed representation of the space itself. In a workshop with students, we observed how, at one point, he felt both types of models at the same time. A student had to explain a house using a number of 3D models she made. One smaller model gave an impression of the outer volumetric of the house, and could be held by Pereira in one hand. The other model was larger and represented the different volumes of the separate spaces of the house. The latter gave him more detailed information about the spatial qualities of the inside of the house, while the former allowed him to put these spaces in the context of the larger whole.

Like Pereira, Downey too had to overcome some particularities of haptic perception when producing his Braille prints. For him, it was not possible to just print out the CAD drawings that his colleagues had produced for an ink and paper plot. As he remarks: 'you need to get the size that is appropriate, and you need to shed some information. [. . .] Visually you can easily separate things, but if all that becomes tactile, it's overwhelming.' He had to find the appropriate scale to be able to read the different plans, sections, elevations and so on with his hands. But also the limitations of the technology to create these drawings have their impact on the chosen scale. The maximum paper size is A3 and the resolution (the distance between the raised dots) is limited. Therefore, Downey needs to discuss with a colleague how to adapt the amount of information in a single drawing and its appropriate output scale. Unlike Pereira, who makes models to the size of his hands, Downey chooses to print out the drawings as large as possible to incorporate as much detail as possible. He then reads such drawings part by part to get a gradual understanding of the whole.

Haptic design tools and haptic design qualities

In the previous section, we explored how Pereira and Downey had to alter their design practices to keep designing, and how they did so by relying mostly on their haptic sense. In the next section, we will further analyse how this haptic design process relates to haptic qualities of their designs. Their specific interaction with the haptic models they make allows them to investigate certain qualities that are more in line with their ambitions to develop a more multi-sensory architecture, learning from their bodily experience of the built environment.

Since Pereira lost his sight, he started developing a new understanding about aesthetics in architecture. Before, he was searching for a strong visual image, much in line with contemporary Portuguese architecture: clean surfaces meeting in distinct sharp edges, making for a clear visual composition and interplay of lines. Now he rather explores shapes that are more comfortable to touch, no sharp edges that cut the hand, but shapes that are better adapted to the hand and invite to touch (Vermeersch and Heylighen 2010). Very important for him in this sense is how he can gain an adequate understanding of the haptic qualities he is trying to pursue in his design. As described above, haptically representing architectural concepts about, for example, location, approaching a site, general layout and so on, is one thing. However, actually representing the haptic qualities of a building is something different. One point of departure for both Downey and Pereira is that certain places in a building are more likely to be touched than others, and when designing for the haptic sense you should first and foremost pay attention to those spots.

To begin their exploration of a building's haptic qualities, Pereira and Downey concentrated first on discrete points in space where people are already touching (parts of) the building. Downey mentions doorknobs, handrails, table tops and so on; Pereira pays considerable attention to the design of handrails and also mentions doorknobs, window sills and so on. The small size of these parts allows them to explore these on a scale of one to one, which is a very appropriate scale to get haptic feedback. For instance, Pereira makes clay models to explore the haptic aspects of a particular shape, such as the ending of a handrail (Figure 3). In such models, the material is of less importance for him, and is dictated by the ease of working and the shape he wants to test, rather than by the tactile aspects of, for instance, the texture. Even on a scale of one to one, they still work with models and not with prototypes.

In this same sense, Downey reinterpreted a tool already in use in the design firm he joined. The interior designer there used to work with material palettes to get a feeling of the visual composition of materials in future spaces. At one meeting they discussed the difference in texture between two flooring materials, which were chosen by the interior designer to contrast with each other. But this choice was mostly informed by the visual sense. In the discussion, which usually proceeded verbally and visually, Downey put the materials on the floor and tried to distinguish between these materials by moving his cane over them, and found no such contrast. In this example, the shapes of the material samples are less important; rather, it is all about the difference in textures of flooring materials and the differences that are perceivable through a cane.

When Boudon (1971) studied the question of scale in architecture, he was still discussing the design process in architecture as a mental matter. However, architects have distributed their design and building processes over multiple artefacts from as early as 2100 BC, increasingly so as history progressed (Porter 1997). So when Boudon defines scale as the rule of transition between real space and mental space, we should

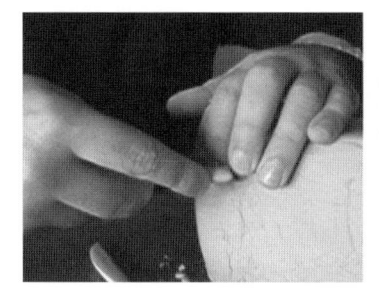

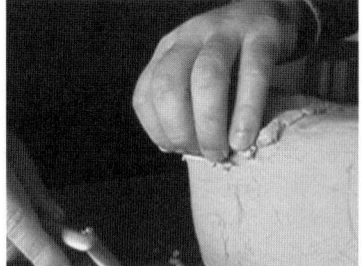

Figure 3
Carlos Pereira exploring haptic qualities while shaping a clay model.

regard the mental space as only partly playing out inside our minds and for the other part being distributed over the different externalized representations produced in a design process. How the conceived architectural space relates to the perceived architectural space then becomes apparent in the design process of Pereira and Downey. We observe a close similarity between their haptic perception of the models and artefacts they use in their design process and the aspired haptic qualities in the designed building or part of the building.

When Pereira is shaping the end of a handrail using a block of clay (Figure 3), the movements he makes with his hands during that process are analogous to the movements his hands would make using that handrail. During this process he manipulates and interprets the model, both in a haptic way. His haptic reading then informs him of the haptic qualities of the handrail he is designing. Tim Ingold (2000), in discussing the theories of James Gibson and Maurice Merleau-Ponty, reminds us of the importance and the role of movement in the act of perception. We are not motionless observers of our environment, but we are actively seeking out information in that environment. If we perceive a space, we are mostly moving through it and, even if we take a pause in our walk, we still move our heads, scanning the environment with our eyes, while sounds and smells come to us informing us of our next steps. Therefore, the relation between the movements Pereira and Downey make during their reading of their respective haptic models and the movements they make in the built environment allows them to anticipate haptic qualities while designing.

Although Pereira and Downey interact in a similar way with their models as with the environment these models represent, this is not a literal translation. When Downey puts the material samples on the floor, he is still limited in his movement by the size of the samples, and focuses specifically on the question of transition and contrast. Also, when Pereira shapes his clay model of a handrail, he still sits at his desk and is not moving down the stairs. Peter Paul Verbeek (2005) uses the concepts of 'reduction' and 'amplification' to discuss how objects, and thus also design tools, mediate our perception of the environment. These design tools allow Pereira and Downey to focus on a certain aspect of a material or a distinct part of a building, but these models are still representations and not the building itself. The interaction with these samples then is also partial in comparison with the eventual interaction with the built environment, but nonetheless brings Pereira and Downey closer to a perception of what it could be.

The models and samples used in the above examples are still on a scale of one to one and thus allow for a direct comparison between the perceptions of the models and of the built environment. They can give an equivalent impression of the haptic qualities in these design solutions. But we also found some more immediate analogues between the haptic reading of a scaled drawing or model and how Pereira and Downey move through a building. Due to Downey's choice of printing his Braille drawings on a larger format of paper, he has to explore that drawing sequentially. The way he then moves his hands over a plan, for instance, follows the same lines and routes as if he walked through that building, and he searches with his fingers for elements he would search for in that space with his cane. In the interview, he refers to the position of columns in a corridor. One idea was to place them in front of the wall, but as Downey went through the plans, he found that this would hinder his movement through that corridor as he would be unable to just follow the wall with his cane (or follow the line representing the wall on the Braille plan with his finger).

We found a similar handling of scaled models in the case of Pereira. He also moves through his larger models, those he intended to go into with his hands, by following the walls with his fingers as if he were exploring that space when built. In a sense, his finger becomes his body, mimicking bodily movements through space, and thus informing him about the perceptual qualities of the design. For Boudon (1971), scale had to do with the relation between conception and perception, but as these examples clearly illustrate, the process of conception cannot take place without perception. For instance, perspective drawings are widely used in architecture to give an impression of the visually perceivable qualities of a design. However, as Porter (1997) remarks, 'perspective was a contradiction to the very nature of visual perception as it caused the viewer to freeze in time and space'. On the other hand, in the design processes of Pereira and Downey, this aspect of motion is crucial to their haptic interpretation of the representations they make in such a way that it relates to their own haptic perception of the environment. Therefore, the decisions they make concerning these haptic qualities, be it through a model on a scale of one to one or on a smaller scale, are informed by a process of perception itself. In that sense, we could state that scale is also a relation between perception in the design process and our perception of the built form.

If movement is crucial in the perception of the (built) environment, as Ingold (2000) pointed out, it is equally important in the perception of tools used in the design process. Although these movements are not entirely the same, as we have argued, in a way they are linked through the architecture of models and building, allowing the architects to use movement within the model to get an impression of what the movement in the built form might be like, and vice versa. Perception of the built environment might colour the way Pereira and Downey perceive their models, and how they relate one with the other. Or, as Boudon (1971) formulates it: 'just like the conception of architectural space makes perception intervene, the perception of the architectural space cannot take place without letting conception intervene'.

In addressing the notion of scale, we studied the design tools of two architects who lost their sight at a certain point in their careers, and who then decided to continue their design practices. Our study focused on the haptic aspects of the tools they use, and how these tools help them to design for haptic perception. Most of these tools in themselves are not so distant from the known tools used in the design process in architecture, but Pereira and Downey use them in a haptic rather than visual way. The power that resides in scale and scaling is explained, in part, by optical consistency. This aspect, however, is not so readily transferrable to further an understanding of how scaled representations can help a design process in architecture based (for the most part) on haptic perception – within this design process, but also in relation to the built environment. Nevertheless, both Pereira and Downey still use scaled models and drawings to design. They scale whole buildings or specific elements to the size appropriate, not for a quick overview but for encompassing or exploring with their hands. Yet also what they want to investigate with these models and drawings is also important in choosing the right scale. First focusing on specific building elements to explore haptic qualities of a design, they work at a scale of one to one, relating their perception of the model closely to the perception of, say, the handrail to be built. But also in smaller-scale models or drawings, we observed how the way in which they move through a raised line plan or a model is not so far off from how they would move through that environment when built.

The study of scale in the haptic tools Pereira and Downey use teaches us that scale has to do not only with the relation between conception and perception, or with moving between representations. Scale also relates perception of models and drawings to the perception of the environment to be built.

Acknowledgements

This study has received funding from the European Research Council under the European Community's Seventh Framework Programme (FP7/2007–13)/ERC grant agreement no. 201673. Peter-Willem Vermeersch received support from the Research Fund K.U. Leuven. We would like to thank Megan Strickfaden and Greg Nijs for their share in the data collection. Last, but not least, we would like to thank Carlos Mourão Pereira and Christopher Downey for their time, enthusiasm, patience and honesty.

Notes

1. The material we base our studies on comes from multiple sources. The study of Chris Downey relies on published materials and a semi-structured in-depth interview we conducted in the office where he works. For the study of Carlos Mourão Pereira, the material comes from published documents (writings, drawings and photographs) and a semi-structured in-depth interview, complemented with observations in his office and observations of a workshop with students. The interviews were audio-recorded and transcribed for further analysis. The observations were recorded in field notes, and photographs and video taken by a collaborator of Pereira.
2. Pioneering work on haptic qualities in the built environment has been conducted by Jasmien Herssens. She studies haptic perception in architecture by working together with blind people and learning from their daily interaction with the built environment (Herssens and Heylighen 2009, 2010, 2011). Her work inspired us to further study aspects of haptic perception in the design process.

Scale adjustment in architecture and music

Richard Coyne

It is well known that Canterbury Cathedral has a bent plan (Barmore and Borst 1969). It also has a pulpitum that separates the nave from the choir. The visitor can see the roof vaults above this ornate stone barrier, but in spite of a narrow central doorway the pulpitum prevents a clear line of sight from one end of the cathedral to the other, and thus occludes the kink in the plan.

This screening device brings to mind the constant necessity to cover over, or otherwise accommodate, discrepancies in architecture. Colin Rowe observes that architecture has to cope with 'the conflict between the absolute and the contingent, the abstract and the natural; and the gap between the ideal world and the too human exigencies of realization' (Rowe 1976: 14). Such accommodation is accomplished by an adjustment of some kind. The need for architectural correctives has several sources: work practices that deviate from some expected standard (that is, 'poor workmanship'), site contingencies, design tolerances, drifts and shifts during and after construction, the deliberate introduction of deviation by workmen and designers, the transposition from one measuring system (scale) to another, and when geometry presents apparent inconsistencies. I will explore this last issue in some detail in what follows, though it is fair to say that these factors are readily conflated or combined in architecture. Architects, builders and regulators have to be concerned constantly with the task of monitoring, controlling, ameliorating and repairing discrepancy, of whatever cause. The processes of such accommodation are brought into sharp relief in the construction of Gothic cathedrals, built in many cases without a plan, and with accretions and corrections over many generations. David Turnbull describes Chartres Cathedral as the product of 'messy heterogeneous practices', and 'the ad hoc accumulation of the work of many men' (Turnbull 1993: 315). Though he is describing pre-modern practices and understandings, Turnbull is quick to point out that the construction of the Gothic is close to the way philosophers of science describe the workings of the modern scientific laboratory. The study of medieval masonry and carpentry reveals something about contemporary practice. As I will show, architecture in general shares with music the need to adjust to discrepancies.

Musical and architectural scales

Architecture and music both have an investment in the issue of scale. In building we think of scale as pertaining to a successive and consistent alteration in size. The metaphor is that of climbing a ladder. Things get smaller or larger to view as you ascend or descend a ladder or series of steps (*escalier*). A musical scale is similar. Ascending the musical scale, accomplished by successively shorter strings or tubes, produces sounds that are of higher pitch. In both architecture and music, the use of scale is regular, calculable and predictable.

Both architecture and music are concerned with the mapping or transposition of one scale system onto another, which again lends itself to calculation. Think of the simple calculation required to transpose drawings or models from a scale of 1:100 to 1:50, especially with CAD (computer-aided drafting) systems. In the early days of metrication, and with less ease, a draughtsman frequently had to transpose drawings from 1/8":1' 0" (or 1:96) to 1:100. Similar scale-based transposition is common in music. Think of transposing a melody up one octave, easily accomplished on a keyboard by moving the fingers to the right by eight white notes on the keyboard, effectively deploying a set of strings of half the length. In Western classical music, an octave is divided into twelve uniformly specified divisions, to make the twelve-note scale. As anyone with a rudimentary knowledge of music knows, the notes of any scale are not laid out as even divisions, as on an architect's scale rule, but into a sequence of notes and half-notes, organised as the white and black keys of the keyboard. Transposing a melody from the C major to the G major scale involves introducing black notes into the transposition (F sharp for the G major scale), and complex musical compositions may incorporate many transpositions across scales.

Le Corbusier begins his book *The Modulor* in praise of classical music's use of its standardised musical scale system, the equivalent of which he hopes to establish for the visual arts (Le Corbusier 2004). For all its ambition, the modulor is not at the acme of proportioning and measuring systems in architecture, but I hope to show how it does exemplify issues of discrepancy in architecture.

Le Corbusier's new system of measurement and proportion was to unite the metric and imperial systems, and relate both to an idealised and abstracted form of the human body through the Fibonacci number series (Figure 1). Of course, the series has no obvious relationship to classical musical scales. The series progresses by adding 1 and 1 to make 2, 1 plus 2 makes 3, 2 plus 3 makes 5, 3 plus 5 makes 8, and so on. The series progresses by adding the last two numbers together to create the next number in the series. As one progresses through the series, the ratio between any two adjacent numbers approaches the ratio of *phi* (φ), ($\sqrt{5}+1$)/2. This ratio is sometimes referred to as the 'golden section' and approximates to 1:1.618. The Fibonacci series begins with a ratio of 1:1, the sides of a square, and progresses to the sides of a rectangle that conforms to the golden section, the classical proportion that keeps cropping up in the construction of the Platonic solids, and that Renaissance theorists thought pleasing and beautiful to the eye (Wittkower 1998).

Figure 1 The modulor system cast into an external wall of Le Corbusier's Unité de Habitation, Marseilles.

As Le Corbusier also indicates, the golden section is more simply constructed from a square divided with a line drawn orthogonally down the middle. By simple manipulation of a compass, the diagonal of the half square can be added to the short side to produce a new rectangle with sides in the ϕ ratio. As analysts of the modulor system point out, there are many practical and theoretical flaws with Le Corbusier's translation of the Fibonacci series into a system for dimensioning buildings (Loach 1998; Padovan 1999). As I shall indicate, it is the flaws and discrepancies in such systems that carry theoretical importance for architecture.

The architecture–music legacy

Interest in relating musical scales to architecture flourished in the Renaissance. Rudolf Wittkower provides a well-known account of how architects such as Francesco di

Giorgio, Alberti and Palladio wrestled with the relationships between proportions in both music and architecture. According to Wittkower, for Alberti, 'music and geometry are fundamentally one and the same; that music is geometry translated into sound, and that in music the very same harmonies are audible which inform the geometry of the building' (Wittkower 1998: 19). The mappings between the domains of architecture and music involved the preservation of ratios, rather than numbers or actual dimensions. Musical ratios pertain to harmonies that Renaissance architects attempted to relate to the whole-number proportioning of rooms and the dimensions of facades (Wittkower 1998: 105).

In less formal terms, architecture and music have been related through the concept of architecture as 'frozen music', a metaphor attributed to both Johann Wolfgang von Goethe, and Friedrich von Schelling in his *Philosophie der Kunst*: '[Architecture] is music in space, as it were a frozen music' (Schelling 1989). More recently, sound theorist Murray Schafer brought the relationship between music and placemaking into sharp relief. In his book *The Tuning of the World*, Schafer suggested that theorists think of the occupants of space as composers and performers, responsible for giving form and beauty to their environment through sound. He refers to Robert Fludd's (1574–1637) famous illustration 'The Tuning of the World', 'in which the earth forms the body of an instrument across which strings are stretched and are tuned by a divine hand'. According to Schafer, we 'must try again to find the secret of that tuning' (Schafer 1977: 6). Tuning is a kind of adjustment.

So attention to music introduces some valuable terms into architecture, namely adjustment and tuning. Rather than harmonies and perfect ratios, I maintain that the theme of adjustment provides the important link between architecture and music. Tuning is a process of adjustment, an activity crucial to the creation of music, and, as I hope to make clear, also to architecture.

The comma

Musicians are familiar with the discrepancies evident in musical scale systems. As I will explain in what follows, the so-called cycle of fifths and the cycle of octaves work together to produce a harmonious and well-ordered system of relationships between notes – though not quite. The superimposition of the two systems that is so essential for free and inventive modulation across musical scales in fact produces discord. By most accounts, advances in the expressive power of music were accomplished with the invention of standardised adjustments to the twelve-tone musical scale system around the time of J.S. Bach (1685–1750) to produce the even-tempered musical scale. It is worth dwelling for a moment on the issue of musical temperament, well explained in authoritative texts (Murray Barbour 2004), and given ample attention on numerous websites. Musical notes related to each other by half an octave produce sympathetic resonances, and sound harmonious. Half an octave above C is the note G. You need to make a string 2/3 of the original length to achieve this ratio. The half octave above G is D, followed by A, E, B, F#, C#, G#, D#, A#, F, and back to C. Musical scales and harmonies

```
C       —
F       —
A#      —
D#      —
G#      —
C#   C  —
F#   C  —
B    C  —
E    C  —
A    C  —
D    C  —
G    C  —
C
```

make use of this so-called cycle of fifths, which encapsulates important relationships. The cycle is a useful way of modulating between scales; that is, it demonstrates relationships between musical scales (or keys). There are twelve keys in this sequence, from C to C (Figure 2). Traversing the musical scale in this way spans seven octaves. However, if you traverse the same octaves by successively halving the length of a string, then you arrive at a slightly different note. You are about a quarter of a note out. The name for this discrepancy is the 'comma' (the Pythagorean or diatonic comma), a comma being a slight pause or gap. This discrepancy or remainder is about a quarter of a semitone accumulated across seven octaves. It is easily calculated as a ratio between a string successively reduced in length by 2/3 (twelve times) and a string successively halved (seven times): $(3/2)^{12}/2^7$. It would be neater, and make the transposition between musical scales more direct, if this ratio turned out to be 1:1. It's close, at 1:1.0136 (to four decimal places). The discrepancy (0.0136 of an octave) is the comma.

To remove the discordant effects of this discrepancy, musical instruments must be slightly detuned across each note to spread the disharmony caused by the progression of octaves when overlaid with the progression of fifths. The ears of most listeners don't pick up these adjustments, but can tell the difference between a piece of classical music played on a modern, even-tempered piano and an early clavichord on which these adjustments have not been made. The latter will sound out of tune. Le Corbusier references the standardised even-tempered musical scale system as a stimulus for his own system of standardisation in architectural dimensioning.

Figure 2
Successive halving of a string length to create an octave series, interlaced with a successive division by 2/3 to produce a series of fifths. The shortest length in each series is the same note C, were it not for the discrepancy of the comma.

Adjustments in architecture and music

What are the parallels between the sources of discrepancy in architecture and in music? Architecture has to deal with standards of workmanship. When detected, error and short cuts require correctives and cover-ups. Standards are obviously a major issue in the manufacture of musical instruments and in performance, requiring correction, adjustment and repair, 'a fundamental category of craftsmanship' according to philosopher and sociologist Richard Sennett, writing in *The Craftsman* (Sennett 2008: 248).

If architecture has to cope with 'the conflict between the absolute and the contingent' (Rowe 1976: 14), then site contingencies in building are comparable to changes in the environment in which music is performed, where instruments have to be adjusted to different temperature and humidity conditions, not to mention adjustment to the acoustical properties of the architectural spaces they occupy.

Buildings and components have expansion joints in any case, as well as built-in tolerances and gaps to enable positioning and securing. Musical instruments are designed in a similar manner to be adjusted, and have tolerances, not least in the deployment of tuning pegs, adjustable mouthpieces and variable tube lengths. Both architecture and music must deal with design tolerances. In the case of architecture, there are changes that occur as window frames and other components are moved to site. The process of transportation loosens joints and puts things out of alignment. These discrepancies have to be corrected, filled in or repaired. So too the pitch and sound qualities of musical instruments drift and shift during transportation, and during performance, corrected by re-tuning.

In architecture, designers and tradesmen may deliberately introduce deviations from design standards and specifications to leave their own individual mark or signature. Musical interpretation involves minor adjustments to the composition and in response to the other players, evident most conspicuously in the case of musical improvisation. The philosopher Alfred Schutz describes the character of ensemble playing in which musicians 'tune-in' to one another's playing (Schutz 1964). This kind of adjustment goes on all the time as participants in musical ensembles adjust to each other's quirks and practices. Something similar occurs in the case of any social grouping, such as a design team or project team on site.

The need for adjustment also appears in architecture in response to errors introduced by moving from one scale system to another, as in the case of converting from imperial to metric units. In music, there are discrepancies in moving from a notational system belonging to the piano to that of the guitar, a sitar to a harp, and, as we have seen, even the relatively simple transposition between the various Western musical scales.

On the issue of geometrical inconsistencies, architectural geometry presents various challenges, such as the task of 'squaring the circle'. Many regular (Platonic) shapes such as an equilateral triangle and a hexagon can be constructed perfectly by means of only a compass and straight edge. Classical geometers thought it ought also to be possible to derive a square from a circle, where the square encloses the same area as the circle from which it is derived. The so-called Vitruvian man, the geometer, ought to exercise mastery over both the circle of the heavens and the square of the earth. 'Squaring the circle' with a compass and a straight edge turns out not to be possible (Jagy 1995), other than as an approximation.

Le Corbusier demonstrates similar faith in a geometrical impossibility. It is well known that in trying to derive the modulor dimensioning system, Le Corbusier thought that by using a simple geometrical extension you could derive a rectangle with sides 1:2 from a rectangle with sides of the ratio 1:φ. After all, adjacent squares make plans and facades that fit a Modernist aesthetic of symmetry and simplicity. In his book on architectural proportion, Richard Padovan explains that a mathematician friend of Le Corbusier confirmed that his constructive method was out by the fraction 0.006 from what he expected (Padovan 1999). In other words, adherence to the rules and methods of geometry does not always produce the results or preserve the simplicity expected. It seems that the blighting of geometrical expectations and the introduction of pragmatic adjustments pervades the modulor (Loach 1998). Though it remains of historical and theoretical interest to architects, the modulor has *not* been adopted in architectural dimensioning. The modulor also provides a further inadvertent link to music.

In music, our intuition tells us that musical scales ought to work in a certain way, that progression along the cycle of fifths ought to lead to harmonisations and smooth modulations. But these can only be accomplished by means of adjustments to create an even-tempered tuning. Though there are standard adjustments that can be made, these are not determined from the mathematics or geometry of music, and have to be introduced from outside. Though less constrained by microscopic arithmetical and geometrical calculation, it seems that architecture is similarly subject to the necessity for adjustment.

There are many differences between architecture and music, of course. Architectural construction is subject to regulation, legislative constraints, quality control, management, a multitude of skills, management systems, an acute division and organisation of labour, and operates over long time scales. But music can be similarly described. I contend that discrepancy has as much entitlement to bridging these two disparate disciplines as concepts of harmony and proportion. The need for adjustments is an embarrassment not only to Le Corbusier's modulor, but arguably to the ancient concept of the 'music of the spheres', that the universe accords with perfect harmonic ratios. At the very least, these problems direct the scholar intent on establishing relationships between architecture and music elsewhere than harmony, beauty and perfect ratios.

Theorising adjustment

The implementation of adjustments, to allow architecture (whether in its craft or idealised proportioning) and music to function, is understandably under-theorised in the classical literature. We are dealing here with deviation from standard and fixed universal methods of making. Any adjustment method cannot easily be generalised and subjected to rule. For the classically trained, geometry is at the pinnacle of theory. So it is little wonder that the classical literature on architecture has little to say about adjustment.

I have already suggested that tuning provides a further metaphor of this process of adjustment. Architects and others in the practical arts make only oblique reference to the language of tuning, detuning, calibration, tolerance, drift, slippage, the gap or the remainder. The Pythagorean comma in music is a remaindered partial note that must be spread among the ordinary notes in a scale series to make them transportable (that is, to facilitate modulation between keys). The remainder is a discomfiture at the margins that after all gets redistributed to bolster the existence of the authorised and the legitimate.

A recognition of the need to make adjustment is, however, nascent in the classical architectural literature. How else could things be brought into alignment but by adjustment? Vitruvius indicates how the construction of buildings necessarily involves fine-tuning (Vitruvius 1960): 'The length of a temple is *adjusted* so that its width may be half its length' (114); 'Order . . . is an *adjustment* according to quantity' (72). It seems that harmony, order and symmetry depend on proper adjustment, as if things need to be brought into alignment from an initial position that is a deviation from the norm or the ideal. Adjustment is an active term, and resonates with processes on a construction site. Blocks of stone do not just fall into place, but have to be manoeuvred. The Latin word rendered as 'adjustment' in English translations of Vitruvius is *temperantur*, a form of the verb *temperare*, to which temperature also relates, and which, according to the *Oxford English Dictionary*, carries connotations of dividing proportionally, combining properly, keeping within limits, regulating, tempering and, of course, even-temperament. Adaptation to local conditions demands such adjustments.

Vitruvius even references a device that aids such fine-tuning, which we can equate to a kind of proto-triangle. In his description of war machines, Vitruvius proffers a device of adjustment: 'Thus with tight *wedging*, catapults are tuned to the proper pitch by musical sense of hearing' (308–9). To the obvious relationship between music and construction, there is a reference here to the inconspicuous wedge, a triangle of wood that holds things in place. Later, there is talk of water clocks that also deploy this adjusting device. The marking out of the hours varies from month to month and 'must be adjusted by inserting or withdrawing *wedges*' (298). Elsewhere, I elaborate on the importance of the wedge (Coyne 2010) as a device for managing space, a theme also developed by Steven Connor (Connor 2004, 2010).

These descriptions from Vitruvius are practical. The ancients knew about *praxis* as a mode of knowing, and it is arguably the case that Vitruvius was aware of Aristotle's teaching about practical wisdom (*phronesis*), the art of knowing when to apply the rule. In her exposition on Vitruvius, Indra McEwen makes reference to Vitruvius's insistence on the importance of *fabrica*, repeated manual activity (McEwen 2003: 61); and in her Ph.D. thesis, Susan Stewart has explained *firmitas* (firmness) as not just 'carrying down the foundations to a good solid bottom', but 'making a proper choice of materials without parsimony' (Stewart 2001). *Firmitas* is about making sound judgement, effective gap management, adjustment, repair and other contingencies of work on site.

So my argument is that the relationships between musical scales and architecture are most compelling when we think of the necessity to make adjustments, in contrast to the orthodox meeting of architecture and music through concepts of proportion, or architecture as participation in the harmony of the spheres. It could be said that architecture and music have long focused on proportion and harmony, but in doing so have inadvertently manifested the remainder, the excluded, the superfluous and the deviant.

Adjustment and empowerment

The assertion of the importance of adjustment has several ramifications. Not least, it boosts the political significance of attending to the marginal, as opposed to the officially sanctioned, which is to say the ideal, the hierarchical, the hegemonic, the powerful and the standardised.

Standardisation is understood in music as well as in architecture. The social theorist Max Weber saw the quest for even-temperament in music as a suppression of the differences that account for regional variation (Weber 1958). Even-temperament is symptomatic of the unfortunate imposition of industrialisation and standardisation onto the arts. Consumers benefit in the age of industrialisation from the transportability of music across national boundaries, but according to Weber's argument, in the process music has lost regional nuance and colour. In fact, even-temperament represents a form of colonial domination and Eurocentrism. Arguably, the licence of musicians to tune and re-tune their playing counteracts these strictures. Much contemporary music, especially laptop and electronic music, operates with alternative tuning systems, even breaking away from the constraints of scale and regular rhythms. Le Corbusier's one-time collaborator Iannis Xenakis deployed mathematical techniques exemplifying this contemporary move from classical formality (Xenakis 1992).

In similar vein, Sennett's book on craftsmanship argues for the importance of tacit knowledge above the theoretical and the industrialised. He illustrates the demoralised state of crafters in the former Soviet Union. Once, when shown around a construction site, Sennett observed empty cartons of caulking compound for sealing around the windows. Their contents had been sold on the black market. Workers filled the gaps around the windows with newspaper and painted over them (Sennett 2008: 403–12). Sennett sees this messiness at the joints as a symptom of material indifference festering within a demoralised workforce devoid of a sense of participation and reward. This failure in workmanship becomes evident at the seams, from which materials are easily pilfered and where there are already tactics of covering over. When visiting a country with inadequate building controls, any tourist is conscious of the mess at the seams, where joints are unresolved, trades are inadequately coordinated, and where there might be little attention to maintenance. These are symptoms of the early adoption of partly industrialised processes. The indigenous structures, where they are retained, exhibit no such degradation at the joints.

Adjustment and invention

Attending to the gaps also amplifies the nature of design, a more positive cast on Sennett's observation about the opportunistic pilfering of caulk.

The various adjustments that have to be made in applying geometry to some schema of expectations often results in the production of a dimension, portion or element that is left over, that does not fit, such as the comma, or the left-over days in the cycle of the calendar. A perfect universe would offer a year of 360 days, divisible into 12 equal months. In his analysis of the Vâstu Mandala, Adrian Snodgrass indicates how the discrepancy evident in calendar cycles, and expressed in rituals and architecture, kept things moving:

> as there is a remainder there is no end, the cycle recommences, and time continues on. The residue is thus the seed of the next cycle . . . No further motion is possible without the discrepancy between one cycle and the next.
> (Snodgrass 1990)

According to Snodgrass, the Aztec calendar gives similar accord to the five uncounted and unnamed days of the year (521). But one has to look hard for a celebration of the remainder in classical architectural discourse.

When Le Corbusier discovered the error in his attempt to derive two squares from the golden section, he rationalised this as a moment for celebration.

> In everyday practice, six thousandths of a value are what is called a negligible quantity, a quantity which does not enter into account; it is not seen with the eye.
>
> But in philosophy (and I have no key to that austere science), I suspect that these six thousandths of a value have an infinitely precious importance: the thing is not open and shut; it is not sealed; there is a chink to let in the air; life is there, awakened by the occurrence of a fateful equality which is not exactly, not strictly equal . . . And that is what creates movement.
> (Le Corbusier 2004: 235–6)

This passage indicates Le Corbusier's relaxed approach to the rigours of mathematics: the amateur's first instinct that measuring a carefully made drawing is a substitute for mathematical proof. It also suggests a lenient attitude to architectural detail and the cumulative effect of errors. A discrepancy of six millimetres over a metre is not insignificant in building. But there is a concession here to the power of this discrepancy, enigmatically indicated through the phrase 'that is what creates movement'. He precedes this with an ellipsis, as if an afterthought, and does not seem to develop the concept further as an impetus to design and invention.

Drawing attention to the interstitial is a recent architectural tactic: those left-over spaces, the non-places, the spaces between unaligned grids, those other spaces that don't conform, the geometrical surpluses (Augé 1995; Graham and Marvin 2001; Koolhaas 2004). This is often where the action is. The remaindered can't necessarily be planned for. Perhaps remaindered spaces carry properties inherited from the enigmatic progenitor of all space, *chora*, 'which is eternal and indestructible, which provides a position for everything that comes to be, and which is apprehended without the senses by a sort of spurious reasoning and so is hard to believe in', according to

Plato in *Timeus* (Plato 1997: 72). This is a theme invoked by Jacques Derrida (Derrida 1997; Coyne 2011), who also denotes *chora* as the etymological root of 'choral', a further elision with music.

There are many relationships between architecture and music. My ambition here has been to show not only that they both have uses for the concept of scale, but that they both rely on informal adjustment to make those scales work. In drawing attention to the margins, adjustment has political importance. It also provides inroads to an understanding of design and invention.

Excursus 3

Complex ordinariness in Oxford

'House after Two Years of Living'

Igea Troiani

In this photographic essay, I deliberately aim to experiment with the image of the house I portray to you visually and textually. The style of writing that I use is purposefully mixed, midway between narrative and academic prose. I aim to explore how academic architectural writing can be made accessible to a wider audience rather than just an architectural one through use of a more expressive, conversational and anecdotal style of prose. This is done also because of my love of hearing spoken words, memories recounted verbally, pauses in speech.

*

Here I am sitting in the house I designed with my architect partner, Andrew Dawson, in which we and our two children live, writing about it. The house is the consequence of Andrew's and my architectural inheritances over the last ten years.

From Alison Smithson and Peter Smithson comes a love of honest materiality; of rough concrete. The beauty of the unsealed beam and block concrete floor/ceiling that supports our green roof lies in the prefabricated imperfections left as bubbles on its surface. From Robert Venturi and Denise Scott Brown comes an interest in *Complexity and Contradiction in Architecture* (Venturi 1983, 1966). From Ray and Charles Eames, a replica video of the film of their house in Los Angeles, 1949, titled 'House after Five Years of Living' (1955). My video, 'House after Two Years of Living', some stills of which are included here, shows our Oxford house at mostly an interior scale so as to underplay it as an architectural object.

*

Soon after it was published, I purchased a copy of Bruno Krucker's book *Complex Ordinariness: the Upper Lawn Pavilion by Alison and Peter Smithson* (2002). I remember

Igea Troiani

Figures 1–12
Stills from the video 'House after Two Years of Living'.

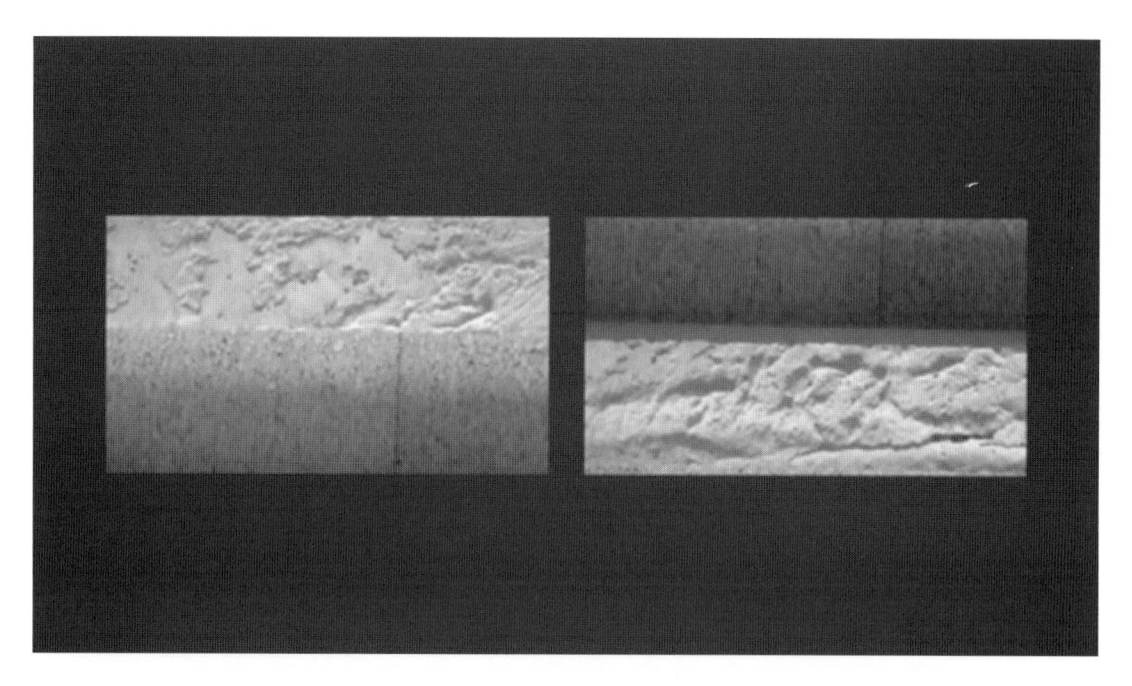

Excursus 3: Complex ordinariness in Oxford

Igea Troiani

Excursus 3: Complex ordinariness in Oxford

Igea Troiani

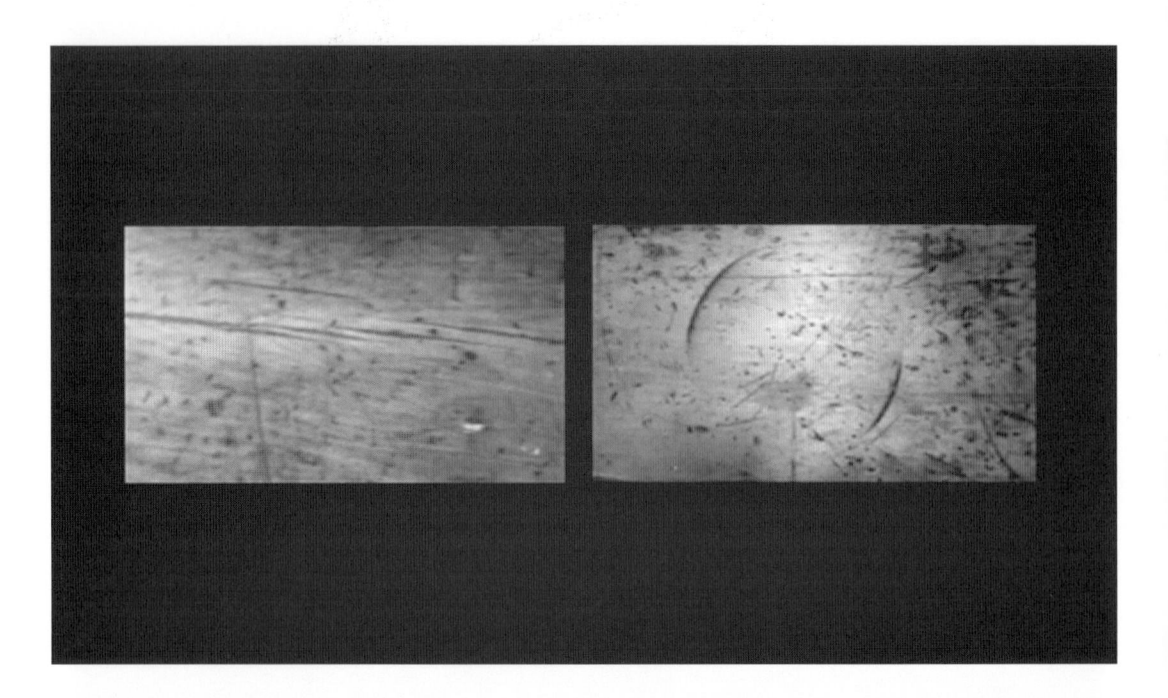

Excursus 3: Complex ordinariness in Oxford

being enamoured with the photographic essay in it by Georg Aerni. It was not until five years later, after I moved to the United Kingdom, that we visited the building. One wintery Sunday afternoon, we had met friends of ours at a pub near the house and after a big roast dinner set off in Wiltshire to visit it.

Andrew and I were both taken by the Upper Lawn Pavilion, by its materiality, its modesty, its unpretentiousness. How tired I am of architecture that is so tightly controlled by the designer that one imagines that the user, another Edith Farnsworth, is unhappily living in their Farnsworth house prison. I quote Edith Farnsworth from Alice T. Friedman's book *Women and the Making of the Modern House*:

> I don't keep a garbage can under my sink. Do you know why? Because you can see the whole 'kitchen' from the road on the way in here and the can would spoil the appearance of the whole house. So I hide it in the closet farther down from the sink. Mies talks about 'free space': but his space is very fixed. [. . .] Any arrangement of furniture becomes a major problem [. . .]
>
> (Friedman 1998: 141)

In Alison and Peter Smithson's book, *Changing the Art of Inhabitation: Mies' pieces, Eames' dreams, the Smithsons*, they elaborate in their preface on how 'three generations of modern architects whose thinking and work have changed our art of inhabitation' (1994: 5). It is not the Miesian components – the transparency or pavilion attributes – of the Upper Lawn Pavilion that intrigue us; it is the relationship the modern addition of the Upper Lawn Pavilion has to its territory, a beautiful existing stone wall. When designing our house in Oxford, the memory and textuality of the Upper Lawn Pavilion's perimeter wall remained with us.

In Mohsen Mostafavi and David Leatherbarrow's book, *On Weathering: the life of buildings in time* (1993), they too undertake a seductive photographic essay of weathered buildings. The 'Casa del Girasole (1947–50), Luigi Moretti, Rome Italy' and 'Palazzo del Tribunale (1512), Donato Bramante, Rome Italy' are of influence. Italy, rough stone plinths under smooth faced stone. Dripping dirt marks caught in that stonework. Like looking at our own skin, I see evidence not only of the architecture but of architecture's relationship to craftsmanship and the elements.

The use of materials with a former life pervades the interior of the house as well. We brought from Australia a 3.8 m-long timber table, which was previously a salvaged chemistry bench. A work of abstract, minimalist art in itself, its surface records the trace of so many students bored in their university lectures or undertaking experiments. It now has nine years of our hands and those of our children eating, drawing and resting on it.

Due to our affection for our table, we set out to create complementary kitchen joinery. Shiny melamine minimalist kitchens bore me. I suspect such a kitchen would make one feel obligated, like Edith Farnsworth, to maintain it. In reaction, everything is exposed in our kitchen and displayed on recycled timber, which we sourced and selected bench by bench.

*

Now if we consider the genealogical scale of our kitchen, it too is generated from the Eameses, in particular what Peter Smithson describes in 'Concealment and Display: meditations on Braun' in *Architectural Design* as

> the 'Eames' Aesthetic'– the 'select and arrange' technique [. . .] This of course, as a design method, is close to flower arrangement and to good taste in the furnishing of rooms with collector's pieces: it uses things for what they are, each object being enhanced and speaking more clearly of itself by virtue of the arrangement.
>
> (Smithson 1966: 362–3)

Our Oxford house is designed to celebrate display in every way possible. The framing of windows, whether large like those in Jacques Tati's *Playtime*, or horizontal like those advocated by Le Corbusier, or vertical as promoted by Auguste Perret; they become shelves on which to considerately arrange the products of our consumption or memory; paper vases, orchids bought by my mother, piles of toys the children have played with, all thoughtfully arranged, all celebrated for their ordinariness.

*

Here I am sitting in the house I designed with my architect partner, Andrew Dawson, in which we and our two children live, writing about it; thinking about those architects before us to whom we are indebted. Like our architectural fathers and mothers before us, the Smithsons, the Eameses, and Scott Brown and Venturi, this complex ordinary house in Oxford exemplifies the scale of historical debts of aesthetic memory and materiality by which post-modern not Postmodernist architectural design can emerge freed from a singular architectural vision.

Scale in the twentieth century and beyond

Ethos pathos logos
Architects and their chairs

Jonathan Foote

In his eighteenth-century treatise on the art of cabinet-making, Thomas Chippendale included several practical offerings on the derivation of the column orders and the good use of perspective drawing in what was a surprising slippage between architecture and the decorative arts. Architecture, he wrote, was 'the very Soul and Basis of the Art [of cabinet-making]', and, although architecture was still clearly distinguished from the craft of domestic furnishings, architectural theory was beginning to be captured and applied in new ways (Chippendale 1754: preface, 1). A generation later, in a handbook by Thomas Sheraton, knowledge of architecture had become fully integrated into the theory of furniture-making, and drawings of chairs, buildings and architectural mouldings were commonly juxtaposed within a single didactic engraving (Sheraton 1802: 309, 321; Figure 1).

By the time that Walter Gropius issued the Bauhaus manifesto of 1919, this affinity between art and craft had been solidified. Furniture-making and architecture were no longer separate disciplines, as they were now subsumed together under the guidance of the 'architectonic spirit' (Bergdoll and Dickermann 2009: 64). Now, as architects concerned themselves increasingly with smaller works as well as buildings, the ability to design among various sizes of construction became embedded within the very notion of architectural knowledge. An interesting point of departure, then, in addressing the scale of works in architecture might be demised from the favoured pastime of Chippendale, Sheraton and, now, countless architects: the design of furniture. Unlike a building, which promises only peripheral contact between the body and the architecture, furniture often joins with the body directly, placing architects intimately in contact with their own architecture. A sometimes painful test of the *Gesamtkunstwerk*, whereby the entirety of architecture, as 'total design', would encompass a paradigm for modern life, furniture is often an anatomical challenge to the spiritual ascendance of the body through reason alone. Frank Lloyd Wright problematised the matter quite succinctly when he lectured to Princeton undergraduates in the autumn of 1938. In discussing the integrity of organic architecture, certain complications nevertheless emerged:

> I soon found it difficult, anyway, to make some of the furniture in the 'abstract'; that is, to design it as architecture and make it 'human' at the

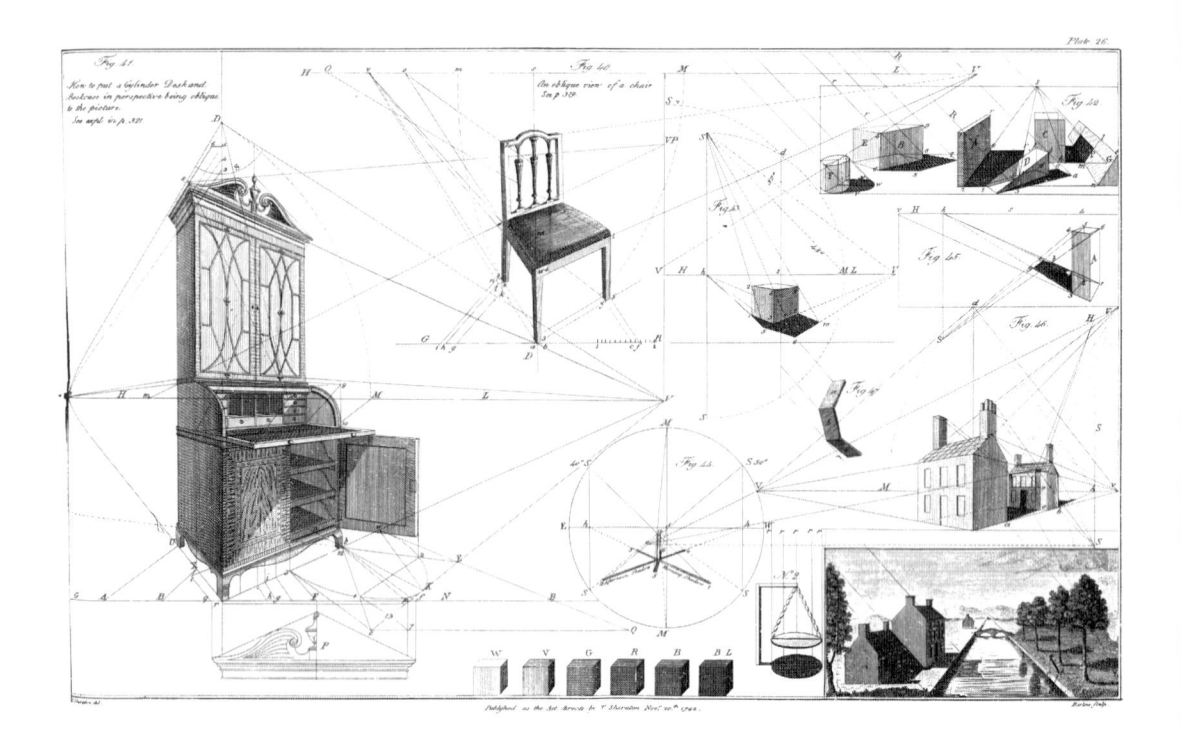

same time – fit for human use. I have been black and blue in some spot somewhere almost all my life from too intimate contacts with my own furniture.

(Wright 1987: 45)

Here, the transference between the various sizes of Wright's constructions is taken as an ethical problem, where architecture is a direct challenge to that which is 'human'. In complaining about the incommodious nature of his own furniture, Wright reveals one of the fundamental difficulties embedded in thinking of large works in the same way as small ones. When furniture is considered as a kind of miniature architecture, unable to be revealed as a world in itself, there is a problem of scale. For Wright, the scaling between various objects of practice is reduced to a static system of measure, where both small and large works are judged in the 'abstract': that is, in their specific adherence to the principles of the organic. However, in the argument proposed herein, scale is not a static relationship of proportional measures, relying on universal principles. Played out in the realm of human situations, rather, scale relies on the ability to interpret and transfer certain modes of thinking between various sizes of works. In this way, scale may be thought of as a realm of practice where the character embodied in the design of large and small works may be transferred between each other. As in the practice of architecture every situation is unique, scale emerges as a key mode of thinking in the transference of ethical thinking between projects of various sizes and scopes.

Figure 1
Drawing by Thomas Sheraton, from Thomas Sheraton, *Cabinet-Maker and Upholsterer's Drawing-Book*, London (1793).

Architecture as overseeing both furniture and buildings

Origins and early problems

It would not be possible to revisit such a notion of scale without the erasure of the traditional disciplinary distinctions between architecture and cabinet-making that played out during the style debates of the eighteenth and nineteenth centuries. The rise of historicism opened the door for small objects of cultural production (such as furniture) to lose their previous grounding in craft tradition and gain increasing intrigue as objects of speculative knowledge. The treatises on cabinet-making by Chippendale and Sheraton highlight this trend from the point of view of the crafts, where the science of perspective, from architectural theory, becomes an integral supplement to traditional craft knowledge. The amalgamation of furniture and buildings under 'architecture' parallels this larger push toward general theorisation within the field of cultural production. Here, the writings of Gottfried Semper provide a poignant point of departure for architecture, as his nineteenth-century tome, *Der Stil*, is still regarded as one of the most comprehensive attempts at the theorisation of cultural production under a universal system of practical aesthetics.

Since the publishing of his *Die vier Elemente der Baukunst* in 1850, Semper had worked to upend the prevailing theories of architecture as originating in the imagined primitive hut, favouring instead a mode of understanding based on human action or making. In *Der Stil*, the meticulous study of furniture provided a valid method for exploring 'primitive' or 'natural' architecture, as was demonstrated in his famous musings over style in Assyrian stools (Hvattum 2001: 537–46). In establishing an evolutionary connection between the origin of architecture in craft motifs and monumental architecture as exemplified in Greek temples, Semper relied on the separation of the tectonic realm into movable and immovable. Here he offered a new characterisation of furniture as a kind of portable tectonic that pre-dated architecture:

> tectonic root forms are *much older than architecture* and had already in premonumental times . . . achieved their fullest and most marked development in *movable domestic furnishings*. From this it follows, according to the general laws of human creation, that the monumental framework as art-form was necessarily a modification of what tectonics had developed on its own in its earlier objective.
>
> (Semper 2004: 623, emphasis in original)

This division between architecture and furniture is a potent example of how the traditional authority of craft knowledge was being replaced by architectonic theory. Now, furniture could be removed from its cultural situation and theorised within a larger notion of architectural production. Because large and small were no longer differentiated by their disciplinary relationship, such as architecture or cabinet-making, the distinction between movability and immovability allowed Semper to subjugate cultural objects of all sizes under a more general aesthetic theory. No longer taken as products intrinsic to cultural production, the study of these objects thus became a valid field of inquiry for architects. Unlike traditional cabinet-making, where the craftsman and the client entered into a situational dialogue surrounding the work's particular needs, circumstances and concerns, the making of furniture was now appropriately 'designed' (possibly by an architect) before it entered the hands of the craftsman.

Semper's work was part of an intellectual tradition that participated in the unification of the arts under various theories of universal knowledge. In the German tradition, one of most striking was certainly the well-espoused theory of the *Gesamtkunstwerk*, if only for its encompassing every aspect of spiritual, intellectual, and productive life. Popularised by Richard Wagner in the *Art of the Future*, the ideal of the *Gesamtkunstwerk* sought to unify the various domains of art as a bastion against the nihilism of the modern, fragmented, industrialised existence. Here, Wagner formalised the principles of 'the great *Gesamtkunstwerk* that comprises all artistic forms, in order to use all individual forms as a means, to annihilate them in order to arrive at the *Gesamtpurpose*, that is, the absolute, immediate representation of the perfect human nature' (Bryant 2004: 156–72). Architecture would lead this transformation, as led by early German Modernists such as Peter Behrens (Bryant 2004: 156–57). Taken in the context of the *Gesamtkunstwerk*, scale is a mode of transference whereby the total, Hegelian Idea finds itself manifest in small and large works, with the expectation that spiritual transcendence will accompany the life of a totally controlled, harmonious environment. In design strategies that embrace abstract, non-situational unity, scale is a mode of transferring between small and large works, whereby the synthetic idea is manifest in different measures as related to a unified continuum of experiences. A building, chair or object is thus 'small-scale' or 'large-scale' depending on its measured relationship to a formal concept, often relegating the primacy of human accommodation to a secondary role.

The Viennese architect Josef Frank protested against the difficulty of foregoing the fundamental differences between large and small, however, writing in 1923 that he was 'of the opinion that anyone who has the desire to rest his posterior on a rectangle is in the depth of his soul filled with totalitarian tendencies' (Frank 1981: 215). The rectangle, belonging to buildings, is contrasted with the human body in repose, conjuring an image of utter contempt towards human accommodation. By invoking the straightness of the rectangle, Frank highlights the danger of abstract, speculative thinking as acted out in the practice of small objects made for human accommodation. In this context, architects, seduced by rational theories and methodologies, could easily lose touch with the original notion of furniture: to accommodate the body. This would be tersely satirised by another Viennese, Adolf Loos, in his short essay 'Poor Little Rich Man', where we learn of the disastrous consequences of the complete and totally designed existence (Loos 2003: 18–22). As with Wright's musings over the difficulty of making furniture fit for human use, Loos exposed the fundamental opposition of total design approaches to the pragmatic affairs of daily life. Ultimately, for our purposes, Loos's essay magnifies the question of scale as an ethical concern. If large and small are unified at the expense of human accommodation, then there is an ethical problem. It is not difficult to uncover disturbing instances of architects putting total design into practice: Wright designed dresses for the women who dwelled in his houses, a natural extension of the total transfer of domestic life under the premises of the organic, for example; and Behrens, in an effort to release workers from the hegemony of industrial production, dictated that they should be exposed to the salvation theme from Wagner's *Parsifal* once every hour (Bryant 2004: 162).

As the control of furniture design was increasingly distanced from those who actually made it, the creep of speculative thinking into the production of furniture became a fundamental ethical consideration. Total design strategies, as pointed out by Loos and Frank, tended to neglect the situational nature of practice and the necessary consideration of size in understanding the relationship of the work to human use. Scale, at this point, had lost its potential to act as an imaginative space between large and small works, and had been reduced instead to a system of measures based on a universal design concept. Such a tension between the abstraction of design and the design of abstraction seems present still today, and perhaps an overly formal understanding of scale is embedded in this hostility. In returning briefly to older notions of practice, however, perhaps we may discover alternative modes of conceptualising scale as a unifying principle between the design of various sizes of works.

Scale as a medium for prudent practice

One common bond between the production of various sizes of works in architecture might be what Aristotle called *phronesis*: the principal intellectual virtue of adapting universal principles to concrete situations. Often translated as 'prudence' or 'practical philosophy', *phronesis* denotes how the architect is able to deliberate properly upon particular situations encountered in daily practice. It is a sphere of non-formalised, yet coherent, knowledge that prepares and guides the architect along the shifting circumstances of practice (Aristotle, *Nicomachean Ethics*: VI.viii.9). As an intellectual virtue, rather than a capability or aptitude, such as judgement, *phronesis* governs one's actions toward 'the good life in general', and includes not only practical shrewdness but also that which is proper and improper, which Cicero and Vitruvius would later call *decorum* (Garver 1994: 41–3).[1] *Phronesis* relies on a keen knowledge of practical affairs, but is not wholly pragmatic.[2] It is rational, yet cannot be justified through logical or universalising propositions; it exemplifies the problem of mastering practice without being mastered by it (Hariman 1991: 26–35; Garver 1987: 14–15).

The rubric of *phronesis* was espoused in classical theories of rhetoric, most of which find their origin in Aristotle's *Rhetoric*. Here, Aristotle provided a concrete programme of how one may act prudently within the shifting and circumstantial realm of oratory, and it would not be difficult to imagine how such an approach could serve as a possible model for a broader interpretation of practice. In Book I, he elucidates what would be one of the most lingering guides in all of classical rhetorical theory: the three 'proofs' of good oratory – *ethos, pathos, logos*. Taken together, the three edicts could be envisioned as a kind of rhetorical programme, as a guide for judgement within the realm of various scales of practised activities. Briefly stated, *ethos* originates in the character of the speaker, in his or her virtue, one might say. Aristotle claims that one possesses *ethos* when the 'speech is delivered in such a manner as to render [the speaker] worthy of confidence'. *Pathos* is that element of a speech that persuades through the arousal of the emotions, 'for the judgments we deliver are not the same when we are influenced by joy or sorrow, love or hate'. And finally, according to Aristotle, a persuasive speech depends on *logos*, or logical argument, which is the interpretation of the speech through one's faculties of reason (Aristotle, *Rhetoric*: I.ii.4–6). *Ethos*, then, acquires primary importance for Aristotle, with the *pathos* and the *logos* taking on a subordinate role to the larger question of how the work of oratory projects the ethical character of the author.[3] This is why *phronesis* is Aristotle's chief intellectual virtue – because, in its ability to determine one's actions within contingent and shifting circumstances, it governs the ethical life in general (Aristotle, *Nicomachean Ethics*: II.vi.15). Aristotle's rhetorical programme is a demonstration of how architecture as a practised activity might be subsumed under the general principles of *phronesis*.[4] As *ethos/pathos/logos* is a guide for situational judgement rather than universal principles, the three proofs offer a concrete example of how non-formalised thinking may be transferred between works of various sizes. Such a transference occurs through a keen awareness of how the object is situated within its context of large and small. Scale is a mode of thinking that relies on prudent thinking and facilitates the transference between large and small without the kind of abstraction present in formal design strategies. In the same way that a scaled drawing facilitates an imaginative inhabitation of the unseen work, scale enables an embodied connection between small and large objects of practice.

It is in the situational nature of practice that scale emerges as the crucial link between size, ethics and meaningful building. An object taken out of situation is an ethical problem, which is why Frank and Loos satirised the tendency of total design strategies to remove works from the realm of human situations. However, with the notion of scale offered herein, one may subvert the hegemony of the synthetic idea and recapture the malleable, situational theorisation that leaves open the deliberative reality of human affairs, desires and reason. With a model such as Aristotle's *ethos/pathos/logos*, we may speak of scale as a metaphorical procedure that makes use of certain commonalities between small and large works hidden beneath their apparent visual or formal properties.

In the context of total design strategies, the allure is in the possibility of the embodiment of a singular design principle or principles within the intimacy of a work of furniture. With Wright, for example, furniture lies along a continuum from object to building, and eventually to the city, the totality of which ought to demonstrate the principles of organic architecture (Wright 1987: 73–5). In the rhetorical context, however, the possibilities are in the transference of *ethos/pathos/logos*, a model of invention through practice, which frees the architect from hegemonic formal principles. Furniture, from this perspective, allows the architect to *perform at a small scale*. As the multiplicity of decisions present in a building project are reduced significantly in a work of furniture, the architect has the ability to control all levels of design and production, should he or she choose to do so. As studies for architecture, then, they are highly productive, as one may demonstrate the principles of practice without actually producing a complex building project. It thus is a revelation of the entirety of one's character, or *ethos*, within a single, intensely tangible work.

Why practise between large and small?

The case of Carlo Mollino

As a discipline that is practised, the ethical principles exemplified in a work of architecture may be studied no matter what its size. In this way, one embodies *phronesis* by acting prudently through a work of architecture of any size, from silverware to buildings. The possibility of *ethos/logos/pathos* as a scaling procedure may be demonstrated quite well in the case of Carlo Mollino, a mid-twentieth-century Italian architect who practised within a wide range of scales. In a recollection of Aristotle's *ethos*, Mollino often emphasised the direct connection between the work and character of the maker, stating in one text that 'every work of art reveals its creator; an exact image and likeness of the person who made it' (Mollino 2007b; Brino 2005: 10). For him, each work is a synthetic response to a wide range of circumstances that often lead to unpredictable results (Mollino 2007a: 212).[5] The possibility of *phronesis*, then, emerges as a guide for practice, allowing him to unify a wide range of works through contextual, rather than strictly formal, undertakings. In this way, a recent publication on Mollino shied away from a traditional typological organisation of his oeuvre, preferring instead to present his work by categories of 'obsessions': flying, skiing, photography, cars and architecture (Brino 2005). Certain formal preoccupations are no doubt detectable throughout his work, but they do not reveal themselves with clarity; rather they are veiled in metaphor. They remain mysterious to definition and open to interpretation. Even while working at many scales, he is able to subvert the total design strategies, and one clearly detects a consistency of inquiry into the virtues of *phronesis* through the ethical dimensions of the human accommodation. We therefore understand the work through a revealing of the synthesising context, which is the basis of *phronesis* and of Aristotle's *ethos/logos/pathos*.

      His studies of the grace and balance of the alpine skier provide a fruitful rhetorical metaphor, for example, which guided his hand among several sizes of works (Figure 2). Here one can observe how an architectural analysis of the skier's body in motion is expressed in the subtlety of the Fürggen cableway station, where the stability of the stone structure, embedded in the mountain face, is juxtaposed with the reach of a delicate steel structure. In contrasting the dynamism of the skier's body with the architectonic/vertical dashed line and centre dot, Mollino suggests a rhetorical procedure for dealing with an alpine architecture: eloquence of both skier and building resides in-between motion and stability (Figure 3). A similar practice may be observed in a work of a different size: his three-legged chair, inspired by the motion and rest of the human body while sitting. Here one imagines how a detailed attention to the balance of the body might easily have derived from his sensibilities developed in skiing, racing cars, and flying acrobatics. The combination of a narrow back along with three legs provides utmost stability among many floor surfaces; yet the careful attention to the curve of the chair back, as belonging to the body, suggests that the chair is an invitation for the sitter to presence the balance of the body within the act of sitting (Figure 4). This stands in contrast to Wright's three-legged chairs, long a matter of derision among his clients, which were viewed by the architect as an extension of organic simplicity.

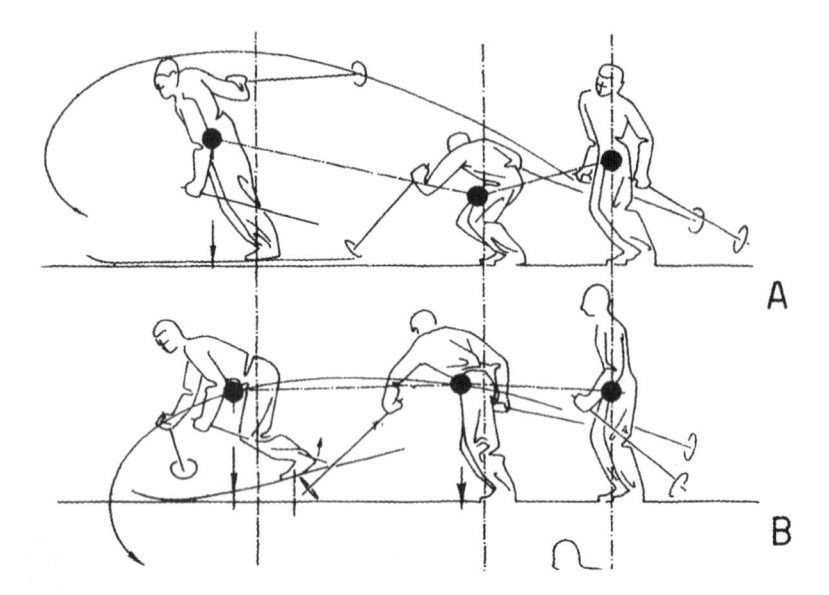

Figure 2
Carlo Mollino's studies of a skier.

Figure 3
Carlo Mollino's design for a cable station.

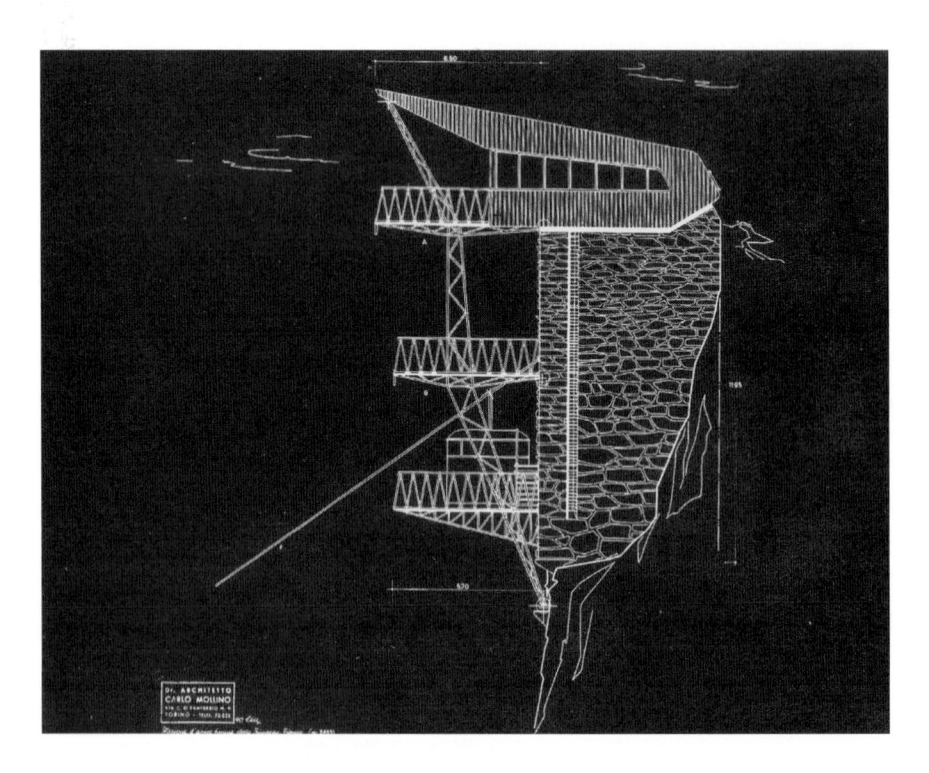

Figure 4
Chairs designed by Carlo Mollino.

For Wright, the active balancing by the sitter was seen as a gentle encouragement of good bodily and spiritual posture.[6] In Mollino's case, however, the chair was primarily a device of human accommodation rather than a tool for moral rectitude. Unlike chairs that are placed within the spectrum of an abstract 'idea', the chair for Mollino cannot be separated from its primacy as an anthropometric device. It is in this way that scale, as a rhetorical procedure rather than a formal one, facilitates the fluidity between the skier, building and chair.

The transference of prudence between various sizes of works is activated through the metaphorical procedure of scale, as is demonstrated through the work of Mollino. Large and small are means of metaphorical inquiry into a prudent practice. All of this discussion, however, raises the question – why do architects design furniture anyway? Perhaps it is in the benefit of smallness that a work of furniture holds the potential to be an embodiment of the entire process of the construction of a building. Unlike a model of a building, which requires that one imagines a future building of a larger size, a chair is already fully sized, present and available for integration into the sphere of human activity. While the multiplicity of decisions present in a building project are reduced significantly in a work of furniture, one may still present the entirety of the poetic and tectonic realm within a single, small work (Figure 5). Mollino's thumbscrew for a brass lamp recognises formal sensitivity as well as the use of the human hand, two principles of architecture that would be transferrable to all sizes of works. As a mode of practice, then, the design of small objects is highly productive, as one can live out the principles of prudent practice without actually producing a complex building. Because one must practise in order to be better at practice, the chair or other small object is often undertaken – it shows its didactic and demonstrative purpose within the discipline of architecture.

But this does not tell the whole story. In terms of total effort, a chair appears to be a relatively simple matter compared to the construction of a building, but perhaps it is not as straightforward as it appears. Architects have often commented on the great

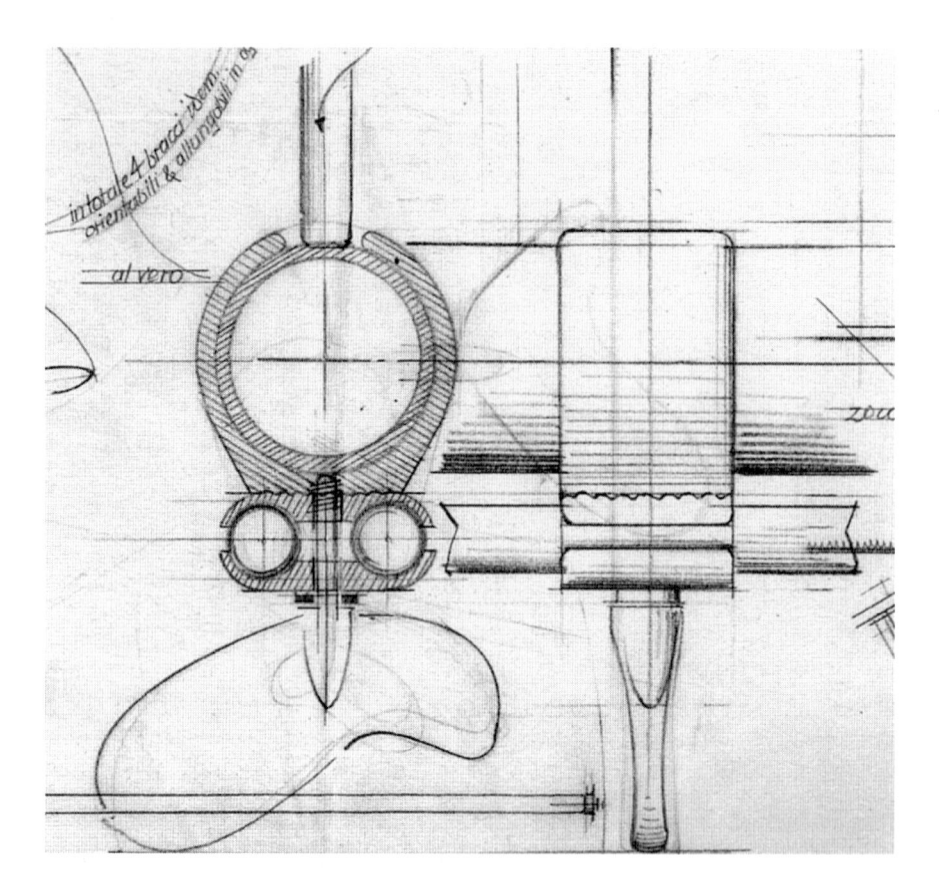

Figure 5
Carlo Mollino's thumbscrew for a brass lamp.

difficulty of designing chairs, for example, since in the experiencing of a chair, one confronts the tangibility of the architecture immediately and directly.[7] A chair may be touched in its entirety, providing a dialectic between that which is at hand and the demonstrability of *phronesis*. The chair as a small object is often thought of as more difficult quite simply because it more openly and tangibly displays its virtues. One can easily imagine Mollino confronting such a difficulty in his three-legged chairs, and, like a building project, would address these questions through drawings, prototypes and models. In confronting the complexity of chair design, we understand the transparency of *phronesis*, which accompanies something sized to be inhabited by the human body. A building hides many secrets among the millions of joints; yet the chair willingly offers itself to any person eager to sit in it and perform an examination of its materials and construction.

      Compared to a building, which is immovable and large, the entirety of a work of furniture is tangible, within reach and at hand. The work itself, through a prudent practice, displays its qualitative principles no matter what the size. Scale provides a method of theorising this metaphorical transference, which occurs between large and small without becoming trapped in the formal modes of total design. Scale, as a virtuous enterprise, will continue to be a powerful aid to the imagination as long as it is not reduced to mathematical relationships of measurement, where size and scale are used more or less interchangeably. Although the process of furniture production might be a mirror of building, as remote and industrialised, the work is nonetheless 'closer', as one imagines that the architect had control over every word, every detail, and how they were pronounced. The confrontation of furniture design by architects seeking meaningful, ethical constructions will remain a potent and fruitful undertaking.

Notes

1. See in particular Cicero, *De officiis* 1.96 and Vitruvius, *De architectura* I.2.5–7. On the classical reciprocity between *decorum* and prudence, see Kahn (1985: 12–22).
2. Aristotle claims that one may excel in *techne*, but not in prudence. One may be either good or bad at rhetoric, taken as a *techne*. Prudence, however, denotes excellence within itself, indicating its status as a virtue (cf. *Nicomachean Ethics*, Vi.v.7).
3. The relationship of the three proofs has never been a settled matter. See, for example, Garver (1994: 109–10).
4. Ernesto Grassi offers a compelling challenge to the supremacy of philosophy over rhetoric. See Grassi (2001: 18–34).
5. 'Le più robuste e sistematiche estetiche, e perciò insieme la critica, sono nate dal "compartimento" della poesia' (Mollino 2007a: 212).
6. The three-legged chair was intended to encourage good posture, a moral proposition based in 'uprightness', both in the body and in the spirit. See Ehrlich (2003: 63).
7. The most famous anecdote is from Ludwig Mies van der Rohe, who was quoted as saying 'A chair is a very difficult object. A skyscraper is almost easier. That is why Chippendale is famous' (Mies van der Rohe 1957). On the difficulty of furniture in another Modernist icon, see Le Corbusier (1990: 105–21).

'Halfway between the electron and the universe'
Doxiadis and the Delos Symposia

Simon Richards

The architect–planner Constantinos Doxiadis (1913–75) is not well known nowadays. There is a trickle of articles covering details of his career and projects, part of a shift in the last two decades to rehabilitate forgotten or vilified Modernists. There is also the 'World Society for Ekistics', which seeks to advance Doxiadis's agenda by lobbying the United Nations. Nonetheless, Doxiadis remains something of an unknown. From the late 1950s through to his death in 1975, however, he seems almost to have been inescapable, and featured regularly not only in professional journals and lecture circuits but in the popular media as well. His public profile at this time might have been higher than any other figure associated with the values of the Congrès Internationaux d'Architecture Moderne (CIAM). *Life* magazine christened him the 'Busy Remodeller of the World' in 1966 (Lurie 1966: 55), and the following year Walter Cronkite sought his opinions for a CBS special on 'Cities of the Future'.[1]

Probably the reason for the current neglect of Doxiadis is the perception that, being preoccupied with building at the grandest scale in accordance with a questionable 'science', and with arrogating total power to the architect–planner, he should rightly be forgotten. But what passes almost unnoticed is that Doxiadis was committed to the smallest, most intimate scales of architecture as well. It was only these that could affect people and enrich experience. Aesthetics applied to the small. Dealing with big things like the planet was about species survival. I would like to argue that Doxiadis was perhaps a more nuanced thinker than he is given credit for, and that he might have something to contribute to the falsely polarised positions – the bi-scalar disorder – of much contemporary architectural discourse. We shall start, however, with some background, and Doxiadis tipping towards the largest end of the scale.

It is easy to see why Doxiadis used to be such a celebrity. He was already chief town planner of Greater Athens prior to Greece's entry into the Second World War in 1940, and continued to have a prominent role in the reconstruction of Greece after 1945, holding several ministerial positions. He advised governments, the United Nations and the World Health Organization on matters of planning and Third World infrastructural development. His international reputation grew after he established his private firm, Doxiadis Associates, in Athens in 1951, and over the next quarter-century their design and consultancy work covered dozens of countries, administered from their branch offices abroad. Doxiadis's projects were usually vast in scale, such as his master plan for the new capital city of Islamabad, a multinational new towns programme covering the River Plate Basin in Latin America, and his regional transport plan for greater Detroit.

But if his projects were vast, Doxiadis's ideas, ambitions and rhetoric were larger still, and these were motivated by a sense of crisis that was tied to his own life experiences. His father, Apostolos Doxiadis, was a distinguished paediatrician based in Athens, who in 1922 was given the role of Minister of Relief to coordinate housing, healthcare and welfare for 1,500,000 Greek refugees fleeing Asia Minor, after the occupying Greek forces were defeated that year in the Turkish War of Independence (Kyrtsis 2006: 303–5). Earlier, the family had fled Bulgarian Thrace when Apostolos was sentenced to death for his part in an insurgency to reclaim it for Greece (Rand 1963: 58–60). And these experiences were followed up by Doxiadis's work with refugees after the war. He was obsessed with managing populations, their growth and migrations. Interviewed by the *New Scientist* in 1975, when he was close to death, Doxiadis noted that in the fifth century BC the poet Pindar had already been worried about Athens, with its population of around 50,000 situated on less than half a square mile of land, as an uncontrollable 'megalopolis'. With the exception of medieval Peking, it was not until the mid-nineteenth century that cities sustained and exceeded populations of 1,000,000 inhabitants; by the mid-twentieth century there were about one hundred, and by the year 2000 – so they predicted – there might be more than one thousand such cities. Humanity was on course to perish under the weight of its own numbers, the excessive drain on natural, industrial and financial resources, and the psychological and social pressures of urban overcrowding and the accelerating pace of life. This was irreversible (Cohen 1975). How, then, could future cities be reconciled with these forces while maintaining a good quality of life for their inhabitants?

The crisis required a new, holistic way of thinking about how to build and manage what Doxiadis called 'the global city'. The sociologist Saskia Sassen is credited with popularising the term in the 1990s, famously defining it as one of a handful of interlinked cities with global economic influence. 'There is no such entity as a single global city', however, nor would there ever be one (Sassen 2001: xxi). Doxiadis would have disagreed, which suggests that his ideas might be out of step with some areas of current discourse, although as we shall see this is not entirely the case. The world of 2100 was imagined as a single planetary city that would comprise newly built and old cities replanned and networked together. Doxiadis saw no alternative and presented his projects as stepping-stones towards this goal. The decision to site Islamabad towards the north of Pakistan, for example, was made because it formed a natural transport route – an 'Asian highway' – towards Lahore, Delhi and Calcutta in the east, and Kabul, Tehran, Baghdad and Ankara in the west. Thus, Islamabad became a pre-emptive 'link in the greatest city that man has ever seen, which is going to cover regions and continents with its branches – the universal city, or ecumenopolis' (Doxiadis 2006 [1965]: 178).

The architect–planner who would bring this about would have to expand his or her professional role. 'The architect can no longer remain a fashion designer or tailor for suits made to order', Doxiadis stated, 'he cannot speak of architecture as the architecture of buildings, much less the design of them' (Doxiadis 2006 [1963]: 250, 254). The architect must become the 'Ekistician', a master of the new 'science of human settlements'. Ekistics was an attempt by Doxiadis and his associates to determine systematically the optimum future-proof building solutions for the planet by combining environmental design with data on medicine, hygiene, nutrition, ecology, demographics, meteorology, sociology, as well as on mass production building technologies. In order to process this vast amount of data, Doxiadis introduced a computer centre to his Athens headquarters in 1964, packed with state-of-the-art IBM 1620 machines. By the end of the decade, computer operatives worked in shifts around the clock to enter the endless stream of data via typewriter and punch cards (Wigley 2001: 98).

But what was the Ekistician to concern himself with, if not buildings? The answer was as simple as it was bewildering: every object, activity and system that takes place on the 'thin layer on the crust of the earth'. Doxiadis counted 'five elements which shape man and are shaped by him': 'nature', as delicate ecosystem, food and leisure resource; 'man', prey to obesity, respiratory problems, alienation and depression; 'society', family and community; 'networks', including transport, telecommunications, utilities and service mains; and finally 'shells', or buildings. The new architect had a duty of care towards preserving these elements in optimum balance with each other, and to do so across all scales of the built environment, from the room to the globe. To that end, in 1965, Doxiadis proposed the 'Ekistic Grid', in which the five Ekistic elements were crossed with the 15 'Ekistic Units', with the individual person and room at one end and the ecumenopolis of 30 billion – predicted for some time in the twenty-first century – at the other (Bell and Tyrwhitt 1972: 21–8).[2] 'It will be very big', Doxiadis said.

Doxiadis was not alone in these thoughts, the main barometer of which were the 'Delos Symposia' that he convened in 1963 and held annually until 1972. They attracted many of what *Time* magazine called the 'glamour intellectuals' of the day, such as Margaret Mead, Barbara Ward, Conrad Waddington, Arnold Toynbee and Jean Gottman, as well as politicians, industrialists, psychiatrists, architect–planners and many other professionals. But it was not only the world-saving agenda and the superstar brains that excited the media, as the format of the symposia was extraordinary as well. After a pre-conference gathering at Doxiadis's apartment overlooking Athens, the delegates would take a chartered cruise around the Aegean. With no telephone, telex, newspapers or mail being allowed aboard to distract them, the delegates would combine brainstorming sessions during the day with island-hopping, shopping, swimming, dancing and drinking in the evenings. A week or so later, the event would be closed with a formal ceremony at the ancient amphitheatre in Delos, where the 'Declaration' of the symposium would be read aloud in a torchlight ceremony (Various 1963). The *Time* reporter who attended Delos VII in 1969 characterised the discussions as 'unfailingly prolix, sententious and jargon ridden', but found it hard to dismiss the potential impact of such a high-powered gathering; besides, while it 'may be pretentious; it is also fun' (Ludson 1969). Running alongside these symposia was the journal *Ekistics*, edited by the urban planner Jacqueline Tyrwhitt, who as the 'sole raconteur' of Delos cleaned up the intellectual dead-ends, spats and ambiguities to try to deliver a coherent vision to the world (Shoskes 2006: 193). Indeed, without Tyrwhitt's organisational genius and extensive connections from CIAM, the Architectural Association, Toronto, Harvard, the United Nations and elsewhere, it is unlikely that Delos would have happened, and Doxiadis's fame would have been diminished hugely.

It is understandable, then, that Mark Wigley believes that Doxiadis's importance was in helping to create a forum for the exploration of planning at the most ambitious scale: the scale of the totally networked planet. The main drivers of this within Delos were the inventor, architect and poet R. Buckminster Fuller, and the media theorist Marshall McLuhan. Again, Tyrwhitt's connections proved invaluable, as she had worked with McLuhan in Toronto from 1953 to 1955 as part of a Ford Foundation grant into the effects of new media. Fuller and McLuhan met for the first time aboard the *New Hellas* for Delos 1 in 1963. The story Wigley tells is of a couple of mavericks who, in a condition of mutual respect and competitiveness, bullied the symposium agenda towards the idea of a comprehensively networked global city. They discoursed on the proliferation of transport and telecommunications, and the way they alter our experience of space, and indeed society, and interpreted computing and communications technology as prosthetic extensions of the human brain and body that would lead to the evolution of a new species. 'The global city is the global body', Wigley contends: 'We inhabit our own hyperextended body.' This rhetoric was ratcheted up through subsequent symposia until 'Networks were . . . the beginning rather than the end point of city form.' Envisaging an imminent future where all these networks are connected globally, the importance of 'house' as a secure enclosure and of cities as places where socialising occurs, ideas are exchanged and business is transacted, becomes undermined. Consequently, Doxiadis had to reconceive buildings as 'minimal form, a single thick semicircular line defining a shelter . . . that is extended out by the wandering tentacles of different forms of circulation. Buildings are but "shells" for movement patterns that reach out far beyond them.' Henceforth, 'The architect elaborates the human body rather than houses it. Designing networks has become a biological necessity.' Traditional cities and intimate spaces were obsolete (Wigley 2001: 83–92, 94, 104–5).

Wigley is correct to note that the Delians delighted in pushing each other to extremes. In Delos 4 in 1966, for example, the political activist Roger Grégoire argued that different types of information, such as education, advertising and propaganda, had become so readily available that there was 'nothing to gain (or lose) by living in big cities'. Indeed, the face-to-face exchanges that might lead to collective political action, or indeed to sex, were no longer that important either. Sure, both 'assume *some* physical relations', but 'Close distance is not indispensable. A voice (even on a record) may suffice.' In the same symposium the astrophysicist Fritz Zwicky argued that while humankind had 'blundered and bungled' the cities on the surface of the planet, there was no reason why these errors should be reproduced elsewhere:

it is of the greatest importance to avoid bungling into the *space age*, including *inner space* (the interiors of the earth and of the planets), and *outer space* (interplanetary and interstellar space) as well as the surface of the bodies of the solar system which are destined to harbour human activities.

But in the meantime, Ekistics should focus on trying to stop conditions on our planet from deteriorating further: smog would be alleviated through the use of jet-propelled cars (Zwicky was an inventor of jet engines, too) running in underground tubes and emitting harmless (sic) CO_2; airline congestion would be tackled through the development of nuclear-powered passenger submarines; and so on. Against ambitions like these, McLuhan's remarks about technology leading to the 'global extension of the human brain' feel tame. Fuller was not to be outdone, though, and he used his slot to define the nature of the universe: 'Universe is the aggregate of all humans' consciously apprehended and communicated [thoughts, dreams and] experiences.' Satisfied with his definition, the work of gathering knowledge could for the first time in history begin, for 'men . . . had not been able to start logically before' (Various/Delos 4 1972 [1966]: 522–3, 525–7). Clearly there was a strain within the Delos symposia that matches Wigley's account, but some of the more significant elements were ignored. Why were they ignored, and what were they?

Bernard Tschumi and Matthew Berman published *INDEX: Architecture* in 2003, which is an encyclopaedia of the issues that were driving debate at the architecture school at the University of Columbia in the transitional period between Tschumi stepping down as dean and Wigley taking the role. The book is packed with statements and images of networks, flows, computing and telecommunications, of nature rendered artificial, of globalisation, man–machine symbiosis and so on (Berman and Tschumi 2003). A conference was convened to mark this moment in Columbia's history and it was dominated by precisely the same themes.[3] Wigley sought in Delos the same things he valued at Columbia and among like-minded colleagues in other East Coast universities; those who relished the pithy provocations of McLuhan and Fuller that real buildings were obsolete, along with the 'architect as stabilizer . . . a figure of order, of pattern within chaos, of comfort'. 'If modern architects are serious', Wigley says, 'they will have to reduce their fixation on shells and become responsible for networks' (Wigley 2001: 88, 114). By which point, Wigley is not writing architectural history, but appropriating Doxiadis into the manifesto of his school.

Ali Madanipour recently took a contrasting view of the large-scale ambitions of Doxiadis. Writing about the 'Tehran Action Plan' that Doxiadis provided for Iran in the early 1970s, Madanipour criticises the apparent disregard for the local conditions of life and building practices of the Iranian people, which reflect his own broadly grassroots and vernacularist agenda:

> [A city] is formed of human agents who look for a range of different options to choose from. Rather than seeing settlements as collections of intelligent humans, who can and should be involved in determining the future of their settlement in new ways, Doxiadis has already worked out a set of principles, which he intends to apply everywhere to this end.
>
> (Madanipour 2010: 496)

Doxiadis, with his blinkered notion of 'the future [as] a giant metropolis covering the globe', ignores the dense 'multi-dimensionality' of cities at the smallest end of the scale (Madanipour 2010: 501).

But whether Doxiadis is celebrated or attacked on these grounds, whether they are used to recruit him into one professional orthodoxy or ostracise him from its alternative, something important is overlooked. Not everyone at Delos ran headlong into the networked sci-fi future, thinking only of design at global scales. Some did, but Delos was a party, and guests do not always behave in the way the hosts intend. Trying to set the agenda for discussion in Delos 4, Tyrwhitt pressed the speakers to reflect on the idea that a distance of '20–30 inches [works best] for verbal communication', whereas 'A distance of 5½–8 feet discourages discussion'. She stated provocatively that 'There is at present a misuse of high-powered means of communication for reasons of snobbery', and encouraged the delegates to reflect on what might be lost: 'Old fashioned written letters gave one time to consider the answers to them' (Various/Delos 4 1972 [1966]: 517, 519). And then, as we have seen, some of them wanted to play at cyborgs and colonise space.

Significantly, when Tyrwhitt and Gwen Bell took a break from editing *Human Identity in the Urban Environment*, which was published in 1972 as a compendium of Ekistic-related research into the megalopolis, their account ran as follows:

> We retired to the solitude of the rock-perched monastery of Kastriani, joined only by a narrow thread to the sparsely settled Aegean island of Kea. Here we seemed to have found refuge from all the effects of urbanization. The sky was the clearest blue, the air fresh with the scent of aromatic bushes. Then one day we clambered down the buff to enjoy a swim. Great black globs of greasy oil scum fouled the shore. The residue of urbanization lay at our feet.
>
> (Bell and Tyrwhitt 1972: 15)

With a population of only 5,000, Kea was tied into the global economic web to manufacture Christmas tree decorations for America using plastic imported from Germany, which linked them in turn with the oil-rich nations of the Middle East. Development came at the cost of 'destroying all that we believe makes life worth living' (Bell and Tyrwhitt 1972: 15). Tyrwhitt was interested in the global network that enmeshed Kea, but only because the run-off from the factories had turned the seashore oily and spoiled her swim. For those at the very centre of Delos, the big was a problem that had to be dealt with in order to try to preserve the traditional, sensual activities and lifestyles – and indeed the building practices – of human beings at the other end of the scale. Wigley's fixation on 'networks' causes him to forget that Doxiadis was concerned with four other 'elements' as well.

Also in 1972, Doxiadis published *The Formation of the Human Room*: 'Today we take the form of the room as a given. We forget how long it took to create it, and at times we try to change it without realizing the forces that shaped it and without considering whether these forces still operate today.' Doxiadis argued that the compact, orthogonal room and its typical furnishings are a product of 2,000,000 years of human evolution, perfected according to 'space-formative principles' rooted in biological and psychological need: round rooms appeared first, out of the need to huddle together for warmth, and the orthogonal type of room evolved later and assumed dimensions that were neither too large nor too small (Doxiadis 2006 [1972a]: 224–6). Doxiadis's description of how this came about gives a good example of his 'science' at work:

> This may sound strange, but after Man came down from the trees and started walking, he found that he did not like walking on uneven ground, because of the many problems that it creates, and he chose to walk on horizontal floors. Even if he has to change its levels, Man still wants to walk on horizontal floors. Such a decision led to the movement of his head on a horizontal level. This movement makes Man feel uneasy under a cupola . . . It is probably for the same reason that he felt uneasy under a pitched roof and why, finally, he preferred to live in spaces covered by horizontal ceilings. Nobody likes to sleep under a big dome in a cathedral. [And w]hen man started sleeping with his body stretched out, he was led to form rectangular sleeping places which were incompatible with round huts. This led to the creation of rectangular rooms.
>
> (Doxiadis 2006 [1968]: 61–2)

Doxiadis's insistence that these ideas reflect hard science and anthropological truth are questionable and occasionally bizarre, such as his insistence that orthogonal rooms evolved in the same way as animal and plant cells, which he illustrated with a collage that suggests that honeycombs traced a direct line of evolutionary descent back via sunflower seeds and yeast to water-borne algae (Doxiadis 2006 [1972a]: 232).

Doxiadis's various other attempts to define scientifically the nature of human beings and their environmental needs are equally strange, even comical. We must build for 'Total Man', he said, which was an extension of Leonardo da Vinci's so-called 'Vitruvian Man': 'Man's body occupies the smallest sphere; then comes the sphere of his senses; then the sphere of his mind; and then the unknown sphere of his soul' (Figure 1). The reach of the mind could be calculated at precisely 10^{27} metres beyond the body. We might also point to Doxiadis's ambition 'to measure [happiness] by standard operational methods' and make 'the formula of feasible happiness', which he outlines provisionally as 'time multiplied by satisfaction multiplied by safety'. Many of these scientific observations and sketches clearly are played for laughs, but even so they give an interesting indication of a set of priorities that contrast strongly with the networked futures and body–brain augmentation programmes advocated by some in Delos. 'The task is hard', Doxiadis admits: 'People have to learn how to be . . . very revolutionary when dealing with new systems and networks . . . [but] very conservative when dealing with man.' 'Of course we have telecommunications', he went on, 'but how can a telephone replace a father at bedtime, and how can television replace the contact of the two sexes?' (Doxiadis 1972 [1966]: 152, 156, 160, 162).

Figure 1
'Man is the measure'.

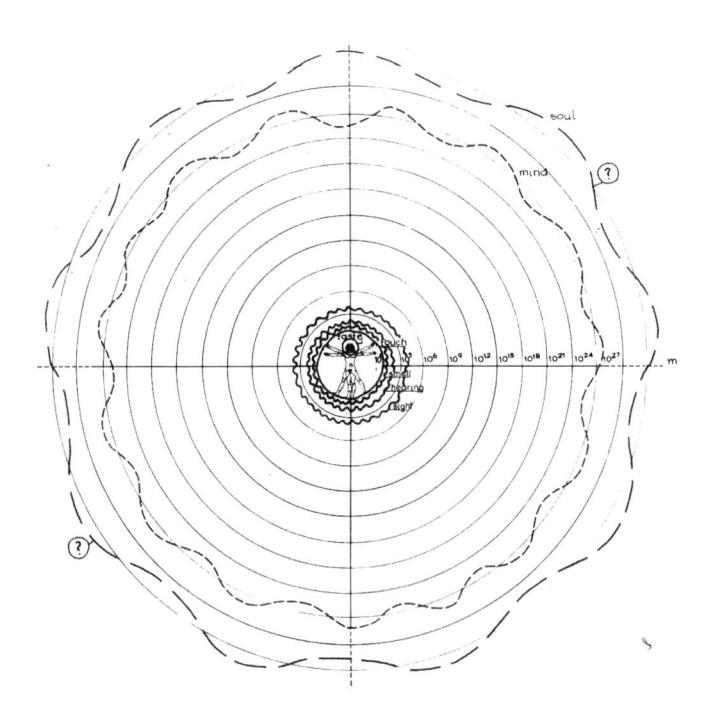

Total Man

Interestingly, though, Doxiadis did not demand that rooms and buildings at the smallest end of the scale should be uniform, to cater to uniform human needs. On the contrary, as the scale increases from the individual man and his room to the global city, 'the number of possible alternatives' diminishes from infinity to zero. 'There are few alternatives for the earth', he said, 'apart from blowing it up at one extreme and saving it at the other' (Doxiadis 2006 [1972a]: 224). Similarly, there are not many alternatives available for the urbanised continent, megalopolis or city. The need to balance all the crisis pressures that Doxiadis and others worried about, such as population growth against natural resources, meant that these larger things had to be designed in a fairly standard way for maximum efficiency. As these pressures diminished lower down the scale, however, the opportunity for architectural variety and creativity increased. Beauty, expression and local architectural interest could be found only in the small, within the perceptual limits of the human body and sensations. The mind reaches further and, with the help of the science of Ekistics, is able to comprehend and control settlements at the largest scales. But the mind does not furnish pleasure. Pleasure is located only within the immediately perceptible, at a scale perhaps no larger than the small town (Kyrtsis 2006: 21–6). It is questionable whether Doxiadis managed to realise this in built work such as the industrial village of Aspra Spitia (1961–65), although the retreat of 'Apollonion', a project that obsessed and nearly bankrupted him in his later life, does show a concern for spatial variety and the sensuality of materials that might begin to reflect these ideals (Figure 2).

It has been argued that Doxiadis's commitment to local vernaculars was not quite as sincere as he made out, being a matter rather of plundering only such styles and techniques as matched his pre-conceived ideas of how buildings should be. This was exposed in the years 1957 to 1961, when the Egyptian architect Hassan Fathy worked for Doxiadis Associates on housing projects in Iraq and Pakistan. Tensions arose between the two men, as Doxiadis pushed Fathy towards abstracting the local vernaculars that fascinated him into broadly applicable 'types': 'Fathy's commitment to the craftsmanship of design, detail, and tectonics remained at odds with the development firm's preference for generalization, repetition and mass production' (Pyla 2007: 32). But criticisms about plundering the vernacular could be levelled at any number of champions of the vernacular at this time, not least at Fathy himself.

The question of the sincerity and extent of Doxiadis's application of these principles remains valid, but does not undermine the fact that they featured heavily throughout the Delos symposia and *Ekistics* journal. In Delos 3, in 1965, for example, discussions about 'density' ended up pointing towards a similar gradation of scales. The report said that it was misleading to consider density in terms of the number of people on a given piece of land. Taking a swipe at Jane Jacobs, they asserted: 'Density is only one, limited and mechanistic, measure of community life which does not mean much on its own.' Instead, one should combine considerations of density with considerations of 'tempo' (the pace of life) and 'interference' (such as radio waves, noise pollution and obtrusive neighbours), and combine these into a measure of 'intensity'. But this measure could not be absolute. A person's desire and tolerance for different levels of intensity changed over 'a twenty-four-hour day, a week, a year, and possibly a lifetime'. Moreover, the tolerance of different nations and races at different stages of prosperity, cultural and technological development was likely to vary as well. All possible variations must

Figure 2
Apollonion: houses. Porto Rafti bay, approx. 40 km south-east of Athens. Conceived from 1958 and built from 1969, Apollonion was intended by Doxiadis to become a perfect village of artists and intellectuals. His health deteriorating rapidly, he nearly bankrupted his company in the rush to bring this project to completion before his death in 1975. It is now a holiday village for wealthy Athenians.

be accounted for in the future built environment. The authority on this topic within Delos was the anthropologist Edward T. Hall, who discussed the 'six different sensory modalities' that he 'used as measuring scales' in his research: 'visual, auditory, kinaesthetic, olfactory, thermal, tactile'. These 'receptor systems' mean that 'each of us carries around with him a concentric series of bubbles which vary in size'. Naturally, 'different cultures have different mixes of these'. Hall challenges the homogenising approach to building derived from 'the visual mode', saying that architectural space should reflect the position of different cultures on the 'continuum of sensory involvement'. This included the 'visual–auditory' world of the Italian, the 'thermal–olfactory' world of the Arab, and so on (Various/Delos 3 1972 [1965]: 214–15).

These ideas were followed up in 1968 with the Delos 6 report focusing on how best to regulate human development, and describing it as a process of stimulus management that has its roots in infancy as the child is introduced to more experiences beyond the mother. Given the increasing stimuli resulting from 'megalopolitan complexity', it was urgent that planners regulate the dangers of 'overstimulation': we have 'to learn to live in an environment in which TV and the aeroplane co-exist with the intimacies of the physical neighbourhood'. Criticizing the intensely networked future of McLuhan, who was not in attendance at this symposium, the report asserts that planning must provide for the extremes of stimuli, for 'peak points as well as isolation points', a 'wide spectrum of interconnections', which takes account of the calm and quiet moments too – 'the Sundays of our lives' (Various/Delos 6 1972 [1968]).

In Delos 7, the following year, which explored 'The Scale of Settlements and the Quality of Life', the discussion turned to the idea of a 'lattice of settlements', villages that were networked together in order to increase their economic prospects, but which remained resolutely villages in order to preserve their 'quality of life'. This report contained also a memorable observation about how changes in scale are not merely quantitative in their effect:

> If you take a steel needle seven feet tall and put it into water it will sink to the bottom. If you shorten it to an inch long, with the same slenderness ratio, it is a sewing needle. If you put this in the water it will float . . . Changes in dimensions create changes in the properties of the object.
>
> (Various/Delos 7 1972 [1969])

In other words, if the thing gets too big, its nature and value is destroyed. Doxiadis illustrated this point with an image that might be mistaken for a painting by Kasimir Malevich. He has filled in all points of the *x* and *y* coordinates on a graph to create a black square (Figure 3). It is a Surrealist graph, perfectly useless, and demonstrating powerfully Doxiadis's belief that the everywhere-city represents death. Ecumenolopolis was never intended as a high-tech 'metropolis covering the globe', transforming our bodies and brains and destroying our values with the density of its data and stimuli, as celebrated by Wigley and condemned by Madanipour. It was not a single global village, but a globe of villages.

Human Identity in the Urban Environment, ostensibly the definitive Ekistics statement on megalopolis, was dedicated in fact to mitigating the harmful effects of

The death of the human city.

Figure 3
'The Death of the Human City'.

megalopolis on settlements, buildings and activities lower down the scale, from 'small town' through 'neighbourhood', 'dwelling' and 'room'. As well as the examples given already, it included Arnold Toynbee on the psychological nourishment that people got from the countryside and the dangers of too much build-up; J.M. Richards on how, with a little re-adjustment, we could console ourselves by imagining the city was an exciting wilderness to explore, with the cars as wild beasts; and W.H. Auden on the need to counterbalance the pressures of metropolitan life through the 'secular prayer' of attending to great art and literature (Auden 1972 [1966]; Richards 1972 [1969]; Toynbee 1972 [1972]). This, I think, is the central agenda of Ekistics and Delos.

Doxiadis has been dismissed as little more than a showman with a good line in pseudo-scientific jargon and a keen eye for business (Rand 1963: 49). It has been suggested also that his main talent was in being in the right place at the right time, ready to exploit the openings and ideas offered him by influential, well-connected friends like Barbara Ward and René Dubos (Adler and Shoskes 2009: 207–13). Some attributed his best ideas to plagiarism, in response to which Doxiadis was disarmingly frank: 'What is original? I'm not a creator' (Lurie 1966: 55). The 'science' of the Ekisticians may have been dubious, their hoped-for influence was certainly arrogant, and Doxiadis was arguably the last dinosaur of the Modernist age. Nonetheless, the attempt to preserve the S against the XL was admirable. Doxiadis was attuned to the sufferings and pleasures of human beings across all scales of the built environment, because he felt the negotiation of scale was what it meant to be human – left dangling as we are 'halfway between the electron and the universe' (Doxiadis 1972 [1966]: 152).

Notes

1 'Cities of the Future', aired as part of 'The 21st Century' series, CBS, 16 April 1967.
2 UN data from 2004 predicted that the population of 2100 will be somewhere between 5.5 and 14 billion.
3 'The State of Architecture at the Beginning of the Twenty First Century', conference held at the Graduate School of Architecture, Planning and Preservation, University of Columbia, New York, 28–29 March 2003.

Little boxes

Gerald Adler

> There is a kind of play common to nearly every child; it is to get under a piece of furniture or some extemporized shelter of his own and to exclaim that he is in a 'house' [...] This kind of play has much to do with the aesthetics of architecture.
>
> (Summerson 1963: 1)

The British architectural historian John Summerson (1904–92), writing in 1946, bases these psychological transferences from child's play to the 'adult' world of aesthetics on Freudian and Jungian interpretations.[1] Summerson's subsequent readers in 1963, when the essay was first published in his *Heavenly Mansions* collection, might have been aware of the writings of the French philosopher Gaston Bachelard (1884–1962), and in particular his seminal book *The Poetics of Space*, first published in French in 1957, although Anglophones would have to wait until the following year to read the first English translation. When Summerson wrote these words, which opened his essay 'Heavenly Mansions: an interpretation of Gothic', he was being prescient about the wave of phenomenological thinking subsequently applied to architecture.[2] His aim, though, was modest: to bring the word 'aedicule', from the Latin *aedicula*, or little house, into architectural discourse. Although he used the aedicule to help elucidate certain characteristics of medieval Western European architecture, in particular the decorative, spatial and structural schemes of Gothic churches, he suggests that it may be extrapolated to all periods and styles. I would like to continue Summerson's musings on the subject while moving without any more ado to the world of contemporary architecture, or at least to that of the recent past of a generation or so ago. My principal examples will nonetheless be focused on the church, a building type weighed down by the tradition of received architectural forms, but one in which the 'little box' looms large and where considerations of scale play a crucial role.

Let us move, then, to modern churches, in particular to those groundbreaking ones from the 1950s to the 1970s designed for the Church of England by Robert Maguire (b. 1931), and from 1959 in partnership with Keith Murray (1929–2005). Beautifully scaled little houses, baldachinos or ciboria, sit over the altars; they render human the space of prayer and ritual, mediating between the human participants on the one hand and the heavenly aspect of the frame of the church and its ceiling above. To borrow from the German art theorist Wilhelm Worringer (1881–1965), as cited by Summerson in *Heavenly Mansions*, one may substitute 'modern man' for his Gothic forebear, such that

> [modern] man seeks to lose himself not only in the infinity of the great, but also in the infinity of the small [. . .] The crown of a pinnacle is a cathedral in miniature, and anyone who has sunk himself in the ingenious chaos of a tracery can here experience on a small scale the same thrill in logical formalism as he experiences in the building system as a whole.
> (Worringer 1927: 165–6, quoted in Summerson 1963: 26)

I will deal with the aedicule in twentieth-century architecture and will suggest that it has a key role in producing carefully scaled sequences of space. I will investigate the specific scaling device that the aedicule offers in these churches – St Paul, Bow Common, London (1955–60), most famously, but also All Saints, Crewe (1962–67). Following Summerson's lead, I categorise this use of the aedicule as ceremonial, an instance of what he apostrophises as the 'architectural subjunctive'. Maguire and Murray, like any architectural practice, also availed itself of the aedicule – the 'little box' of this paper's title – for straightforward reasons of commodity, for reasons of function or psychological fit, characterised by Summerson as 'cosiness'. I confine myself to contemporaries of Maguire and Murray in the 1950s and 1960s who would have had an influence on their architectural practice, and to historians and theorists such as Summerson and Rudolf Wittkower, who taught Maguire at the Architectural Association in the early 1950s. It is only in the section on 'Buildings within buildings' and the concluding excursus that I venture beyond this historic frame to the present day, in order to see what lessons have been learned – or ignored – by contemporary architects in their understanding of scale.

Classic versus Gothic scale

One idea developed from Summerson is that whereas Gothic buildings maintain a single scale throughout their fabric, so that, spatially, the Gothic church is an addition of compartments, many of which are aedicules in their own right. Classical architecture on the other hand has a variety of scales, carefully calibrated adjustments to the sizes of neighbouring components. There is, particularly in the great English Gothic churches, a certain relentless energy in the piling up of forms, or rather the horizontal repetition of motifs. Imagine standing in the nave of Norwich Cathedral (main part, 1096–1150); its sheer length, almost disproportionate to its height, gives one the sense that its master-masons strove to break some sort of record, rather than aiming to produce a balanced whole, where vertical and horizontal parts come to together in harmonic proportion. Nikolaus Pevsner was there:

> The interior is at its most powerful when one first sits down in the nave. [. . .] The palisade of closely crowding masts in the Norman walls, in spite of the arches between them, is as relentless as the bundles of closely crowded staffs that make the ribs, and the three parallel lines of bosses along the ridge shoot into the distance with the same straightness and the same never-halting tempo as the arcades.
>
> (Pevsner and Wilson 2002: 188)

One is reminded of the skyward strivings of the modern office tower, where, even today, height is a quality trumpeted above all others. The situation is not quite so stark in the case of continental Gothic; French medieval churches, for instance, have more rounded forms (contrast the semicircular *chevet* of Notre Dame, Paris with the boxy, almost crenellated plan at either end of Norwich); here the conception of the whole is clearly greater than the sum of the parts.

It is when the forms of the Italian Renaissance are encountered that a truly 'organic' architecture is evident; by this, I mean one whose carefully sized parts have prescribed scale – and formal – relationships with their neighbours. Alberti's church of Sant' Andrea, Mantua (1470–93) has a precisely delineated build-up of pilasters, arches, and vaults, where each of these elements stands in perfect proportional relationship with its immediate, adjacent forms, as well as prefiguring the final, largest-scaled element visible inside: the barrel-vault over the nave. Not for Alberti the clustered column, shedding its colonnettes as and when medieval vaulting demanded. Instead, as Wittkower rephrased Alberti's definition of beauty, it 'consist[ed] in a rational integration of the proportions of all the parts of a building in such a way that every part has its absolutely fixed size and shape and nothing could be added or taken away without destroying the harmony of the whole' (Wittkower 1998: 18). Wittkower ended his book on a wistful note, citing the French architect Julien Guadet, doyen of the *Ecole des Beaux Arts* in Paris, in his *Eléments et théorie de l'architecture* (Guadet 1910):

> 'Les proportions, c'est l'infini' – this terse statement is still indicative of our approach [at mid-twentieth century]. That is the reason why we view researches into the theory of proportion with suspicion and awe. But the subject is again very much alive in the minds of young architects today, and they may well evolve new and unexpected solutions to this ancient problem.
>
> (Wittkower 1998: 137)

Indeed it was, and they did.

In short, and as a generalisation, the Gothic cathedral tends to aggregate elements of varying size, whereas the Italian Renaissance church seems to adjust the overall scheme as a result of judgements made about the relative sizes of all its principal parts. St Paul, Bow Common has this attribute of classical design, where the external form is simple, bold and of a size that has sufficient civic presence in its locale to signal its communal role. If the altar table, located for all the right liturgical reform reasons near

Figure 1
Robert Maguire, St Paul, Bow Common, London (1955–60). Altar, ciborium, and hanging corona.

the centre of the church, had no ciborium above it, in addition to the hanging corona, then architecturally it would be lost in the large-scaled volume of the church (Figure 1). This has nothing to do with engendering a feeling of cosiness for the communicants – the 'functional–psychological' aspect of the aedicule outlined by Summerson – rather it has the heightened aspect of the ceremonial, the 'architectural subjunctive' case of 'as if'. What St Paul, Bow Common presents, in terms of scale, is a big box with phenomenal presence in its neighbourhood, containing within itself a series of scaled virtual boxes, culminating in the 'box' of the altar table itself. The ciborium at St Paul, then, is not unlike that of San Clemente, Rome (main building *c.* 1099–1120), which is monumental (monumental, that is, in Adolf Loos's sense of commemorating the dead) insofar as it marks the place of the shrine of the saint buried below.[3]

Cosiness and ceremony

For Summerson, the aedicule has attributes that engender feelings of cosiness on the one hand, and of ceremony on the other; the ciborium falls into this latter category. It concentrates attention on the act of sacrament: it symbolises it without facilitating it. The altar has undergone a radical change of significance from the Catholic medieval period to the Reformation and the Puritan period that succeeded it. What began life in the early Church as a stone altar, raised up on three steps to commemorate Calvary, the hill where the Crucifixion took place, became after the Reformation a place of symbolic re-enactment of the Eucharist, the commemorative meal depicted by Leonardo da Vinci in the *Last Supper* (Comper 1950). Protestants tend to re-imagine the (stone) altar as a (wooden) altar table; like its antecedent it, too, is generally raised up, but here the allusion is to a dais, the raised dining platform where the gentry sit. The bread becoming the messianic body is a kind of religious subjunctive akin to Summerson's architectural subjunctive, where the domestic qualities of the house, its cosiness, get transferred in order to provide the ceremonial setting for a rite.[4]

Maguire and Murray's ciboria do this in quite distinct ways. For a start, they are not just 'houses', but miniature houses – gabled tents made of striped material – whose diminutive size contrasts starkly with the noble stature of the church enclosure itself (Figure 2).

The similarity of the ciborium to a tent is reminiscent of the heightened sense of safe enclosure mentioned by Summerson, while the striped material recalls Karl Friedrich Schinkel's design for the 'Tent Room' at Schloss Charlottenhof, Potsdam (1826–29), itself an elaboration of the cosiness imparted by the hangings around a four-poster bed. The tent alludes to a history preceding the Christian era, namely that of the Israelites wandering around Sinai after the exodus from Egypt. It suggests that the divine presence may be found anywhere, and is not restricted to 'religious' buildings such as temples or churches.[5]

Figure 2
Robert Maguire and Keith Murray, All Saints', Crewe (1962–67). View of altar and ciborium.

Garden structures

The aedicule is a diminutive version of the archetypal house; a house of the gods, no less, a temple form. In this way it represents the hearth, the place of burned offering to the god's image. Lisa Heschong, author of *Thermal Delight in Architecture*, has talked about the aedicule in the following terms:

> The inglenook, the gazebo, and the porch swing [also] have strong definitions of their spaces. They are each a bit like a little house set off for a special thermal purpose. They might be termed 'thermal aediculae'. Although the term aedicula is most often used in conjunction with a sacred or ceremonial little house, it can also be used to describe any diminutive structure used to mark a place as special.
>
> (Heschong 1979: 40, citing Summerson 1963: 2)

Before the aedicule came indoors and began to structure interior, heated space, it had a life outside, one that began with the myth of the primitive hut. We see it in garden structures either free-standing, as in the gazebo, or, in the pergola, attached to (and dependent upon) the house.

Buildings within buildings

Garden structures are generally smaller than the main buildings to which they are subservient. When it comes to buildings within buildings, then those within are necessarily smaller than their hosts, although again differences of scale can come into play. An example where the 'house within' has a greater scale than that of its surrounding enclosure is Charles Moore's own house at Orinda, California (1962). The giant order columns frame spaces suggestive of ritual, and render them as 'spaces apart', as if they were religious sanctuaries (Bloomer 2000; Bloomer and Moore 1977). The 'house within', as a far more literal idea of domestic architecture, may be found in the German Architecture Museum, Frankfurt-am-Main (1979–84), designed by the neo-Rationalist architect Oswald Mathias Ungers (1926–2007). Placing a full-size house in the centre of the rear glazed atrium of the museum is quite startling in its scale contrast. This eidetic image of the house, albeit one shorn of its smoking chimney, roses trailing around the front door, and curtains to glazed windows, puts the dwelling at the heart of architecture: a kind of cartoon version of the Abbé Laugier's primitive hut (Ungers 1999, 2002). Instead of the cartoon image we have architectonic reality in the remodelling (1999–2009) of Friedrich August Stüler's *Neues Museum*, Berlin (1843–55) by David Chipperfield with Julian Harrap. This scheme sees the insertion of a spare, reinforced concrete trabeated grid structure into the former 'Egyptian' courtyard. The etiolated columns suggest an extremely abstracted classicism, one in which the vertical dimension is stretched relative to the 'human' scale of the horizontal dimensions. The vertical dimension is critical in determining one's sense of ease within a space, more so than the horizontal. Even minor differences in ceiling height can be unsettling, whereas we take a wide variety of horizontal measures 'in our stride', itself a telling body-metaphor. Stand in the worryingly low-ceilinged spaces of Jean Nouvel's *Institut du Monde Arabe*, Paris (1981–87), and you will see what I mean.

Earlier I berated Gothic architecture, following Summerson, for its maintenance of a single scale throughout; however, this did not prevent the masons and carpenters of the later medieval period, particularly those of 'perpendicular' England, from erecting the 'little houses' of their chantry chapels within the confines of churches (Coldstream 2002: 137–9). For the architectural historian Nicola Coldstream, they were 'the epitome of the controlled space that was at once public and private' (Coldstream 2002: 139). It is this ambiguity between public and private realms that the aedicule is so adept at presenting, even if in medieval buildings the sum of the parts is often greater than the whole, to turn Aristotle's aphorism on its head (Aristotle *Metaphysica*: 10f–1045a). Summerson refers to decorative features of French and English Romanesque architecture (such as arcading applied as a low-relief wall surface) as 'maddening', and complains that they

> do not really lift the architecture off the ground. They have the gaucherie of some would-be aviator who, by fixing wings to his shoulders and looking up to heaven, hopes he may find himself flying. In Romanesque, it is always the grave, sombre rhythm which appeals to us; the aedicular scaffolding grafted on is rarely moving and often tiresome and bizarre.
>
> (Summerson 1963: 10–11)

Summerson appears to be criticising Romanesque architecture for using the aedicule merely as a decorative device, whereas the subsequent Gothic manner incorporated 'heavenly mansions' into the physical, three-dimensional reality of (predominantly) churches.[6] In this way, Gothic architecture availed itself of the aedicule in a thoroughgoing architectural mode, rising above the 'merely decorative'.

The architectural subjunctive

In language, the subjunctive is used in order to present a particular 'take' on one's experience of the world, mediated through emotions such as fear, desire or pleasure, in addition to indicating what *might* be. 'The weather forecast suggested it might rain tomorrow' would be an example of the second kind of linguistic subjunctive, where conjecture and uncertainty come into play. Languages other than English have far more pronounced subjunctive forms, which allow the reported and conjectural parts of speech to be heard more distinctively. The subjunctive questions the content of a clause, rather than asserting its truth, as the indicative does; as such, applying the linguistic analogy to building, we might suggest that the subjunctive is that mood which, in short, denotes architecture. An oil refinery is in the architectural indicative; the Pompidou Centre, the subjunctive. Piano and Rogers's building alludes to industry while being perceived squarely as a cultural building.

You might think that the buildings of the New Brutalism would be firmly in the architectural indicative, and yet Stirling and Gowan's Camberwell school hall, London, of 1958 clearly alludes to a castle keep on its mound, and even Alison and Peter Smithson's Hunstanton School, Norfolk has a *parti* that recalls the English Palladian country house of the eighteenth century (with a nod at Holkham just down the road). The particular aedicules at St Paul, Bow Common and All Saints, Crewe have something of the Orient about them, recalling crusaders' tents, or the relatively insubstantial wooden architecture of the Ottoman kiosk. They contribute, in Maguire and Murray's otherwise functionally orthodox modern architecture, an air of 'oriental fantasy' (to quote Summerson on the effect the Gothic pointed-arch system had on thirteenth-century Western churches), a conceit that coalesces with the dreamy Byzantine-inspired mosaics, depicting angels with arms raised aloft in prayer, executed by Charles Lutyens on the spandrel panels framing the sanctuary at St Paul's.

Excursus: scaly scale

What we call contemporary parametric architecture has curious affinities with the non-finite architectural aesthetics of the Gothic. Medieval architecture tends to produce repeat patterns of aedicules, be they elaborate double-pitched roofs over dormer windows, or blind arcading as wall decoration. This is not to say that good spatial and surface contrasts are not possible with such architecture; it does suggest, though, that meaningful scale contrasts *require* the juxtaposition of discrete architectural elements, and not simply the addition of geometrically cognate patterned parts, as can be seen in 'early English' and 'perpendicular' low-relief wall carving. A grid on its own will only have potential for proper architectural scale relationships, if the intervals between grid components relate to objects of a known size. This is why the Pompidou Centre works at the level of scale (we can see people travelling up and down those transparent escalator tubes), while so many of today's parametric buildings do not.

Looking at, say, Future Systems's Selfridge's store (1999–2003) in Birmingham, one is reminded of the mathematician Benoît Mandelbrot's famous question: 'How long is the coast of Britain?' (Mandelbrot 1967: 636–8). We have no meaningful (meaningful, that is, in terms of known scaled objects) way of knowing the size of Selfridge's since, as Hannah Higgins, author of *The Grid Book*, has said,

> real length proves to be elusive [. . .] Length is a matter of scaling: it turns out to be a dual function of the distance relationship between the observer and the observed and the process of smoothing out curves to arrive at an apparently straight line length.
>
> (Higgins 2009: 268)

When it comes to describing buildings, Mandelbrot's kind of question is trivial: this room is 3.5 m high, not 3,455 mm; or, to put it another way, it is two people high. The metre is close enough to the yard, and we all know that one yard is roughly equal to our stride, and that I am about two yards tall. The unit of measure to be chosen should be one whose principal dimension has some bearing on the human body; the metre manifestly has this, in contrast to the millimetre.

Last thoughts

I have ranged far and wide in our search for the little box in architecture. I began with Summerson's hymn to the aedicule, his essay 'Heavenly Mansions', and I end with some musings on New Brutalist buildings. According to the critic Kenneth Frampton, the late 1950s and early 1960s 'neoplastic' masonry buildings around Cologne designed by Ungers represented 'the last attempt to posit a rigorously modern, normative brick culture for northern Europe, just before the effects of the *Wirtschaftswunder* hit home; that existential moment prior to the advent of the consumer society that broke over Europe to the detriment of its politics and culture' (Frampton 1995: 48). In 'Machine Aesthetes', an essay written three years after the more famous 'New Brutalism' one (Banham 1955), the critic Reyner Banham asserted that

> The Brutalist and *Team Ten* connections have [. . .] been as honest about materials as one might hope an engineer would be, and they have been sufficiently courageous in their mechanistic convictions to build in brick, and to let the brick appear.
>
> (Banham 1966: 28)

The point I am making is that the recourse to the humble brick by the *enfants terribles* of New Brutalism naturally raised questions of scale: it was the ubiquitous building material for housing, as well as for the factory. It is the smallest unit of all building materials at our disposal (while still maintaining its discrete individuality), and brickwork in its bonding, colour and mortar joints can lead to the simplest of functional boxes, or highly elaborate exercises in textural complexity. We can see most clearly the use of this brick box technique, 'letting the brick appear', as Banham put it, in the work of the great German church architect of mid-twentieth century, Rudolf Schwarz (1897–1961). His church of St Anthony's, Essen (1959) possesses the enigmatic scaling device of the rectangular window and corresponding brick infill panel, all set within a relentless reinforced concrete framework. The frame dimensions imply a rather squashed ceiling-to-floor height, suggesting an industrial building from the outside, which instantly assumes a far nobler aspect when you get inside (Pehnt with Strohl 1997).

The challenge faced by thoughtful architects half a century ago was identified by Summerson, as the critic Ellis Woodman has noted in his recent book on the architect James Gowan (James Stirling's partner from 1956 until 1963), in the following terms:

> Summerson recounted how, from Viollet-le-Duc onwards, the modern architect had adopted a quasi-scientific mindset in reaction to his appalled realisation that the discipline was 'almost entirely an affair of copying'. Cool-

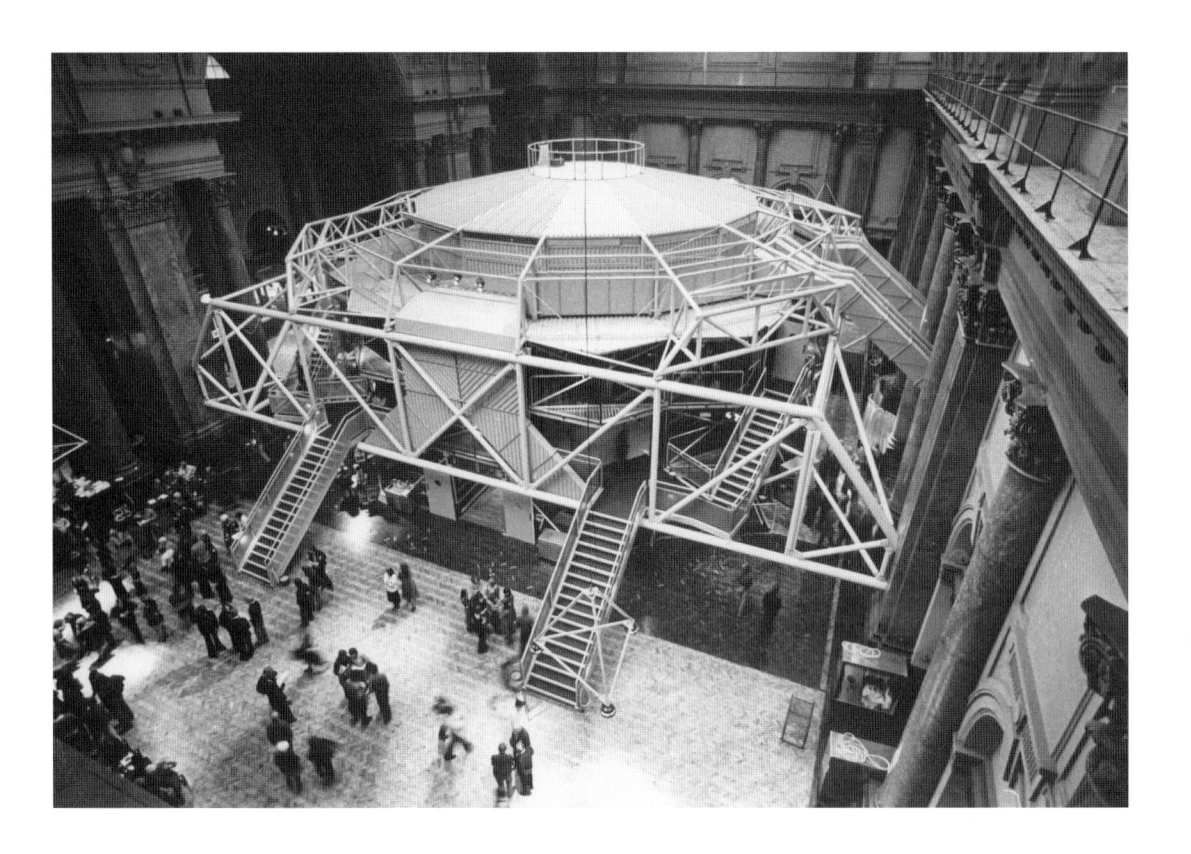

Figure 3
Levitt Bernstein architects, Royal Exchange Theatre, Manchester (1974–76). External view of auditorium.

headed rationalism offered a means of circumventing a reliance on the styles and, as Summerson acknowledged, the best work of the pre-war era was the product of just this sensibility.

(Woodman 2008: 13)

'Cool-headed rationalism', the positivism that made a meal out of a quantifiable programme, together with its counterpart, the bill of quantities, would not be quite enough. The poetics of architectural space also needed to figure, and the scaling device of the little box was one particular way of humanising the space of Brutalism. But it would be too easy to leave you with the impression that humanism would triumph over hard-nosed economics and technology in the scale stakes. Contemporary technology, in the guise of the apparatus to put the first men on the moon, would figure large in my favourite little box of the late-twentieth century. In the case of Levitt Bernstein's Royal Exchange Theatre at Manchester (1974–76), the original 'scale model', an Apollo moon-landing pod, has been scaled *up* to fit the needs of a repertory company, as well as the particular dimensions of the Victorian host building (Figure 3). Man's spindly aedicule, cast off from the mother ship of Apollo 11 and serving as lunar home to Buzz Aldrin and Neil Armstrong for three Earth days, was just as capable of re-using and humanising a redundant nineteenth-century commercial structure as any 'bespoke' designed shell.

Figure 4
Robert Maguire, 'Kentlands', near Sevenoaks, Kent. House for Colin and Rosemary Boyne. Rabbit and hutch, with timber frame erected (1959).

I end with another building designed by Robert Maguire, around the same time as Bow Common Church. This was the house for the editor of the *Architects' Journal*, Colin Boyne (1921–2006), his wife Rosemary and their then three children near Sevenoaks in Kent. Even while the house was being built, by Colin and Rose themselves, the rabbit was not forgotten, and was housed in its lapicule, my own neologism for a lapidary aedicule (Figure 4).

Acknowledgements

The research for this paper was carried out in the context of my forthcoming book *Robert Maguire and Keith Murray* in the series 'Twentieth Century Architects', to be published by RIBA Publishing, the Twentieth Century Society and English Heritage. I am grateful to Bob Maguire for the many hours he has spent with me discussing his work, and for allowing me access to his archive. I am also grateful to Duncan Ross, the vicar of St Paul, Bow Common, for sharing with me his love for the building, as well as his knowledge of the ciborium in architecture. Finally, I must thank my colleague Timothy Brittain-Catlin for drawing my attention to the important role played by the architect Sir Ninian Comper in the revival of the ciborium.

Notes

1. This essay was first read as a Sessional Paper before the RIBA in London in 1946.
2. More recently, and cogently, we have Juhani Pallasmaa's book *The Eyes of the Skin: architecture and the senses* (Pallasmaa 1996).
3. I am not attempting to give the history of the ciborium in ecclesiastical architecture; however, Maguire and Murray's revival of it in the twentieth century, in the context of the liturgical movement, owes a great deal to the researches of British architects of the Gothic revival. Most significant to mention is Sir Ninian Comper (1864–1960), who documents the history of the ciborium, and shows how it may be deployed to great stylistic and liturgical effect in his contemporary church designs (Comper 1947, 1950; Symondson and Bucknall 2006). See also Loos 1998.
4. The doctrine of transubstantiation is explained succinctly in Diarmaid MacCulloch's *A History of Christianity* (MacCulloch 2009: 405–6).
5. The tent-like form of the ciborium also uncannily resembles two temporary structures which persist in Jewish ritual: the *chuppah* (the bridal canopy erected for the marriage ceremony) and the *sukkah* (the temporary pavilion put up for the eight days of the festival of Succoth, or Tabernacles).
6. Robert Maguire has commented that '[a]edicular scaffolding' also nicely describes the entire cladding of the Duomo at Pisa, and numbers of other Italian churches like Arezzo: '[If] Summerson thought blind arcading in English and French Romanesque [was] maddening, [. . .] wouldn't it apply just as much to the insistent Italian (only slightly more 3-D) sort?' (Maguire, personal communication, 14 January 2011).

Scale and identity in the housing projects of Coderch

Michael Pike

The Modern Movement, and particularly Le Corbusier, has been criticised for its making of 'complex house-simple city' (Rowe and Koetter 1984: 93), a reference to the way in which the richness of the designs for private houses were lost at the urban scale. As Colin Rowe and Fred Koetter have noted:

> The public world is simple, the private world is elaborate: and, if the private world affects a concern for contingency, the would-be public personality long maintained an almost too heroic disdain for any taint of the specific.
> (Rowe and Koetter 1984: 93)

The housing projects of the Catalan architect José Antonio Coderch display an intense preoccupation with this balance between the scale of the home and the scale of the city. He endeavoured to maintain the complexity and richness of the individual dwelling within his collective schemes. He saw the introduction of variety as a means to reduce the shift in scale between the individual dwelling and the city, essential to assuring that the home remained identifiable. When he presented his Barceloneta housing project to the Team 10 meeting in Royaumont in 1962, Jaap Bakema had commented that: 'In my opinion Coderch's search is towards a morality based on identification in group housing' (Risselda and van den Heuvel 2005: 178). This chapter aims to investigate this question of scale and identity in Coderch's work using the example of one project: the Banco Urquijo housing project in Barcelona, completed in 1972. The intention is to examine the way in which Coderch explores an intermediate scale in this project, a scale that is capable of relating to the historic city and that ensures the identity of the individual homes can be maintained. This size, which is between the detached house and the urban block, allows for a small-scale form of collectivity, enabling an appropriation of the collective domain while maintaining a clear identity and boundaries.

In 1970, the Italian architect Giancarlo de Carlo, a prominent member of Team 10, wrote an essay entitled 'Architecture's Public' that began to politicise the criticism of the Modern Movement inherent in the discussions of Team 10 over the previous fifteen years. He launched a vehement critique of the architects' role in the post-war housing boom that followed 1945 and their complicity in providing 'cultural alibis for the most ferocious economic speculation and the most obtuse political inefficiency'. In response to the urban housing shortage, they had provided remedies that reduced housing 'to the absolute minimum which could be tolerated in terms of surface and space'. They had, according to de Carlo, lost all sense of their wider cultural commitment and had played into the hands of the power structure. The 'brilliant solutions' that they proposed became over the proceeding 40 years 'houses and neighbourhoods and suburbs and then entire cities, palpable manifestations of an abuse perpetrated first on the poor and then even on the not-so-poor' (de Carlo 1992: 207).

This criticism of the massive housing projects undertaken in the name of modern architecture in the post-war period underpinned the dialogues and endeavours of Team 10. The inhuman scale of the resulting environments pointed to the failings of the dictates laid down by CIAM and its promotion of modern, functional, large-scale and efficient housing. At the Otterlo Conference in 1959 Aldo van Eyck declared 'that "rarely" had the possibilities been "so great" for the architectural profession, but "never" had it failed "so badly"' (Lefaivre and Tzonis 1999: 13). The focus of their discussions and debates was therefore how to give meaning to a professional task centred on solving the problems of social housing and the reconstruction of cities affected by the war. In contrast to the optimism and confidence of CIAM, when faced with this problem of 'the greatest number', the members of Team 10 presented a more self-effacing and modest prognosis. As Carles Fochs has described it:

> subjects under debate gradually moved away from the dream of the architect as the creator of a new world for a future society to centre on observation and proposals for intervention in the built environment and the generation of new alternatives compatible with the principles of the traditional city.
> (Correa *et al.* 2006: 118)

De Carlo had argued that the post-war housing architects were too concerned with the problems of 'how' the shortage could be solved as cheaply and efficiently as possible, and neglected the problems of 'why' this was being undertaken in this way. As he stated in the same essay:

> We have a right to ask 'why' housing should be as cheap as possible and not, for example, rather expensive, 'why' instead of making every effort to reduce it to minimum levels of surface, of thickness, of materials, we should not try to make it spacious, protected, isolated, comfortable, well-equipped, rich in opportunities for privacy, communication, exchange of personal creativity, etc. . . . No one, in fact, can be satisfied by an answer which appeals to the scarcity of available resources, when we all know how much is spent on wars, on the construction of missiles and anti-missile systems, on moon projects.
> (de Carlo 1992: 207)

De Carlo had been introduced to Team 10 by the Catalan architect José Antonio Coderch and it is perhaps in this architect's housing projects that the critique of the large-scale post-war housing finds its most eloquent expression. Coderch had initially been sceptical about the architect's ability to successfully address issues of mass housing. In the discussion of the Candilis–Josic–Woods project for Toulouse Le-Mirail at the Royaumont Meeting in 1962, he had thrown serious doubt upon whether projects of such a vast scope could lie within the grasp of the individual designer or design team:

> In my limitations I think that it is very necessary for me, many times, to complete only a little thing within six months; I am able to make one thing. It is a great responsibility to compromise in this way.
> (Smithson 1991: 98)

It is clear, however, that his participation in Team 10 had an increasing influence on his work, particularly in the late 1960s and early 1970s. The consideration within the group given to the importance of the architect's involvement in mass housing and the search for individual identity within these large-scale proposals finds a resonance in the later work of Coderch.

House and city

José Antonio Coderch occupies an unusual position in relation to the prominent European architectural figures of the post-war period. He was a descendant of the Marquis de Sentmenat, a member of the Catalan nobility and had fought for Franco during the Spanish Civil War. He was opposed to the egalitarian ideas of the Bauhaus and of many of his associates in Team 10. He also operated with an essentially non-theoretical approach, being committed primarily to the practice of architecture, and was reluctant to forego his individual role. As Frederico Correa has remarked:

> Coderch was never given to associations and assemblies. His individualism and his mixture of timidity and pride made him wary of categorical group declarations rendering him unable to share any idea that did not coincide exactly with his own.
> (Correa *et al.* 2006: 110)

His work was fundamentally concerned with the design of domestic space, involving a large number of single-family houses and a series of housing projects. The projects for individual houses were used to develop Coderch's ideas about the arrangement of domestic space, and these ideas were then transposed to the larger proposals. As Luis Girbau has described it:

> Coderch's entire work can be read as an uninterrupted and persistent development of his reflections on the one-family home and just as his best

Figure 1
José Antonio Coderch, Banco Urquijo apartments, site/upper floor plan.

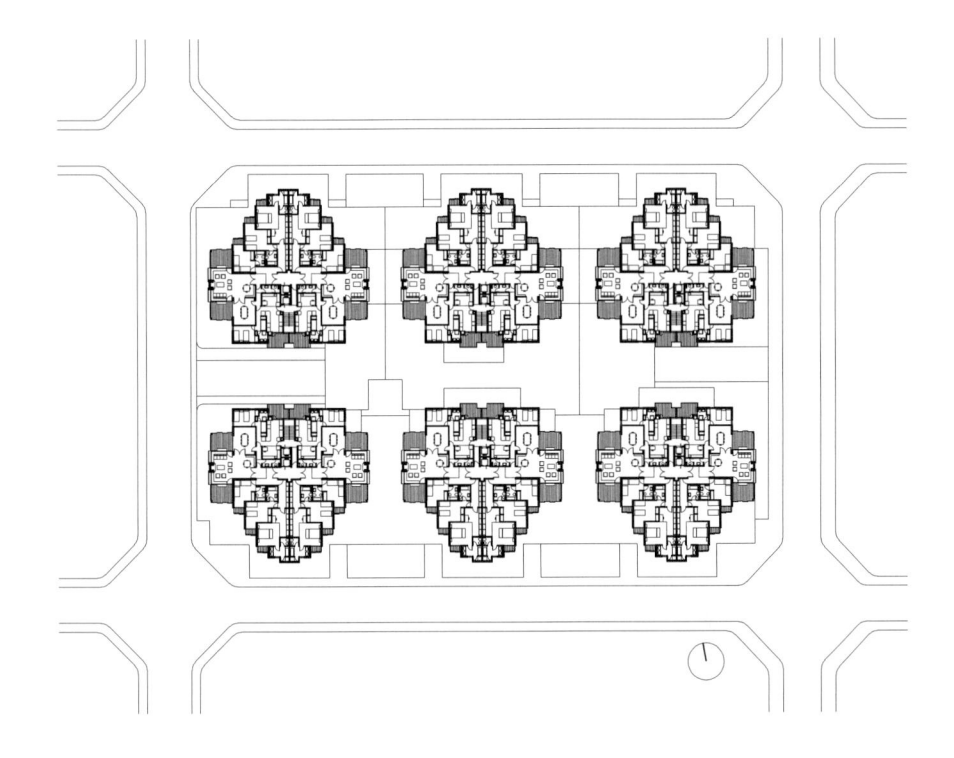

> critics have pointed out, the most complex multi-family dwellings, hotels, touristic groupings, etc. are nothing but a manifest and affectionate edition of individualized cells.
>
> (Girbau 1987: 22)

The project for Banco Urquijo was entrusted to Coderch in 1967.[1] The client was a Madrid-based commercial bank seeking to build it as an investment. The appointment of Coderch was made after the director and architect of the bank visited the Hotel del Mar in Palma, completed in 1964. The project involved the construction of 54 apartments and other facilities in the affluent Sant Gervasi district of Barcelona. The site occupies a full street block and is located on the crest of a hill between the Via Augusta and the Ronda del General Mitre, with a steep slope towards the south-west. The area was formerly occupied by large villas, some of which remain. The newer buildings are typically five or six storeys. Although not part of the Eixample district, the block has the chamfered corners of Cerda's plan.

Urban scale

Coderch's preoccupation with scale and his critique of the post-war approach to housing is clearly evident from the initial strategy adapted for the project. The approved planning scheme for the site showed two free-standing tower blocks occupying the northern side and this was quickly rejected by the architect in favour of a medium-rise solution that would relate to the scale of the surrounding buildings. Coderch was strongly opposed to high-rise housing and declared in 1972:

> Perhaps because I suffer from vertigo, I find the idea that people should live at great heights repugnant. Nor do I agree with the type of urban developments now being built, practically all of them inspired by Le Corbusier's ideas about urban planning. I consider an error the construction of tall rectangular blocks among green spaces, for two reasons: firstly due to what I have already said about vertigo and secondly because I consider it inhuman to sit on a bench looking at what are usually monotonous blocks of 10, 20 or 30 storeys.
>
> (Coderch 1972: 16)

This criticism of Le Corbusier and his urban planning ideas is expressed even more overtly in an interview given in 1982: 'My obligation before I die is to say that Le Corbusier was a very mediocre architect, as was Walter Gropius, and their followers even more so' (Correa et al. 2006: 118).

Coderch therefore begins the project with a critique, a direct prejudice against the thinking that had dominated architectural discourse over the previous 40 years. The alternative strategy involved the making of six blocks of between five and six storeys that rise up from a plinth that adapts the scheme to the slope and provides the space for a range of offices and communal facilities. The six residential blocks are all accessible from the two longitudinal streets and the space in between becomes a series of shared gardens. In this way, the buildings take on the scale of a series of villas and relate directly to the surrounding fabric. As Xumeu Mestre has described it: 'Coderch did not give in to the temptation of the gigantic; the street block contains a series of buildings that do not stand out for their dimensions' (Mestre 2006: 137). The staggered form of the six buildings allows them to remain identical, while adapting to the chamfered corners of the block. This repetition is critical in establishing the urban scale, allowing the separate buildings to read as a coherent ensemble.

The intermediate spaces play a crucial role. The entrances to the blocks are subtly separated from the street by small lawns and are accessed from curved passageways that set up a generous sense of arrival and threshold. These passageways have views through to the adjacent entrances, making the experience a shared one. The semi-private gardens between the buildings are deliberately half-open rather than closed to the public realm. In this way the urban block becomes visually, if not physically, permeable. These glimpses through the depth of the block and the alternations in light and shade give a sense of indeterminacy to the dimensions. The project takes on the scale and intricacy of a village, and in this sense feels very different from the experience of its surroundings.

An appropriate urban scale is reasserted through the use of a very limited palette of materials – terracotta tiles and vertical timber slats in front of the openings. These materials are disposed in large uninterrupted vertical planes. The language is one

Figure 2
José Antonio Coderch, Banco Urquijo apartments, elevations and section.

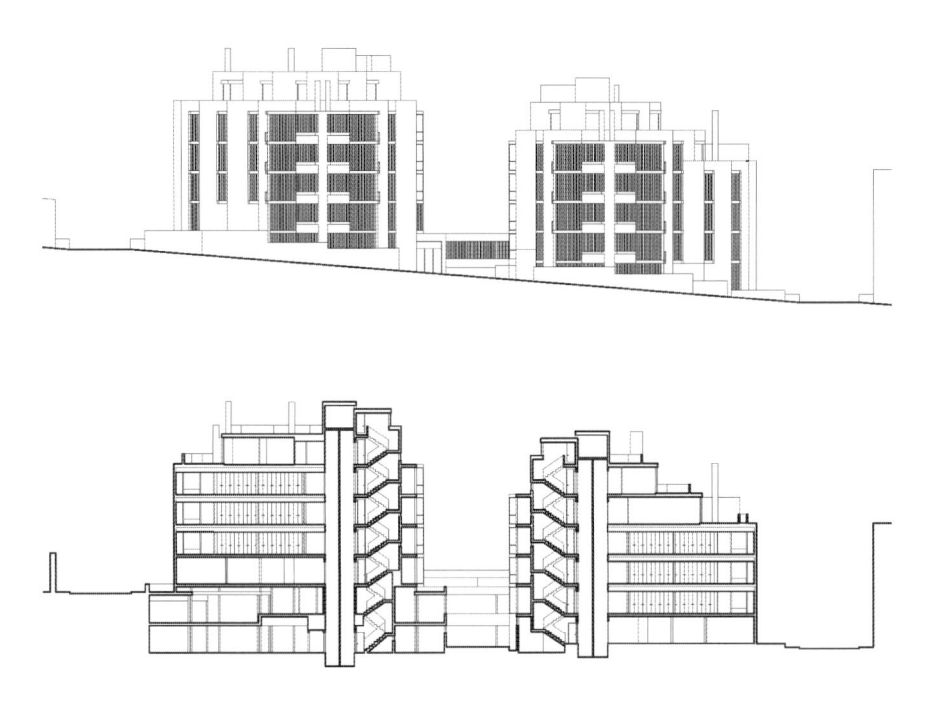

of wall and the absence of wall, rather than a language of individual windows and openings. This gives the elevations a more abstract and unified quality:

> Their zigzag floor plan breaks them down into vertical elements, some opaque, smooth, abstract and closer to the street, others, with openings, presenting a slight vibration, a break-down into closely related planes that illustrate the measure of the domestic, the scale of life.
>
> (Mestre 2006: 138)

These smooth vertical planes bring coherence to each element and to the whole, and establish a balance between the scale of the individual room and the scale of the city block. Without these unifying planes, the architectural composition would be too fragmented and would read only at the scale of the domestic. The arrangement and materiality of the elevations act to conciliate repetition and irregularity, as well as privacy and openness.

Dwelling scale

The plans of the dwellings in Banco Urquijo are direct adaptations of a number of Coderch's single-family houses, principally the Uriach House, built in L'Ametlla del Valles outside Barcelona in 1961. These houses are characterised by a clear organisation of the house into functional zones – living, sleeping and service. Each of these zones is then allowed its own individual character without being dominated by a strong unitary concept, but are sequentially linked to create a spatial continuum. The L-shaped plan of the Uriach house forms an outdoor room, a patio that nonetheless remains half-open to its surroundings. The living areas then relate directly to this patio. The plan is also notable for the staggered arrangement of the bedrooms, providing oblique and democratic views for each of the rooms, as well as creating a more dynamic and less monotonous corridor.

Figure 3
José Antonio Coderch, Banco Urquijo apartments, exterior view.

In Banco Urquijo, this plan is then paired and stacked to make an apartment layout. This recalls Aldo van Eyck's phrase, 'a house is a tiny city, a city a huge house' (Hertzberger 1991: 126). The private patio of the Uriach house becomes in this version an in-between space, a threshold between the public realm of the street and the private world of the apartment. The apartment is reached vertically by lift and this gives access to a generous hallway. From here, there is a direct connection to each of the three functional zones. It is a plan of rooms that slip past each other, with the openings located in the corners, creating diagonal views and a rich sequence of spaces. The blocks are constructed using a Domino-type structural system, with columns and rigid slabs, making it possible to free the space of load-bearing walls and create this loose arrangement of rooms with an expressive plan outline.

The staggered arrangement of the bedrooms allows the apartments effectively to turn sideways to the street, exploiting the depth of the plot and avoiding the need for the interior lightwells that are commonplace in Barcelona. This plan also gives expression to each bedroom in the form, treating them as autonomous cells, identifiable units of habitation. The scale of the dwelling and the block is therefore determined by the scale of the room. This extreme articulation is tempered, however, by the recurrence of modules and by the suppression of the individual windows in the elevations. The three main bedrooms, despite differences in plan, have the same frontage dimension, and identical external openings and terraces. This makes the independent cells read within an overall visual system.

Through this transposition of a plan for a tried and tested single family dwelling into a grouping of apartments, Coderch attempts to overcome the dilemma posed by the disappearance of the client from these projects. This dilemma is described by Adrian Forty through the phrase 'user', common to the architectural discourse of this period:

> the 'user' was always a person unknown – and so in this respect a fiction, an abstraction without phenomenal identity . . . its merit is to allow discussion of people's inhabitation of a building while suppressing all the differences that actually exist between them.
>
> (Forty 2004: 312)

Coderch does not have direct access to the 'user' and therefore relies on the previous creation of a home for a private client in attempting to meet their future needs.

This dilemma at the heart of housing design is also addressed through flexibility. From the outset, Coderch considered how the arrangement of the apartments

Scale and identity in the housing projects of Coderch

could allow for subdivision or for the acquisition of part or all of a neighbouring dwelling. In this way, the apartments can adapt to the changing circumstances and requirements of the households. The scale of the dwellings can shift and change according to their occupancy. The buildings become organisms and allow the 'users' to create identity through their modifications to the fabric. He sees this flexibility as essential to avoiding the monotony he so strongly opposes:

> We must emphasize this solution to prevent the rigidness imposed by other solutions and to allow, in a single volume and building, diversification in the sizes and layouts of dwellings, which adapt freely to the differing needs of future users.
>
> (Correa et al. 2006: 123–4)

Detail scale

The preoccupation with scale is also carried through to the detailed construction of the building. In Banco Urquijo, as has been previously mentioned, the window, in a traditional sense, disappears. It becomes simply an absence of wall, a floor-to-ceiling glazed opening that is then protected by a balcony and a screen of vertical timber slats. The window is almost always in the corner of the room, opening up a diagonal view as described by Coderch:

> I use corner windows for two reasons: first of all to avoid the wall–wall trauma, that sensation of bouncing from one to another. This also makes it possible to look at the street diagonally, thus avoiding the monotonous front view of the street's full width and providing a chance to make the most of different orientations.
>
> (Soria 1979: 84)

The timber screens are made from triangular teak sections and held in thin steel frames, with the same dimensions and spacings on all the elevations. These are then used in different ways; some are hinged and can be pivoted outwards to create different levels of openness and privacy, others are fixed in front of glazing. The vertical arrangement provides the occupants with better views of the exterior, while at the same time ensuring privacy by inhibiting transparency in the required direction.

These layered openings create rooms that are filled with light and yet closed, recallling the wood strip lamp designed by Coderch in 1952. Through this emphasis on the design of the intermediate spaces, these dwellings become like 'a half-open organism', as the architect Sáenz de Oiza has described it (Abalos 2001: 98). Coderch combines the privacy of the traditional Mediterranean courtyard house and the Modernist transparent apartment to make a new form of dwelling, capable of accommodating the physical and psychological needs of the modern household in dense urban contexts.

Close to the ground

Team 10 presented themselves as rebelling against what they saw as 'the 'mechanistic' approach of the older generation of modern architects – Le Corbusier, Gropius, Giedion – and the post-war reconstruction schemes carried out in their name' (Lefaivre and Tzonis 1999: 9). They wished to replace what they saw as the mechanistic doctrines of CIAM applied during the post-war reconstruction with a more humanistic architecture. To this end, the Smithsons had proposed the replacement of the strict 'CIAM grid' functional categories of housing, work, recreation and traffic with the more phenomenological categorisation of house, street, district and city:

> one lives in a place where the core group is obviously the family, traditionally, the next social group is the street (or square or green space, or any other element which by definition represents shelter or permanency), then comes the neighbourhood and, finally, the city.
>
> (Correa *et al.* 2006: 113)

On examination of the built production of the Team 10 members, however, it is clear that many of the housing projects still bear a close attachment to the avant-garde of the Modernist period, particularly Le Corbusier. Proposals such as the Smithsons' Golden Lane or Candilis–Josic–Woods's Toulouse Le-Mirail are cloaked in a new terminology, but remain ostensibly loyal to the compositional methods of their predecessors. As Kenneth Frampton has noted:

> Opposed to the deterministic rationalism of the European Modern Movement, the Smithsons were at once caught in their Golden Lane project by the subliminal presence of a very similar rationalism and, what is worse, by an identical rationalizing process; that is, the self-same process as that which had long since been used to vindicate the deterministic projections of CIAM, which were then the ostensible target of the attack.
>
> (Frampton 2002: 139)

Coderch, as has been mentioned, was not influenced by Le Corbusier in the same way. He emerged from a tradition different from many of the other Team 10 members, and his direct influences were Spanish, Italian and Scandinavian. The influence of Alvar Aalto provided Coderch with an escape from the rationalising process that inhibited the Smithsons. Alan Colquhoun has described Aalto's distinct approach, which was rooted in the practice of architecture:

> The Modern Movement in its early phase was concerned with the general schemata by which both society and architecture could be reconstructed according to rational principles. Apparently Aalto never concerned himself with such universalism. He was content to remain 'close to the ground' and to follow where his instinct for form led him.
>
> (Colquhoun 1981: 75)

For Coderch, as for Aalto, this capacity to remain 'close to the ground' is based on the central role given to the drawing in their design practice. The drawing becomes the means of connecting to the real circumstances of the future inhabitants; it is as Ernst Gombrich has described it: 'the means to probe reality and to wrestle with the particular' (Gombrich 1969: 173). The sketch drawings for Banco Urquijo that are held in the Coderch Archive all show this concern for the small-scale, with the dimensions and use of rooms, and with the layering and control of the rooms' enclosures. A process of constant overlay is used to make alterations and adjustments. For Coderch, drawing was a process of discovery and enabled a close connection to the contingencies of everyday life. Aalto used the dictum 'to include everything', and Coderch responds to this challenge: 'All those casual and temporal aspects that originate in the necessities of practical, real life, and which Mies eliminates or hides, are for Coderch genuine sources of inspiration' (Montaner 1998: 29).

In this way, it is evident that the Banco Urquijo has been designed from the inside out. The staggered form of the buildings is sufficiently loose-fit to enable it to adapt to the developing intricacies of the interior layout. As Coderch himself described it: 'Houses are made from the inside out, with the subconscious working on the outside, but always from the inside out' (Soria 1979: 84).

Through this inside-out strategy, Coderch endeavoured to maintain the complexity and richness of the individual dwelling within a collective scheme. He strove to make the apartments into homes in the same way as he had approached his designs for single-family houses.

In the subsequent years the *parti* of the Banco Urquijo project was tested at a series of larger scales, first in the Las Cocheras development on a nearby site and then in an unbuilt project for the Gran Kursaal in San Sebastian. These show both the strengths and weaknesses of the approach. Whereas in Las Cocheras the predominance of the interstitial pedestrian streets gives a scale and order to the fragmented blocks, in San Sebastian this middle scale is lost and the housing becomes a kind of monumental landscape. Even in Las Cocheras, where the scale and density is significantly increased from that of the Banco Urquijo project, there is a loss of the richness of the facades and the intricacy of the dwellings. This poses the question as to ultimately how transferable this could be to addressing the real issues of mass housing and 'the greatest number', so important to Team 10. Asked about this by Aldo van Eyck at the Otterlo meeting, Coderch had responded: 'This may be an inspiration for the poor house in future. The houses for the rich are important because they become a kind of example for everybody' (Risselda and van den Heuvel 2005: 329).

This is a somewhat unconvincing answer – a kind of architectural version of Reaganomics. Considered on its own terms, however, Banco Urquijo presents a very compelling example of an intermediate scale, of a counter-proposal to the vast post-war projects, which instead addresses the specificity of its location and that can relate to an existing urban context. By operating at this critical scale, between the dwelling and the urban block, Coderch develops a proposition where the coherence of van Eyck's city and house is perceptible, and where each can be a vital and tangible cultural force. At this intermediate scale, Coderch comes closest to this equilibrium between the home and the city, and achieves perhaps the most convincing embodiment of the ideas of Team 10 in relation to housing design. As van Eyck remarked in an interview in 1991:

> For example, what should I say about Antonio Coderch? Except that he was the most gifted architect of the lot. A great architect. He was very emotional, he didn't argue much, a solitary figure; he was severe, morally severe, but not dogmatic; he was a puritan and catholic. He was a genius architect. He wrote the article 'It isn't geniuses we need now', but he really was a genius, a fantastic architect, an artist.
>
> (Risselda and van den Heuvel 2005: 329)

Note

1. A letter from J.A. Coderch to Sr D. Bartolme J. Buadas of the Hotel del Mar, dated 14 June 1967 and held in the Coderch Archive, describes how the director of the bank and his architect had visited the hotel and had given Coderch this commission as a result. He writes to Sr Buadas to thank him for the trust he has always shown in him.

Politics and the deliquescence of scale

The Columbaria of Brodsky and Utkin

Michael J. Ostwald

In the wake of *glasnost*, the projects of a number of young Russian architects came to light that had been produced, allegedly at least, as a form of rebellion against the authoritarian Soviet State. Two of the better-known proponents of the underground Paper Architecture movement were Alexander Brodsky and Illya Utkin. In the 1980s, Brodsky and Utkin ignored laws forbidding them to practise architecture outside the state system and produced a series of dark etchings of unbuildable fantasy designs. A recurring theme in their work, and indeed in the work of all of the Paper Architects, is the dissolution of scale. This chapter traces the origins of their fascination with subverting scale to the strategies employed in the state architecture of Stalin and Brezhnev. Drawing on the philosophy of Jacques Rancière, this chapter investigates the use of scale in two closely related projects by Brodsky and Utkin: 'Columbarium Architecture' (1984) and 'Columbarium Habitabile' (1986). Finally, the chapter offers some notes about the problems of the dissolution of scale as a political tactic.

Identifying the void

According to Mikhail Belov (1988: 6), 'the history of Russian Architecture came to an abrupt end', at least as far as the Western world was concerned, in the 1930s. For Belov, 'the last names of any note' recorded by Western historians 'were Leonidov and Melnikov' (Belov 1988: 6). A review of the canonical histories of architecture supports Belov's assertion that, in the aftermath of Constructivism, Russian architecture almost completely ceased to exist. For example, *Sir Banister Fletcher's A History of Architecture* (Cruickshank 1996) devotes almost three-quarters of its coverage of twentieth-century Russia to Constructivism, and thereafter a fifty-year gap occurs until a new movement is tentatively singled out for praise: the Paper Architects.

The title 'Paper Architects' was originally used by the Soviet academy as a derogatory designation for a loose group of graduates who had declined positions in government offices but still continued to design. By renouncing such positions, these graduates effectively accepted the possibility that their works would never be constructed. However, rather than limiting their outlook, this restriction liberated the Paper Architects, encouraging them to produce designs for a range of unbuildable structures. From optical illusions of utopian cities to romantic urban bridges, avian cathedrals and inhabitable dolls' houses, the Paper Architects designed projects that consistently blurred the distinction between scales.

According to Brian Hatton (1988: 40), if there is a unifying theme in all of the Paper Architecture 'it is a recurrent theme of the infinite'. Regardless of whether the Paper Architects used fractal geometry, mirrors or simply denied graphic conventions, their work embraced the endless and the scaleless (Ostwald 2010). A key metaphor that Hatton uses to describe this quality of their work is 'a kind of matryoshka (the familiar toy of concentrically enclosing dolls)' (Hatton 1988: 60). This observation prefigures a recurring theme in the present chapter, where the matryoshka is both a seemingly ideal symbol for the Paper Architects purposes, but also a poorly understood one.

The matryoshka was historically seen as a symbol of fecundity (Soloviova and Marder 1993), but over time its meaning began to change, and for a while it represented the hidden family unit, divided, exiled and imprisoned at the hands of a Stalinist purge. By the mid-1980s, matryoshka dolls depicting communist leaders, nested within each other, were available on the black market; a case of a child's toy being repositioned to parody the state (Ertl and Hibberd 2003). It is no doubt the range of meanings, including the subversive, that attracted the Paper Architects to the matryoshka's apparent ability to operate at multiple scales simultaneously; but what was the underlying catalyst for their obsession with scale?

In the following section, Jacques Rancière's theory of the *distribution of the sensible* is introduced to provide a structure for the analysis of the relationship between politics, scale and representation. Thereafter, the chapter provides an overview of Belov's 'blank' years in Russian architectural history, emphasising the architectural and representational practices used by the state to affirm its power over the people. Finally, the chapter describes and interprets the Columbaria projects of Brodsky and Utkin – two projects exploring the same theme, but using different approaches to scale and leading to divergent political outcomes.

Politics and resistance

According to Banister Fletcher, the Paper Architects used design to 'attack [...] the defeatism and complacency' (Cruickshank 1996: 1444) of the state's architectural establishment. It is this desire for subversion and resistance that narrows the range of possible analytical frameworks for the historian to interpret the work. Most studies of architecture and politics are actually focused on questions of power. This is because architects have established theories connecting space, form and power, by way of surveillance, agency, control and hierarchy. Such theories are most useful for explaining what Dovey (1999: 15) calls 'power over': the architectural expression of control. In contrast, theories of politics and aesthetics that acknowledge the capacity for resistance are relatively rare. For example, Neil Leach fundamentally rejects the notion that 'architectural form is in and of itself political' (Leach 1999: 6). Fredric Jameson agrees, although he notes that, from a political perspective, a building 'can serve as a history lesson if its public and its viewers still have a sense of history' (Jameson 1999: 74). One of the few theories that is useful in this context has been developed by the French philosopher Jacques Rancière.

Rancière is not concerned with whether the ideological values of a system of governance are socialist, democratic or fascist; rather he is interested in the capacity of such systems to remain in a steady state. Rancière is similarly unmoved by arguments that specific works of art and architecture (or even large-scale protests and strikes) are necessarily subversive or disruptive. Instead, he offers a meta-framework to explain stability, volatility and politics. Rancière (2004) commences his meta-theory with the division of the traditional concept of politics into the binary set 'police' and 'politics'. The term 'police' (*la politique/police*) is used to describe the myriad controls that define what is lawful, right or expected in a society. The 'police order' includes everything from the media and social mores to laws and cultural practices. Rancière reserves the use of the word 'politics' (*la politique/politique*) to describe only those actions that disrupt the police order. The ultimate purpose of the police order is to maintain a type of equilibrium (a state where all of the elements are appropriately distributed) and thereby limit the potential for politics.

The capacity for politics to occur in this meta-system is reliant on the 'distribution of the sensible' (*partage du sensible*), a notion that divides any society into a system of organisation (a *distribution* of elements) and a measure of the extent to which an individual or group is apparent in this system (a capacity to be seen, heard or otherwise *sensed*). Rancière argues that all social systems are constructed upon a 'system of self-evident facts of sense perception that simultaneously discloses the existence of something in common and the delimitations that define the respective parts and positions within it' (Rancière 2004: 12). That system is the distribution of the sensible; a way of locating each element in its equilibrium state and of understanding the capacity of that element to be seen, heard or felt. Significantly, the sensible is scale-dependent; it is a measure of the visibility of an event, the audibility of a protest or the smell of a burning building. However, being sensible does not necessarily equate to being political; for politics to eventuate, a specific type of *disagreement* must occur.

Rancière proposes that actions, events or representations that conform to behaviours anticipated in the police order, even if they disagree with or break that order, are examples of 'dissent'. Actions, events or representations that actually alter or reconfigure the distribution of the sensible are examples of 'dissensus' (Rancière 2010). However, the distinction between dissent and dissensus is context-sensitive, and it is possible for an aesthetic object to be framed in multiple different ways. For example, in Russia in the 1980s the act of producing an unauthorised architectural design may have been illegal, but it was an anticipated form of dissent. If the designs satirised or critiqued the state, that too was dissent, because such actions were also anticipated in the police order. However, if the same Paper Architecture was published in the Western media and praised for its critical stance on the Soviet state, it was now an instrument of dissensus. Thus, in Rancière's theory, it is the way in which the event or object is positioned, framed or made visible that is important, not the event or object itself (Rancière 2004; Ostwald 2007). Once the Paper Architecture had the potential to alter the distribution of the sensible, then the state was forced to act. Their solution was elegant in its efficiency: they embraced the work of the Paper Architects as the product of Soviet ingenuity and even sponsored a modest exhibition. In this way, a potential ripple in the distribution of the sensible was swiftly accommodated, and reframed, to minimise the impact of any dissensus (Ostwald 2007).

Rancière's theory may be applied in several ways; most often it is used to analyse the politics *of* aesthetics, but it can also be used to illuminate the politics *in* aesthetics. The former involves particular types of post-production framing of the aesthetic object that can encourage political dissensus. The latter is concerned with the pre-production strategies embodied in the aesthetic object that might, at best, cause dissent. While Rancière regards the latter category – politics *in* aesthetics – as necessarily ineffective, it nevertheless provides an insight into local conditions.

Examining the void

By the early years of the twentieth century Russia had been transformed from an agrarian economy into one reliant on heavy industry. The Communist Party had put in place 'five-year plans'; it had established 'collective farms' and 'worker schools', and constructed many 'state offices' (Paperny 2002). Although millions of Russians were forced into Siberian labour camps in the 1930s, and the Nazi invasion of 1941 had a devastating impact on the populace and the economy, design and construction continued to occur throughout this period. By the late 1940s, Russia had begun to plan new urban centres, develop new districts and construct many hundreds of buildings (Kosenkova 2009; 2010). Nevertheless, despite the number and size of these designs, few were to earn the respect of the Western architectural media. In the 1930s, Joseph Stalin's professed enthusiasm for a type of extravagant historicism led to the state embracing 'Socialist Classicism' as the only legitimate approach to architectural design (Tarkhanov and Kavtaradze 1992). As a result of this decision, almost all of the buildings produced from the 1930s to the early 1960s featured similar hypertrophic facade profiles, lined with repetitive engaged columns and surmounted by Renaissance lanterns beneath a roofscape of golden spires (Aman 1992). These ornately finished buildings towered above the surrounding urban fabric, typically ten storeys higher than most of the nearby housing stock and, in the case of Moscow's famous 'Seven Sisters', over thirty storeys higher (Kiernan 1998). These oversized structures were typically sited on new urban piazzas, empty except for similarly overwrought 'Socialist Realist' statues. Such statues depicted heroic industrial workers, or indefatigable farmers often completed at four times human scale (James 1973). A large number of statues of Stalin, several up to fifteen storeys high, were also constructed across Russia and the neighbouring communist states, and several gigantic Mother Russia statues (*Rodina-mat'*) were completed, including three that rivalled, or surpassed, the scale of New York's Statue of Liberty (Boobbyer 2000).

It is a combination of the vast scale of the buildings, the magnitude of the labour embodied in their construction and the wealth invested in their ornamentation that raises the sensibility of the state; an act of overt political oppression. While the state-owned media and similar propaganda outlets existed, the Stalinist buildings, and particularly the Seven Sisters, permanently altered the sensibility of the Soviet State. Similarly, the hundreds of gargantuan statues, each athletic of build, square-jawed and perfect, reinforce this reading. These statues make sensible the state's aspirations for the worker, in much the same way that the Stalinist architecture makes sensible the limitless power of the Communist Party.

All of this was to change when, in February 1956, Nikita Khrushchev famously denounced the excesses of Stalinism and the cult of personality that had grown around him. In the following year, Khrushchev called for the Communist Party to reject the neo-classicism of Stalin and to endorse a new state architecture; a type of utilitarian Modernism. However, rather than heralding a new era in architecture, one state style was simply replaced by another and, in the hands of Khrushchev's successor Leonid Brezhnev, this directive resulted in the production of huge perimeter slab blocks, with endless standardised rooms and corridors, constructed of mass-produced industrial materials. As Alexander Rappaport notes in his reflections on Russia, the problem 'lies not only in gigantism or in the cult of power' of Stalin's era, 'but also in [the] normative monotony' of Brezhnev's era (Rappaport 1989: 12). The shift from the hyper-scale to the scale-less, from the ornate and handmade to the industrial and mass-produced, had a similar stultifying impact.

While Stalin's grand-scale works were concerned with heightening sensibility – reinforcing the police order – the operations of Brezhnev were focused on altering distribution. The process of constructing hundreds of scaleless urban blocks directly undermined the individual's capacity to locate themselves in their own world. This sense of the loss of place was exacerbated through the process of forced repatriation wherein returning workers were accommodated in new, but identically sized rooms, each with the same furniture. Through this process of enforced radical equity, the distribution of the system was altered, a political act driven by the state, to ensure that the workers had less capacity for differentiation than they did under the previous regime. However, the single factor that enabled the state to so effectively revise the police order was its *tabula rasa* town planning practice. Relatively few of the hundreds of buildings and urban squares constructed in Russia between 1930 and 1980 were built on vacant sites. Where once a rich mixture of housing, churches, shops, meeting halls and markets filled each urban street, they were all swiftly demolished to make way for the sprawling office building or worker-housing block. This process brutally undermined the old distribution of the sensible by erasing people's past connection to the land, to individual homes, to specific family structures and places of worship.

It is against this backdrop that, in the late 1970s and early 1980s, a small group of architectural graduates found themselves unwilling to continue to work for the government design office. Instead, and without official sanction, these graduates chose to spend their time designing dark, satirical works as a critique of the state. As Heinrich Klotz records:

> Prevented from building and attacked by the party architects, suspected of being reactionary and under pressure of not being able to act, they withdrew into their little offices – sketched, and invented stories. It was here, in shabby basement rooms, that [they produced] a cornucopia of sketches, plans, large format presentation boards and models.
>
> (Klotz 1989: 8)

These architecture graduates submitted their clandestine work to international competitions, where they gradually won both prizes and recognition in the West.

Among the most successful of the Paper Architects, winning eight international prizes for unbuilt work between 1978 and 1988, were Brodsky and Utkin. Their work was produced, initially at least, 'without official endorsement or recognition [and] under a regime fundamentally hostile to individual expression' (Nesbitt 2003: n.p.). In response to these circumstances, many of their designs can be read as direct criticisms of the Soviet state and its attitudes. Possibly the most famous of their early works was their 'Columbarium Architecture' project.

The Columbaria projects

In 1984, in a deliberate and provocative act, Brodsky and Utkin submitted a design entitled 'Columbarium Architecture' to the Union of Architects of USSR Competition, a state-sponsored and state-judged award. Their design, a criticism of the *tabula rasa* planning approach, was for a Museum for Disappearing Buildings. In their competition entry, Brodsky and Utkin observe that:

> It's hard to say how many old buildings [. . .] have disappeared from our city in recent years. It's even harder to say how many of them will disappear in the near future. Some were torn down in order to build new ones in their place; others because they stood too close to a new construction site [. . .]
>
> (Brodsky and Utkin 1984, n.p.)

The Museum for Disappearing Buildings is a four-storey, largely hollow volume with a facade to a Moscow street. It is sited near the intersection with an unnamed public square centred on a grand statue. The facade incorporates a slice through the building that was demolished to make way for it. To enter the museum, a visitor must travel further down the street, away from the public square, and then through an alley and hidden arcade. After crossing the threshold, the visitors find themselves within:

> An enormous concrete honeycomb [housing memorials to] all urban structures, significant and insignificant, beautiful and homely, loved or barely acknowledged, that are destined to destruction under the steamroller of modern urban renewal. The structure's niches are labeled like tombstones with the dates of each building's life span.
>
> (Nesbitt 2003: n.p.)

A metal ramp spirals up into the space, allowing visitors to view replicas of each lost building. A single translucent globe hangs in the centre of the void, amplifying the last rays of the afternoon sun, turning the museum into a *tableau vivant* to the destruction of Moscow's built heritage. In contrast, each morning the globe at the centre of the now-darkened Lilliputian cityscape resembles a wrecking ball, a reminder of the process that transformed the full-size buildings into rubble.

While ostensibly without a specific site, the diagrammatic plan provided by Brodsky and Utkin bears a strong resemblance to a particular public square – defined by several intersections, a street configuration, subway station and statue – that existed in Moscow until 1983 (just before their competition entry was completed). At the time, this particular space was colloquially known as Dzerzhinsky Square, in honour of the 17-metre-high statue that was at its centre (see below). However, the real name of the square is Lubyanka (*Lubianskaya*) and it is named after the headquarters of the KGB, which dominates its entire east side. That Brodsky and Utkin's 'Columbarium Architecture' is, covertly at least, sited on such a square is significant. This location features one of the most subversive transformations of scale in the urban and social fabric of Moscow, and the siting of the 'Columbarium Architecture' serves to accentuate this transformation.

If ever there was a space that unwittingly promulgated the deliquescence of scale, it would be Lubyanka Square. Starting from the east, the KGB headquarters is positioned against a backdrop of Muscovite housing. The Lubyanka building itself – a massive wall of offices above a subterranean prison – was euphemistically and somewhat grimly known as 'the tallest building in Moscow' – 'because Siberia can be seen from its basement' (Miller *et al.* 2010). In the centre of Lubyanka Square is Iron Felix, a giant statue of Felix Dzerzhinsky, the original founder of the secret police in Soviet Russia. His oversized presence, in front of the similarly hyper-scaled facade of the Lubyanka building, serves as a reminder of the night-time raids and the tens of thousands of adult prisoners who were last seen entering Lubyanka's doors. But across from Iron Felix, partially bisecting his gaze, and sited in opposition to the Lubyanka building, is the facade of Aleksei Dushkin's Detskiy Mir; better known as Children's World, the home of the Moscow Toy Company. While the window displays of Detskiy Mir are regularly changed, they almost always feature, celebrated in one of the many traditional scenes, a matryoshka. Behind the facade, another scale change occurs; inside, the building is dominated by children, many of whom will be clustered around Detskiy Mir's beloved centrepiece: a human-sized teddy bear, reminiscent of Misha, the icon of the 1980 Moscow Olympics. Finally, behind Detskiy Mir's rear facade, Brodsky and Utkin proposed a different sort of urban backdrop: a mausoleum wall, lined with miniature

Politics and the deliquescence of scale

Figure 1
Brodsky and Utkin,
Columbarium
Architecture
(Museum of
Disappearing
Buildings), 1990.
From 'Projects'
portfolio,
1981–90, 35
etchings, ed.
of 30, 43 x 31¾"
(F).

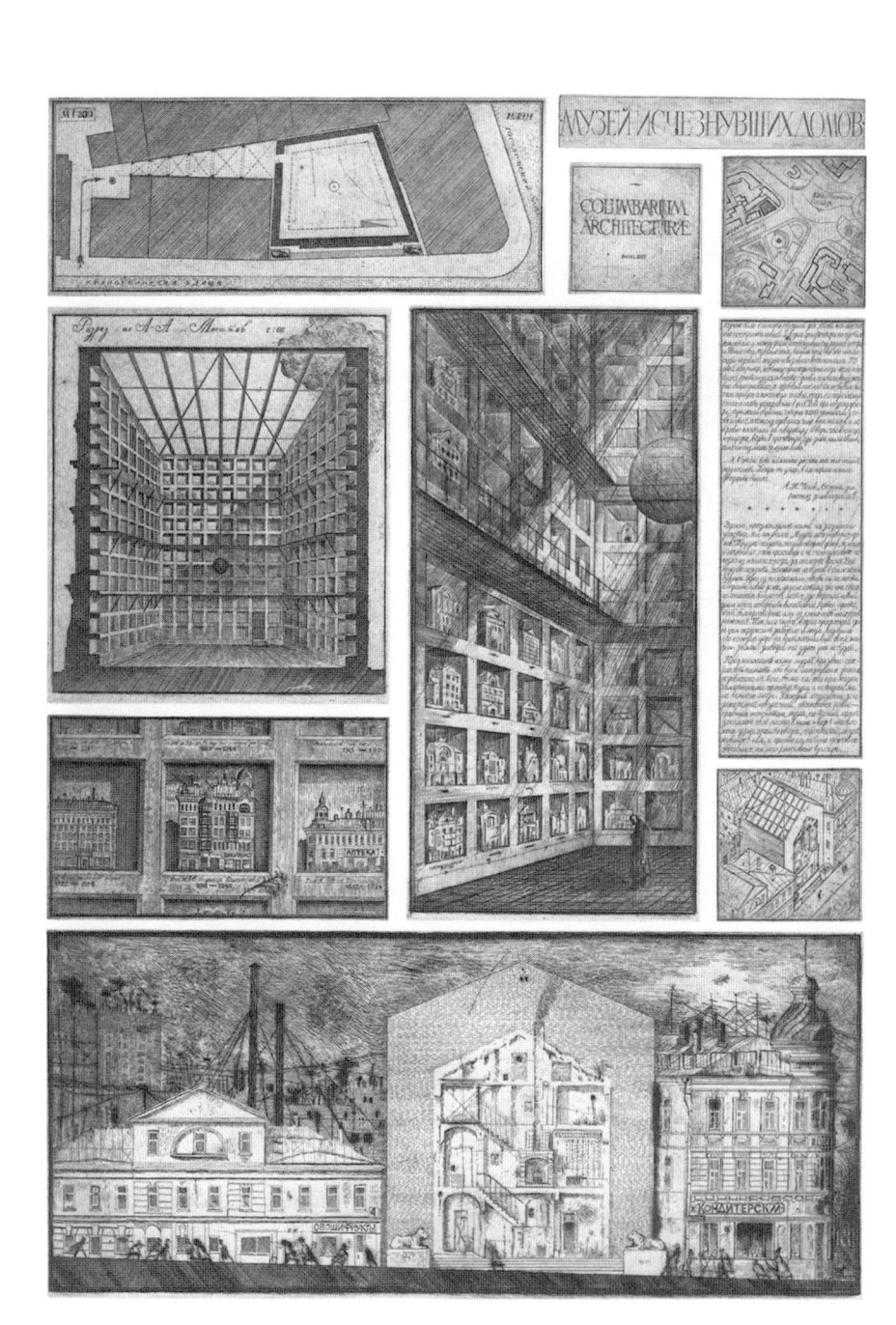

213

dwellings. In this vignette, the matryoshka is the scale hinge, the transformative device that critically pairs children in opposition to adults, plush Misha against Iron Felix, the KGB headquarters against Detskiy Mir, and, finally, the miniature city in Brodsky's and Utkin's museum against the full-scale city of Moscow.

From the perspective of the politics *of* aesthetics, the 'Columbarium Architecture' was ideally positioned to promote dissensus. Being entered into a state competition ensured that the design would have a heightened level of sensibility, and, being both an unauthorised design and one that was the product of excessive and selfish labour, was enough to provoke a potential political reaction. Conversely, the content of the design in relation to its context, supporting a reading of the politics *in* aesthetics, is less compelling. Without a more overt recognition of the relationship between their project and Lubyanka Square, the viewer is left with a depiction of a private space for the mourning of lost architecture; a strangely understated reading of the adverse impact of the destruction of Moscow's historic building stock under the directive of the Communist Party.

Two years later, Brodsky and Utkin returned to the same theme, producing a design for a 'Columbarium Habitabile'. This project was submitted, if not with state support, then certainly without sanction, to the *Japan Architect* journal's annual ideas competition. The new design had many similarities to the first, but with one key difference: the buildings housed in the new Columbarium are full size, so the museum has become the size of a small city to accommodate them.

The new Columbarium design is set in an unnamed city where historic buildings are destroyed to make way for modern ones. Brodsky and Utkin then offer the curious postulate that a house is only worth saving if it is inhabited. Thus, once the government decides to relocate people to new, modern flats, the inhabitants of the soon-to-be-demolished houses are given a choice.

> There is only one possibility for the owner of such a house to save it: let them take the house from its place and put it into a Columbarium – a huge concrete cube standing in the center of the city. But they do it only if the [. . .] family continue living in their house – now standing on a shelf in a concrete box. While they live in it the house lives also[;] but if they cannot live in these conditions any more [then] their house is destroyed.
>
> (Brodsky and Utkin 1986: n.p.)

According to Nesbitt (2003: n.p.), the 'Columbarium Architecture' consists of a 'mammoth rectangular courtyard building with niches to store buildings' – full size houses – 'slated to be torn down'. At the core of this Columbarium design is a wrecking ball, hanging from the centre of the roof as a reminder of the inevitable future. When a house becomes deserted, the wrecking ball is used to demolish it, making way for a future displaced structure. Brodsky and Utkin's submission depicts an elderly man drinking tea, as he looks forlornly across the cube at his soon-to-be-destroyed neighbours and wonders about the future of his own home.

Politics and the deliquescence of scale

Figure 2
Brodsky and Utkin,
Columbarium
Habitabile,
1989–90.
From 'Projects'
portfolio, 1981–90,
35 etchings,
ed. of 30, 43 x 31¾"
(F).

Whereas the 'Columbarium Architecture' design was clearly a reaction against the *tabula rasa* approach, and deployed scale as a mediating device, the political intent of the 'Columbarium Habitabile' is more ambivalent. As Nesbitt observes, it 'represents a triumph of Modernist uniformity' (Nesbitt 2003: n.p.). It is almost as if Brodsky and Utkin were setting out to propose an alternative, satirical solution to the state's housing problem; a solution that, somehow having lost all irony through its execution, is almost as destructive as those of the previous generations of Russian architects. Here, Brodsky and Utkin have forgotten to dissolve scale to enable resistance, and have, perhaps unwittingly, produced a project that supports the very police order they were seeking to undermine.

Conclusion

In the hands of the Communist state, scale was the architectural strategy *par excellence*. It allowed successive Soviet regimes to modify the police order, altering the distribution of the sensible to favour the state for over six decades. It is not surprising, then, that Brodsky and Utkin should be drawn to subvert the very design strategy that was at the heart of the state's power. Thus, from their earliest projects, the dissolution of scale, the breakdown of its fixed and seemingly immutable relationship with the world, was a central strategy in their work. From the point of view of the politics *of* aesthetics, the dissolution of scale was (initially, at least) a potent subversive force, and from 1979 to 1986 the Paper Architects deployed it with some success. However, by the time the Western world had begun to celebrate the Paper Architects' resistance, the last vestiges of the Iron Curtain were already rusting away and Mikhail Gorbachev's 'perestroika' had been superseded by a fledgling free-market economy. By the early 1990s, the Communist Party had been banned, democratic elections were being held and the distribution of the sensible was forever changed.

Ultimately, the dissolution of scale is a contrary and slippery proposition that is just as likely to usefully support an agenda as it is to undermine it. This is certainly the case with the 'Columbarium Habitabile', with its threatening message and themes of incarceration. This problem with the predictability and stability of scale is not just limited to architecture.

Since the 1980s, several disciplines, including geography, politics and sociology, have begun to reject fixed scales as useful ratios for the interpretation of facts, figures, events and objects (Taylor 1982; Marston *et al.* 2005). But these disciplines are equally wary of the complete dissolution of scale, a practice they view as contrary and ultimately unpredictable. Instead, scholars have offered several new models for working with scale; models that are relative but not fixed, flexible but not fluid. The foremost model developed in these fields to accommodate such needs has been described as a 'nested hierarchy', or more fittingly as a 'matryoshka system' (Herod 2009, 2010). Contrary to the Paper Architects' romantic reading of the matryoshka as a symbol of the breakdown of scale, it is actually a tightly controlled, hierarchical system; the ideal chiastic device to provide a hinge between one scale and another. Appropriately, this is the very role the matryoshka plays in the window of Detskiy Mir: quietly signalling, through its capacity to transform scale, the ability to resist the overwhelming power of the state.

Bibliography

Abbreviations

CW: *Critical Writings of Adrian Stokes*, London: Thames & Hudson, 1978.
SE: *Standard Edition of the Complete Psychological Works of Sigmund Freud*, London: Hogarth, 1974.

Aarsleff, H. (1982) *From Locke to Saussure: essays on the study of language and intellectual history*, Minneapolis, MN: University of Minnesota Press.
Abalos, I. (2001) *The Good Life*, Barcelona: Gustavo Gili.
Adler, G. (2011) *Robert Maguire and Keith Murray*, London: RIBA Publishing in association with the Twentieth Century Society and English Heritage.
Adler, S. and Shoskes, E. (2009) 'Planning for Healthy People/Healthy Places: Lessons from Mid-Twentieth Century Global Discourse', in *Planning Perspectives*, 24.2 (April): 197–217.
Alberti, L. (1988) *On the Art of Building in Ten Books*, translated by Rykwert, J., Leach, N. and Tavernor, R., Cambridge, MA: MIT Press.
Alberti, L. (2004) *On Painting*, translated by Grayson, C., London: Penguin.
Aman, A. (1992) *Architecture and Ideology in Eastern Europe during the Stalin Era*, Cambridge, MA: MIT Press.
Andrews, H. (1948) *Westminster Retrospect: a memoir of Sir Richard Terry*, London, New York and Toronto: Oxford University Press.
Aristotle, *Metaphysica*.
Aristotle, *Nicomachean Ethics*.
Aristotle, *Rhetoric*.
Arnheim, R. (2004) *Art and Visual Perception: a psychology of the creative eye* (1954/74), Berkeley, CA: University of California Press.
Aubrey, J. (1898) *Brief Lives*, Clark, A. (ed.) 2 vols, Oxford: Clarendon Press.
Auden, W.H. (1972) [1966] 'Culture and Leisure', in Bell, G. and Tyrwhitt, J. (eds) *Human Identity in the Urban Environment*, Harmondsworth: Penguin.
Augé, M. (1995) *Non-places: introduction to an anthropology of supermodernity*, translated by Howe, J., London: Verso.
Bachelard, G. (1957) *La Poetique de l'Espace*, Paris: Presses Universitaires de France.
Bacon, F. (1605) *Of the Advancement of Learning*, Oxford: Henrie Tomes.
Bagenal, H. (1919) 'Acoustics of Churches: choral music', in *Architects' Journal*, 24 December: 772, 777.
Bagenal, H. (1920) 'Acoustics of Churches and Choral Music', in *Architectural Association Journal*, February: 245–7.

Bagenal, H. (1921) 'Some Notes on Auditoria for Large Choirs', in *The Builder*, 8 January.
Bagenal, H. (1922) 'Acoustics and the Vatican Choir', in *The Builder*, June: 841.
Bagenal, H. (1927) 'Influence of Buildings on Musical Tone', in *Music and Letters*, 8: 437–47.
Bagenal, H. (1954) 'Cathedral Acoustics', in *RIBA Journal*, April: 223–6.
Bagenal, H. and Wood, A. (1931) *Planning for Good Acoustics*, London: Methuen.
Bagenal, J. (1984) Lecture: Hope Bagenal, *The Art Worker's Guild*, London: RIBA Archives.
Bagenal, P. (ed.) (2010) *Letters to a Niece and Letters to a Brother: two autobiographical fragments by Hope Bagenal*, San Francisco and London: Blurb.
Bagenal, R. (ed.) (1983) *Letters to a Niece*, Oxford: Oxford Polytechnic.
Ballard, J. (2001) 'The Thousand Dreams of Stellavista', in *Vermillion Sands*, London: Vintage.
Banham, R. (1955) 'New Brutalism', in *Architectural Review*, December, 354–61.
Banham, R. (1966) 'Machine Aesthetes', in Banham, R. *A Critic Writes: essays by Reyner Banham*, Berkeley, Los Angeles, CA and London: University of California Press.
Banham, R. (1984) *The Architecture of the Well Tempered Environment*, Chicago, IL: University of Chicago Press.
Barmore, F. and Borst L. (1969) 'Canterbury Cathedral: an alternate explanation of its plan', in *Science*, 166: 772–4.
Batchelor, D. (2000) *Chromophobia*, London: Reaktion Books.
Bell, G. and Tyrwhitt, J. (eds) (1972) *Human Identity in the Urban Environment*, Harmondsworth: Penguin.
Belov, M. (1988) 'Children of the Stagnation', in *Nostalgia of Culture: contemporary Soviet visionary architecture*, London: Architectural Association.
Benedikt, M. (1987) *For an Architecture of Reality*, New York: Lumen.
Bennett, J., Cooper, M., Hunter, M. and Jardine, L. (2003) *London's Leonardo: the life and work of Robert Hooke*, Oxford: Oxford University Press.
Bergdoll, B. and Dickerman, L. (2009) *Bauhaus 1991–1933: workshops for modernity*, New York: Museum of Modern Art.
Berlin, B. and Kay, P. (1969) *Basic Colour Terms: their universality and evolution*, Berkeley, CA: University of California Press.
Berman, M. and Tschumi, B. (eds) (2003) *INDEX: Architecture*, Cambridge, MA and London: MIT Press.
Bicknell, P. and Munro, J. (1988) *Gilpin to Ruskin: drawing masters and their manuals, 1800–1860*, Cambridge: Fitzwilliam Museum.
Bion, W.R. (1967) 'A Theory of Thinking', in *Second Thoughts*, London: Heinemann.
Bloomer, K. (2000) *The Nature of Ornament: rhythm and metamorphosis in architecture*, New York and London: Norton.
Bloomer, K. and Moore, C. (1977) *Body, Memory and Architecture*, New Haven, CT and London: Yale University Press.
Bochner, M. (2008a) 'An Interview with Lisa Haller (1973)', in Bochner, M. (ed.) *Solar System and Rest Rooms: writings and interviews, 1965–2007*, Cambridge, MA: MIT Press.
Bochner, M. (2008b) 'Excerpts from Speculation (1967–1970)', in Bochner, M. (ed.) *Solar System and Rest Rooms: writings and interviews, 1965–2007*, Cambridge, MA: MIT Press.
Bochner, M. (2008c) 'Three Statements for Data Magazine (1972)', in Bochner, M. (ed.) *Solar System and Rest Rooms: writings and interviews, 1965–2007*, Cambridge, MA: MIT Press.
Bois, Y-A. (1995) 'The Measurement Pieces: from index to implex' in Field, R. (ed.) *Mel Bochner: thought made visible 1966–1973*, New Haven, CT: Yale University Art Gallery.
Bois, Y-A., Bonnefoi, C., Clay, J., Damisch, H. and Troy, N. (1979) *Architecture, arts plastiques: pour une histoire interdisciplinaire des pratiques de l'espace*, Paris: Corda.
Boobbyer, P. (2000) *The Stalin Era*, London: Routledge.
Borges, J.L. (1998), 'On Exactitude in Science' ['Del rigor en la ciencia'], translated by Hurley, A., in Borges, J.L. *Collected Fictions*, New York: Penguin.

Bibliography

Boudon, P. (1971) Sur l'espace architectural: essai d'épistémologie de l'architecture, Dunod, Paris, translated in: Heynen, H. et al. (2004) Dat is architectuur: Sleutelteksten uit de twintigste eeuw, Rotterdam: 010.

Bourdieu, P. (1986) Distinction: a social critique of the judgement of taste, Abingdon: Routledge.

Boyer, C. (1987) The Rainbow: from myth to mathematics, Princeton, NJ: Princeton University Press.

Bray, R. (1995a) 'Music and the Quadrivium in Early Tudor Music', in Music and Letters, 76: 1–18.

Bray, R. (1995b) 'Music and Musicians', in Bray, R. (ed.) The Blackwell History of Music in Britain: the sixteenth century, Oxford: Blackwell.

Brino, G. (2005) Carlo Mollino: architecture as autobiography, London: Thames & Hudson.

British Council (2010) Villa Frankenstein. The Journal of the British Pavilion, 12th International Architecture Exhibition 1 (August).

Brodsky, A. and Utkin, I. (1984) 'Columbarium Architecture,' in Nesbitt, L. (2003) Brodsky and Utkin: the complete works, New York: Princeton Architectural Press, pl. 2 n.p.

Brodsky, A. and Utkin, I. (1986) 'Columbarium Habitabile,' in Nesbitt, L. (2003) Brodsky and Utkin: the complete works, New York: Princeton Architectural Press, pl. 3 n.p.

Brothers, A. (1998) Worlds in Miniature: the etchings of Jacques Callot and Wenceslaus Hollar, Sydney: National Gallery of Victory.

Brougher, K. and Mattis, O. (2005) Visual Music: synaesthesia in art and music since 1900, London: Thames & Hudson.

Bryant, G. (2004) 'Timely Untimeliness: architectural modernism and the idea of the Gesamtkunstwerk', in Hvattum, M. and Hermansen, C. (eds) Tracing Modernity: manifestations of modern in architecture and the city, Abingdon: Routledge.

Bryon, H. (2008) 'Revolutions in Space: parallel projections in the early modern era', in Architectural Research Quarterly, 12: 3–4.

Buchloh, B. (1999) 'Conceptual Art 1962–1969: from the aesthetic of administration to the critique of institutions (1989)', in Alberro, A. and Stimson, B. (eds) Conceptual Art: a critical anthology, Cambridge, MA and London: MIT Press.

Bullen, J. (1992) 'Ruskin and the Tradition of Renaissance Historiography', in Wheeler, M. and Whiteley, N. (eds) The Lamp of Memory: Ruskin, tradition and architecture, Manchester: Manchester University Press.

Camus, A. (1942) L'Étranger [The Outsider], Paris: Éditions Gallimard.

Carpenter, N. (1958) Music in the Medieval and Renaissance Universities, Norman, OK: University of Oklahoma Press.

Chapman, A. and Kent, P. (eds) (2005) Robert Hooke and the English Renaissance, Leominster: Gracewing.

Chippendale T. (1754) The Gentleman and Cabinet-maker's Director: being a large collection of the most elegant and useful designs of household furniture, in the most fashionable taste, London: for the author.

Choisy, A. (1873) L'art de bâtir chez les Romains, Paris: Ducher.

Choisy, A. (1883). L'art de bâtir chez les Byzantins, Paris: Société anonyme de publications périodiques.

Choisy, A. (1899) Histoire de l'architecture, 2 vols, Paris: Gauthier-Villars.

Cicero, De Officiis.

Coderch, J.A. (1972) 'Un Proyecto de Viviendas', in Arquitectura, 162: 16–21.

Cohen, D. (1975) 'Diagnostician for Cities', in New Scientist, 30 January: 262–4.

Coldstream, N. (2002) Medieval Architecture, Oxford: Oxford University Press.

Collingwood, W. (1893) The Life and Work of John Ruskin, London: Methuen.

Collins, H. (1913) 'Latin Church Music by Early English Composers', in Proceedings of the Musical Association, 39th Session.

Collins, P. (1965) Changing Ideals in Modern Architecture, London: Faber and Faber.

Colomina, B. (1994) *Privacy and Publicity: modern architecture as mass media*, Cambridge, MA: MIT Press.
Colquhoun, A. (1981) 'Alvar Aalto: type versus function', in *Essays in Architectural Criticism*, Cambridge, MA: MIT Press.
Comper, J.N. (1947) *Of the Atmosphere of a Church*, London: Sheldon.
Comper, J.N. (1950) *Of the Christian Altar*, London: SPCK.
Connor, S. (2004) 'Edison's Teeth: touching hearing' in Erlmann, V. (ed.) *Hearing Cultures: essays on sound, listening and modernity*, Oxford: Berg.
Connor, S. (2010) Inclining to the View: a talk given at the symposium 'Seeing From Above', Wellcome Trust, London, 6 February, www.stevenconnor.com/inclining/inclining.pdf.
Conrad, J. (1899) *Heart of Darkness*, edition of 1960, New York: Bantam.
Cook, E. and Wedderburn, A. (eds) (1904–13) *The Works of John Ruskin*, London: George Allen.
Cooke, C. (1988) 'A Picnic by the Roadside or Work in Hand for the Future?', in *Nostalgia of Culture: contemporary Soviet visionary architecture*, London: Architectural Association.
Cooper, M. (2003) 'A More Beautiful City': *Robert Hooke and the rebuilding of London after the Great Fire*, Stroud: Sutton.
Correa, F., Fochs, C., Rovira, J., Garnica, J. and Maldonado, J. (2006) *J.A. Coderch a Sarria-Sant Gervasi: Les Cotxeres*, Barcelona: COAC.
Cosgrove, D, (1979) 'John Ruskin and the Geographical Imagination', in *Geographical Review*, 69.1: 43–62.
Coyne, R. (2010) *The Tuning of Place: sociable spaces and pervasive digital media*, Cambridge, MA: MIT Press.
Coyne, R. (2011) *Derrida for Architects*, Abingdon: Routledge.
Crary, J. (1992) *Techniques of the Observer: on vision and modernity in the nineteenth century*, Cambridge, MA: MIT Press.
Cross, N. (1982) 'Designerly Ways of Knowing', in *Design Studies*, 3.4: 221–7.
Cruickshank, D. (ed.) (1996) *Sir Banister Fletcher's A History of Architecture*, Oxford: Architectural Press.
Curtis, W. (1986) *Le Corbusier: ideas and forms*, London: Phaidon.
Dallmayr, F. (2000) 'Exit from Orientalism', in Macfie, A., *Orientalism: a Reader*, Edinburgh: Edinburgh University Press.
Daston, L. (2005) 'Fear and Loathing of the Imagination in Science', in *Dædalus*, 4: 16–30.
Davidts, W. (2008) 'Claes Oldenburg, the Poetry of Scale' (unpublished paper).
Day, T. (1994) 'Sir Richard Terry and Sixteenth-Century Polyphony', in *Early Music*, 22: 296–307.
de Carlo, G. (1992) 'Architecture's Public', in Zucchi, B. (ed.) *Giancarlo de Carlo*, Oxford: Butterworth Architecture.
Derrida, J. (1997). 'Chora', in Kipnis, J. and Leeser, T. (eds) *Choral Works*, New York: Monacelli Press.
Dibble, J. (2002) *Charles Villiers Stanford: man and musician*, Oxford: Oxford University Press.
Dischinger, M. (2006) 'The Non-Careful Sight', in Devlieger, P. et al. (eds) *Blindness and the Multi-sensorial City*, Antwerp: Garant.
Dixon, T. (2003) *From Passions to Emotions: the creation of a secular psychological category*, Cambridge: Cambridge University Press.
Dixon Hunt, J. (2004) *Gardens and the Picturesque: studies in the history of landscape architecture*, Cambridge, MA: MIT Press.
Dovey, K. (1999) *Framing Places: mediating power in built form*, Abingdon: Routledge.
Doxiadis, C. (1968), *Ekistics: an introduction to the science of human settlements*, London: Hutchinson.
Doxiadis, C. (1972) [1966] 'Anthropocosmos: the world of man', in Bell, G. and Tyrwhitt, J. (eds) *Human Identity in the Urban Environment*, Harmondsworth: Penguin.
Doxiadis, C. (2006) [1963] 'A New Role for the Architect', in Kyrtsis, A.-A. (ed.) *Constantinos A. Doxiadis: texts, design drawings, settlements*, Athens: Ikaros.

Doxiadis, C. (2006) [1965] 'Islamabad: the creation of a new capital', The Town Planning Review, 36.1, in Kyrtsis, A.-A. (ed.) *Constantinos A. Doxiadis: texts, design drawings, settlements*, Athens: Ikaros.
Doxiadis, C. (2006) [1968] 'A City for Human Development', in Kyrtsis, A.-A. (ed.) *Constantinos A. Doxiadis: texts, design drawings, settlements*, Athens: Ikaros.
Doxiadis, C. (2006) [1972a] 'The Formation of the Human Room', in Kyrtsis, A.-A. (ed.) *Constantinos A. Doxiadis: texts, design drawings, settlements*, Athens: Ikaros.
Doxiadis, C. (2006) [1972b] 'The Two-Headed Eagle: from the past to the future of human settlements', in Kyrtsis, A.-A. (ed.) *Constantinos A. Doxiadis: texts, design drawings, settlements*, Athens: Ikaros.
Durand, J.-N.-L. (1802–9) *Précis des leçons d'architecture données à l'École Polytechnique*, Paris: for the author.
Eames, C. and Eames, R. (1955) *House after Five Years of Living* [video], Los Angeles, CA.
Edgerton, S. (2009) *The Mirror, the Window, and the Telescope: how Renaissance linear perspective changed our vision of the universe*, Ithaca and London: Cornell University Press.
'Editor' (1926) 'Editorial', in *Music and Letters*, 7: 1.
Ehrenzweig, A. (1967) *The Hidden Order of Art*, edition of 1973, St Albans: Paladin.
Ehrlich D. (2003) *Frank Lloyd Wright: interior style & design*, London: PRC Publishing.
Elson, L. (1915) 'Acoustics: suggestions on behalf of an unpopular subject', in *The Musical Quarterly*, 1: 410–15.
Emmons, P. (2005) 'Size Matters: virtual scale and bodily imagination in architectural drawing', in *Architectural Research Quarterly*, 9.3/4.
Ertl, R. and Hibberd, R. (2003) *The Art of the Russian Matryoshka*, Boulder: Vernissage.
Evans, J., and Whitehouse, J. (eds) (1956) *The Diaries of John Ruskin*, Oxford: Clarendon Press.
Evelyn, J. (1995) *The Writings of John Evelyn*, de la Bédoyère, G. (ed.), Rochester, NY and Woodbridge: Boydell and Brewer.
Falconar Fry, A. (1937) 'Letter to the editor', in *The Gramophone*, 42.
Farish, W. (1822) 'On Isometrical Perspective', in *Transactions of the Cambridge Philosophical Society*, 1: 1–19.
Field, R. (1995a) 'Mel Bochner: thought made visible' in Field, R.S. (ed.) *Mel Bochner: thought made visible 1966–1973*, New Haven, CT: Yale University Art Gallery: 15–74.
Field, R. (ed.) (1995b) *Mel Bochner: thought made visible 1966–1973*, New Haven, CT: Yale University Art Gallery.
Fisher, M. (2009) *Capitalist Realism: is there no alternative?* Ropley: O Books.
Forty, A. (2004) *Words and Buildings: a vocabulary of modern architecture*, New York: Thames & Hudson.
Foster, H. (1996) 'The Crux of Minimalism', in Foster, H. *The Return of the Real: the avant-garde at the end of the century*, Cambridge, MA: MIT Press.
Foucault, M. (1991) *The Order of Things*, first published in 1966 in French, Abingdon: Routledge.
Fowler, H. (1926) 'Acoustics', in Fowler, H. (ed.) *A Dictionary of Modern English Usage*, Oxford: Oxford University Press.
Frampton, K. (1995) 'Between the Project and the Built: three moments in the work of Oswald Mathias Ungers', in Sieber-Albers, A. and Kieren, M. (eds) *Sichtweisen: Betrachtungen zum Werk von O.M.Ungers*, Brunswick and Wiesbaden: Vieweg and Cologne: Ungers Archiv für Architekturwissenschaft.
Frampton, K. (2002) 'Team 10, Plus 20: the vicissitudes of ideology', in *Labour, Work and Architecture*, London: Phaidon.
Frank, J. (1981) 'Die Rolle der Architektur', in Spalt, J. and Czech, H. (eds) *Josef Frank 1885–1967*, Vienna: Hochschule für angewandte Kunst.
Freud, S. (1914) 'On narcissism', *SE14*: 73–102.

Freud, S. (1917) 'Mourning and melancholia', *SE14*: 243–58.
Freud, S. (1923) *The Ego and the Id, SE19*: 13–59.
Freud, S. (2002) *Civilization and its Discontents*, London: Penguin.
Friedman, A. (ed.) (1998) *Women and the Making of the Modern House: a social and architectural history*, New York: Abrams.
Gage, J. (1997) *Colour and Culture*, London: Thames & Hudson.
Gage, J. (1999) *Colour and Meaning: art, science and symbolism*, London: Thames & Hudson.
Garver, E. (1987) *Machiavelli and the History of Prudence*, Madison, WI: University of Wisconsin Press.
Garver, E. (1994) *Aristotle's Rhetoric: an art of character*, Chicago, IL: University of Chicago Press.
Girbau, L. (1987) 'The Cell and the Organism', in *Arquitectura*, 268: 22–33.
Godfrey, M. (2005) 'From Box to Street and Back Again: an inadequate descriptive system for the seventies' in De Salvo, D. (ed.) *Open Systems: rethinking art c.1970*, London: Tate Publishing.
Godfrey, R. (1995) *A Bohemian Artist in England*, New Haven, CT and London: Yale University Press.
Goethe, J. (1982) *Theory of Colours* (first published 1810), Cambridge, MA: MIT Press.
Gombrich, E. (1969) *Art and Illusion*, Princeton. NJ: Princeton University Press.
Graham, S. and Marvin, S. (2001) *Splintering Urbanism: networked infrastructures, technological mobilities and the urban condition*, Abingdon: Routledge.
Grassi, E. (2001) *Rhetoric as Philosophy: the humanist tradition*, translated by Krois, J. and Azodi, A., Carbondale, IL: Southern Illinois University Press.
Graver, M. (2009) *Stoicism and Emotion*, Chicago, IL: University of Chicago Press.
Gray, C. (1934) *Peter Warlock: a memoir of Philip Heseltine*, London: Jonathan Cape.
Griffiths, A. and Kesnerova, G. (1983) *Wenceslaus Hollar: prints and drawings*, London: British Museum Publications.
Gross, D. (2006) *The Secret History of Emotion: from Aristotle's* Rhetoric *to modern brain science*, Chicago, IL: University of Chicago Press.
Guadet, J. (1910) *Eléments et théorie de l'architecture*, 4th edition, Paris: Librairie de la Construction Moderne.
Gubler, J. (2008) *Jean Tschumi: architecture at full scale*, Milan: Skira.
Guy, F., Shaw-Miller, S., Tucker, M. (2007) *Eye-Music: Kandinsky, Klee and all that jazz*, Chichester: Pallant House.
Hammond, P. (1960) *Liturgy and Architecture*, London: Barry and Rockliff.
Hampton, T. (2004) 'Strange Alteration: physiology and psychology from Galen to Rabelais', in Paster, G., Rowe, K. and Floyd-Wilson, M. (eds) *Reading the Early Modern Passions: essays in the cultural history of emotion*, Philadelphia, PA: University of Pennsylvania Press.
Hardin, C. and Maffi, L. (eds) (1997) *Color Categories in Thought and Language*, Cambridge: Cambridge University Press.
Hariman, R. (1991) 'Prudence/Performance', in *Rhetoric Society Quarterly*, 21.2 (Spring).
Hatherley, O. (2008) *Militant Modernism*, Winchester: O Books.
Hatton, B. (1988) 'Voices from the Courtyard', in *Nostalgia of Culture: contemporary Soviet visionary architecture*, London: Architectural Association.
Hays, K. and Miller, D. (eds) (2008) *Buckminster Fuller: starting with the universe*, New York/New Haven and London: Whitney Museum of American Art/Yale University Press.
Herod, A. (2009) 'Scale the Local and Global', in Clifford, N., Holloway, S., Rice, S. and Valentine, G. (eds) *Key Concepts in Geography*, London: Sage.
Herod, A. (2010) *Scale*, New York: Taylor & Francis.
Herssens, J. and Heylighen, A. (2009) 'A Lens into the Haptic World', in *Proceedings of Include 2009*, London: Royal College of Art – Helen Hamlyn Centre.

Herssens, J. and Heylighen, A. (2010) 'Blind Body Language', in Clarkson, P. et al. (eds) *Proceedings of the 5th Cambridge Workshop on Universal Access and Assistive Technology*, Cambridge: University of Cambridge: 109–18.

Herssens, J. and Heylighen, A. (2011) 'Haptic Design Research: a blind sense of place', in *Proceedings of the ARCC/EAAE 2010 International Conference on Architectural Research*, ARCC/EAAE, Washington, DC.

Hertzberger, H. (1991) *Lessons for Students in Architecture*, Rotterdam: 010.

Heschong, L. (1979) *Thermal Delight in Architecture*, Cambridge, MA. and London: MIT Press.

Hewison, R. (2009) *Ruskin on Venice*, New Haven, CT and London: Yale University Press.

Higgins, H. (2009) *The Grid Book*, Cambridge, MA: MIT Press.

Hilton, T. (2002) *John Ruskin*. New Haven and London: Yale University Press.

Hind, A. (1972) *Wenceslaus Hollar and His Views of London and Windsor in the Seventeenth Century*, New York: Benjamin Blom.

Hipkins, A. (1879) in Grove, S. (ed.) *A Dictionary of Music and Musicians*, 1st ed., London: Macmillan.

Hooke, R. (1665) *Micrographia: or some physiological descriptions of minute bodies made by magnifying glasses with observations and inquiries thereupon*, London: Royal Society.

Hooke, R. (1935) *The Diary of Robert Hooke, M.A., M.D., F.R.S., 1672–1680*, Robinson, H. and Adams, W. (eds) London: Taylor & Francis.

Hunter, M. (2010) 'Hooke's Figurations: a figural drawing attributed to Robert Hooke', in *Notes and Records of the Royal Society*, 64.3, 20 September: 251–60, published online and accessed 24 March 2010.

Hvattum, M. (2001) 'Gottfried Semper: between poetics and practical aesthetics', in *Zeitschrift für Kunstgeschichte*, 64.4: 537–46.

Ingold, T. (2000) *The Perception of the Environment: essays on livelihood, dwelling and skill*, Abingdon: Routledge.

Isacoff, S. (2003) *Temperament: how music became a battleground for the great minds of Western civilization*, New York: Vintage.

Jagy, W. (1995) 'Squaring Circles in the Hyperbolic Plane', in *The Mathematical Intelligence*, 17.2: 31–6.

James, C. (1973) *Soviet Socialist Realism: origins and theory*, New York: St Martin's Press.

Jameson, F. (1999) 'History Lessons.' in Leach, N. (ed.) *Architecture and Revolution: contemporary perspectives on Central and Eastern Europe*, Abingdon: Routledge.

Jopling, J. (1842) *The Practice of Isometrical Perspective*, London: M. Taylor.

Kahn, V. (1985) *Rhetoric, Prudence, and Skepticism in the Renaissance*, Ithaca: Cornell University Press.

Kandinsky, W. (2006) *Concerning the Spiritual in Art*, London: Tate Publishing.

Kant, I. (1969) *The Critique of Judgment* (first published 1790), Oxford: Oxford University Press.

Keats, J. (1973) *The Complete Poems*, London: Penguin Books, p. 431.

Kiernan, M. (1998) *Moscow: a guide to Soviet and post-Soviet architecture*, London: Ellipsis.

Kite, S. (2007) 'Watching Palaces: Ruskin and the representation of Venice', in Swenarton, M., Troiani, I., and Webster, H. (eds) *The Politics of Making*, Abingdon: Routledge.

Kite, S. (2008) '"Filled with Thoughts of Flowing Leafage and Fiery Life": John Ruskin's Venice – fragility and flux', in *Architectural Theory Review*, 13.3: 274–87.

Kite, S. (2009a) *Adrian Stokes: an architectonic eye*, London: Legenda.

Kite, S. (2009b) '"Watchful Wandering": John Ruskin's strayings in Venice', in *Journal of Architectural Education,* 62.4 (May): 106–14.

Klein, M. (1925) 'A Contribution to the Psychogenesis of Tics', in *Love, Guilt and Reparation* (1975), London: Hogarth.

Klein, M. (1932) *The Psycho-analysis of Children*, edition of 1975, London: Hogarth.

Klein, M. (1945) 'The Oedipus complex in the light of early anxieties', in *Love, Guilt and Reparation* (1975), London: Hogarth.

Klein, M. (1946) 'Notes on some schizoid mechanisms', in *Envy and Gratitude* (1975), London: Hogarth.
Klein, M. (1948) 'On the theory of anxiety and guilt', in *Envy and Gratitude* (1975), London: Hogarth.
Klotz, H. (1989) 'Introduction', in Klotz, H. (ed.) *Paper Architecture: new projects from the Soviet Union*, New York: Rizzoli.
Knuuttila, S. (2004) *Emotions in Ancient and Medieval Philosophy*, Oxford: Clarendon Press.
Koolhaas, R. (2004) 'Junk Space', in Koolhaas, R., AMO and OMA, *Content*, Cologne: Taschen.
Koolhaas, R. and Mau, B. (1995) *S, M, L, XL: small, medium, large, extra-large*, New York: Monacelli Press.
Korzybski, A. (1973) *Science and Sanity: an introduction to non-Aristotelian systems and general semantics* (first published 1933), Fort Worth, TX: Institute of General Semantics.
Kosenkova, Y. (2009) *The Soviet City of 1940–1955*, Moscow: Librokom.
Kosenkova, Y. (2010) *Architecture of the Stalin era*, Moscow: KomKniga.
Krauss, R. (1993) *The Optical Unconscious*, Cambridge, Mass.: MIT Press.
Krucker, B. (2002) *Complex Ordinariness: the Upper Lawn Pavilion by Alison and Peter Smithson*, Zurich: gta Verlag, ETH.
Kyrtsis, A.-A. (ed.) (2006) *Constantinos A. Doxiadis: texts, design drawings, settlements*, Athens: Ikaros.
Lacan, J. (1948) 'Aggressivity in Psychoanalysis', translated by A. Sheridan, and later published in *Ecrits* (1977), London: Tavistock.
Lacan, J. (1949) 'The Mirror Stage as Formative of the Function of the I as Revealed in Psychoanalytic Experience', translated by A. Sheridan, and later published in *Ecrits* (1977), London: Tavistock.
Lacan, J. (1953) 'Some Reflections on the Ego', in *International Journal of Psycho-analysis*, 34: 11–17.
Lacan, J. (1958) 'The Signification of the Phallus', translated by A. Sheridan, and later published in *Ecrits* (1977), London: Tavistock.
Lagerlund, H. and Yrjönsuuri, M. (eds) (2002) *Emotions and Choice from Boethius to Descartes*, Dordrecht: Kluwer.
Latour, B. (1990) 'Visualisation and Cognition: drawing things together', in Lynch, M. and Woolgar, S. (eds) *Representation in Scientific Practice*, Cambridge, MA: MIT Press.
Lawson, B. (1994) *Design in Mind*, Oxford: Butterworth Architecture.
Leach, N. (1999) 'Introduction', in Leach, N. (ed.) *Architecture and Revolution: contemporary perspectives on Central and Eastern Europe*, London: Routledge.
Le Corbusier (1990) 'The Undertaking of Furniture', in *Precisions: on the present state of architecture and city planning*, translated by Aujame, E., Cambridge, MA: MIT Press.
Le Corbusier (2004) *The Modulor: a harmonious measure to the human scale universally applicable to architecture and mechanics*, Basel: Birkhäuser.
Lefaivre, L. and Tzonis, A. (1999) *Aldo van Eyck: humanist rebel*, Rotterdam: 010.
Lemoine, S., Rousseau, P., Jollet, E. and Rocque, G. (2003) *Aux origines de l'abstraction: 1800–1914*, Paris: Réunion des Musées Nationaux.
LeWitt, S. (1999) 'Paragraphs on Conceptual Art (1967)' in Alberro, A. and Stimson, B. (eds) *Conceptual Art: a critical anthology*, Cambridge, MA and London: MIT Press.
Loach, J. (1998) 'Le Corbusier and the Creative Use of Mathematics', in *The British Journal for the History of Science*, 31.2: 185–215.
Loomis, J. and Lederman, S. (1986) 'Tactual Perception', in Boff, K., Kaufmann, J. and Thomas, J. (eds) *Handbook of Perception and Human Performance*, 2, New York: John Wiley.
Loos, A. (1998) 'Architektur', in *Ornament and Crime*, translated by Mitchell, M., Riverside, CA: Ariadne.
Loos, A. (2003) 'The Poor Little Rich Man', in Samitz, A. (ed.) *Adolf Loos 1870–1933: architect, cultural critic, dandy*, Cologne: Taschen.

Loria, G. (1921) *Storia della geometria descrittiva dalle origini sino ai giorni nostri*, Milan: Ulrico Hoepli.
Ludson, H. (1969) 'Planners: Oracles at Delos', *Time*, 8 August. (www.time.com).
Lurie, D. (1966) 'Close Up / City Planner Constantinos Doxiadis', *Life*, 7 October: 55–60.
Lutz, C. and White, G. (1986) 'The Anthropology of Emotions', in *Annual Review of Anthropology*, 15: 405–36.
Lynn, G. (2005) 'On Calculus in Architecture', in *TED Talks*, www.ted.com/index.php/talks/greg_lynn_on_organic_design.html (accessed 11 April 2011).
Lynn, G. (2011) 'New City', Video. Seedmagazine.com http://seedmagazine.com/designseries/greg-lynn.html (accessed 11 April 2011).
Lyons, J. (1995) 'Colour in Language', in Lamb, T. and Bourriau, J. (eds) *Colour: art and science*, Cambridge: Cambridge University Press.
Lyotard, J.-F. (1994) *Lessons on the Analytic of the Sublime*, translated by Rottenberg, E., Stanford, CA: Stanford University Press.
McCarthy, F. (2008) 'A House for the Mind', in *Guardian Review*, 23 February: 12.
MacCulloch, D. (2009) *A History of Christianity*, London: Allen Lane.
McEwen, I. (2003) *Vitruvius: writing the body of architecture*, Cambridge, MA: MIT Press.
Macfie, A. (2000) 'Introduction', in Macfie, A. *Orientalism: a reader*, Edinburgh: Edinburgh University Press.
Madanipour, A. (2010) 'The Limits of Scientific Planning: Doxiadis and the Tehran Action Plan', in *Planning Perspectives*, 25.4, October: 485–504.
Maggi, G. and Castriotto, J. (1564) *Della Fortificazione delle Città*, Venetia: Borgominiero.
Mandelbrot, B. (1967) 'How Long Is the Coast of Britain?: Statistical self-similarity and fractional dimension', in *Science*, 156: 636–38.
Marsh, N. (1684) 'An Introductory Essay to the Doctrine of Sounds, Containing some Proposals for the Improvement of Acousticks', in *Philosophical Transactions (1683–1775)*, 14: 472–88.
Marsh, L. and Steadman, P. (1971) *The Geometry of the Environment*, London: RIBA Publications.
Marston, S., Jones, J. and Woodward, K. (2005) 'Human Geography Without Scale', in *Transactions of the Institute of British Geographers*, 30.4: 416–32.
Mestre, X. (2006) 'Por la calle Freixa', in *Quaderns*, 250: 136–9.
Meyer, M. and Meyer C. (1863) *Lehrbuch der axonometrischen Projectionslehre*, Leipzig: H. Haessel. First published as *Lehrbuch der Axonometrie* Lief. I (1852), Lief. II (1853), Lief. III (1855).
Mies van der Rohe, L. (1957) 'Art: Architect's Furniture', in *Time*, 18 February.
Miller, F., Vandome, A. and McBrewster, J. (eds) (2010) *Lubyanka (KGB)*, Mauritius: AlphaScript.
Milton, K. and Svasek, M. (eds) (2005) *Mixed Emotions: anthropological studies of feelings*, Oxford: Berg.
Mitchell, W. (1995) *Picture Theory*, Chicago, IL: University of Chicago Press.
Mollino, C. (2007a) 'Architettura arte e tecnica', in *Architettura di parole: scritti 1933–1965/ Carlo Mollini; a cura di Michela Comba*, Turin: Bollati Boringhieri.
Mollino, C. (2007b) 'Il linguaggio di architettura', in *Architettura di parole: scritti 1933–1965/ Carlo Mollini; a cura di Michela Comba*, Turin: Bollati Boringhieri.
MoMA (2009) 'Exhibitions. Performance 4: Roman Ondák', 28 October 2010. www.moma.org/visit/calendar/exhibitions/980
Montaner, J. (1998) *Casa Ugalde*, Barcelona: COAC.
Moore, C. (1976) *Dimensions: space, shape and scale in architecture*, New York: Architectural Record.
Morley, T. (1597) *A Plaine and Easie Introduction to Practicall Musicke*, later published in 1952, New York: Norton.
Morris, R. (1995) 'Notes on Sculpture, Part 2 (1966)' in R. Morris (ed.) *Continuous Project Altered Daily: the writings of Robert Morris*, Cambridge, MA: MIT Press.

Mostafavi, M. (ed.) (2002) *Approximations: the architecture of Peter Märkli*, London: Architectural Association.

Mostafavi, M. and Leatherbarrow, D. (1993) *On Weathering: the life of buildings in time*, Cambridge, MA and London: MIT Press.

Murray Barbour, J. (2004) *Tuning and Temperament: a historical survey*, Mineola, NY: Dover.

MVRDV (2005) *KM3, Excursion on Capacities/MVRDV*, Barcelona: Actar.

Naumann, C. (1830) *Lehrbuch der reinen und angewandten Krystallographie*, Leipzig: F.A. Brockhaus.

Nesbitt, L. (2003) *Brodsky and Utkin: the complete works*, New York: Princeton Architectural Press.

Nietzsche, F. (1909) *Human, All-Too-Human: a book for free spirits*, translated by Zimmen, H., Edinburgh: Foulis.

Ondák, R. (2009) 'Measuring the Universe. Interview by Klaus Biesenbach', in *Flash Art*, 42.268 (October): 78–81.

Orcutt, W.D. (1933) *Wallace Clement Sabine: a study in achievement*, Norwood, MA: Plimpton Press.

Ostwald, M. (2007) 'Rancière and the Metapolitical Framing of Architecture: reconstructing Brodsky and Utkin's voyage', in *Interstices*, 8: 9–20.

Ostwald, M. (2010) 'The Politics of Fractal Geometry in Russian Paper Architecture', in *Architectural Theory Review*, 15.2: 125–37.

Padovan, R. (1999) *Proportion: science, philosophy, architecture*, London: Spon.

Pallasmaa, J. (1996) *The Eyes of the Skin: architecture and the senses*, London: Academy.

Pallasmaa, J. (2005) *The Eyes of the Skin: architecture and the senses*, Chichester: Wiley-Academy.

Paperny, V. (2002) *Architecture in the Age of Stalin*, Cambridge: Cambridge University Press.

Pav, J. (1973) 'Wenceslaus Hollar in Germany (1627–1636)', in *Art Bulletin*, College Art Association, 55.1 (March): 86–105.

Pehnt, W. with Strohl, H. (1997) *Rudolf Schwarz: Architekt einer anderen Moderne*, Ostfildern-Ruit: Hatje.

Pennington, R. (1982) *A Descriptive Catalogue of the Etched Work of Wenceslaus Hollar 1607–1677*, Cambridge and London: Cambridge University Press.

Pérez-Gómez, A. (1983) *Architecture and the Crisis of Modern Science*. Cambridge, MA and London: MIT Press.

Pérez-Gómez, A. (2007) 'Questions of representation', in Frascari, M., Hale, J. and Starkey, B. (eds) *From Models to Drawings: imagination and representation in architecture*, Abingdon: Routledge.

Pérez-Gómez, A. and Pelletier, L. (1997) *Architectural Representation and the Perspective Hinge*, Cambridge, MA: MIT Press.

Pevsner, N. and Wilson, B. (2002) *The Buildings of England, Norfolk 1: Norwich and North-East*, New Haven, CT and London: Yale University Press (first published by Penguin, 1962; 2nd edition, 1997).

Platnauer, M. (1921) 'Greek Colour-Perception', in *Classical Quarterly*, 15: 153–62.

Plato (1997) 'Timaeus', in Cooper, J. (ed.) *Complete Works*, Indianapolis: Hackett.

Porter, T. (1997) *The Architect's Eye: visualization and depiction of space in architecture*, London: Spon.

Pyla, P. (2007) 'Hassan Fathy Revisited: postwar discourses on science, development, and vernacular architecture', in *Journal of Architectural Education*, 60.3 (February): 28–39.

Rancière, J. (2004) *The Politics of Aesthetics*, London: Continuum.

Rancière, J. (2009) *Aesthetics and its Discontents*, Cambridge, UK: Polity.

Rancière, J. (2010) *Dissensus: on politics and aesthetics*, London: Continuum.

Rand, C. (1963) 'The Ekistic World', in *The New Yorker*, 39.12 (11 May): 49–87.

Rappaport, A. (1989) 'Language and Architecture of Post-Totalitarianism', in Klotz, H. (ed.) *Paper Architecture: new projects from the Soviet Union*, New York: Rizzoli.

Raskin, E. (1954) *Architecturally Speaking*, New York: Reinhold.
Richards, J. (1972) [1969] 'Lessons from the Japanese Jungle', in Bell, G. and Tyrwhitt, J. (eds) *Human Identity in the Urban Environment*, Harmondsworth: Penguin.
Risselda, M. and van den Heuvel, D. (eds) (2005) *Team 10: in search of a utopia of the present*, Rotterdam: NAi Publishers.
Rodino, R. (1991) '"Splendide Mendax": authors, characters and readers in *Gulliver's Travels*', in *PMLA*, 106.5: 1054–70.
Roque, G. (2009) *Art et science de la couleur: Chevreul et les peintres de Delacroix à l'abstraction*, Paris: Gallimard.
Rorty, R. (1989) *Contingency, Irony and Solidarity*, Cambridge: Cambridge University Press.
Rowe, C. (1976) *The Mathematics of the Ideal Villa and Other Essays*, Cambridge, MA: MIT Press.
Rowe, C. and Koetter, F. (1984) *Collage City*, Cambridge, MA: MIT Press.
Royer, J. (1960) 'A Propos des Notes de Voyage et Carnets de Croquis d'Auguste Choisy', in *Académie des Beaux-arts: Communications, 1959–1960*: 53–60, pls II–VIII.
Rudofsky, B. (1984) *Architecture without Architects: a short introduction to non-pedigreed architecture*, Albuquerque, NM: University of New Mexico Press.
Ruskin, J. 'First Sketchbook', Ruskin Foundation (Ruskin Library, University of Lancaster), RF 1518.
Ruskin, J. 'Canterbury Tower', Ruskin Foundation (Ruskin Library, University of Lancaster), RF 1189.
Sabine, P. (1936) 'The Beginnings of Architectural Acoustics', in *Journal of the Acoustical Society of America*, 7: 242–8.
Sabine, W. (1902) 'Acoustics' in Sturgis, R. (ed.) *Illustrated Dictionary of Architecture and Building*, New York: Dover.
Sabine, W. (1922) 'Building Material and the Musical Scale', in *Collected Papers on Acoustics*, Cambridge, MA: Harvard University Press.
Saïd, E. (1978) *Orientalism*, London: Vintage.
Sartre, J.-P. (2010) *Sketch for a Theory of the Emotions*, translated by Mairet, P., Abingdon: Routledge.
Sassen, S. (2001) *The Global City: New York, London, Tokyo*, Princeton, NJ: Princeton University Press.
Schafer, R. (1977) *The Tuning of the World*, Toronto: McClelland & Stewart.
Schelling, F. (1989) *The Philosophy of Art*, Minneapolis, MN: University of Minnesota Press.
Scheppe, W. (2010) *Done. Book. Picturing the City of Society*, Ostfilden: Hatje Cantz.
Schneewind, J. (1996) 'Kant and Stoic Ethics', in Engstrom, S. and Whiting, J. (eds) *Aristotle, Kant, and the Stoics: rethinking happiness and duty*, Cambridge: Cambridge University Press.
Schön, D. (1983) *The Reflective Practitioner: how professionals think in action*, London: Maurice Temple Smith.
Schumacher, P. (2010) *The Autopoiesis of Architecture*, Chichester: Wiley.
Schutz, A. (1964) 'Making Music Together', in Brodersen, A. (ed.) *Alfred Schutz, Collected Papers II: studies in social theory*, The Hague: Martinus Nijhoff.
Semper, G. (2004) *Style in the Technical and Tectonic Arts, or, Practical Aesthetics*, translated by Mallgrave, H., Los Angeles, CA: Getty Research Institute.
Sennett, R. (2008) *The Craftsman*, London: Penguin.
Sheraton, T. (1793) *The Cabinet-maker and Upholsterer's Drawing-book. In four parts.* London: for the author.
Sheraton, T. (1802) *The Cabinet-maker and Upholsterer's Drawing-book. In four parts.* 3rd edition, London: for the author.
Shoskes, E. (2006) 'Jacqueline Tyrwhitt: a founding mother of modern urban design', in *Planning Perspectives*, 21 (April): 179–97.

Smithson, A. (ed.) (1962) 'Team 10 Primer 1953–1962', *Architectural Design*, 12 (December), special issue: 559–600.

Smithson, A. (1966) 'Concealment and Display: meditations on Braun', in *Architectural Design*, 36: 362–3.

Smithson, A. (ed.) (1991) *Team 10 Meetings*, New York: Rizzoli.

Smithson, A. and Smithson, P. (1994) *Changing the Art of Inhabitation: Mies' pieces, Eames' dreams, the Smithsons*, London: Artemis.

Snodgrass, A. (1990) *Architecture Time and Eternity: studies in the stellar and temporal symbolism of traditional buildings*, I, New Delhi: Aditya Prakashan.

Soloviova, L. and Marder, M. (1993) *Russian Matryoshka*, Ann Arbor: Interbook.

Soria, E. (1979) *Coderch de Sentmenat: conversations*, Barcelona: Blume.

Springell, F. (1963) *Connoisseur and Diplomat: the Earl Arundel's embassy to Germany in 1636 as recounted by William Crown's diary, the earl's letters and other contemporary sources with a catalogue of the topographical drawings made on the journey by Wenceslaus Hollar*, London: Maggs Bros.

Steadman, P. (2001) *Vermeer's Camera: uncovering the truth behind the masterpieces*, Oxford: Oxford University Press.

Stewart, S. (2001) 'Gathering, Disposing and the Cultivation of Judgement', in Sir Henry Wotton's The Elements of Architecture', in *Architectural Theory Review*, 6.2: 81–94.

Stokes, A. (1925) *The Thread of Ariadne*, London: Kegan Paul, Trench, Trubner.

Stokes, A. (1926) *Sunrise in the West*, London: Kegan Paul, Trench, Trubner.

Stokes, A. (1929a) 'Oxford' in *The Rugbeian*, 1.11 (July): 173.

Stokes, A. (1929b) 'The Sculptor Agostino di Duccio', in *Criterion*, 9.34 (October): 44–60.

Stokes, A. (1932) *The Quattro Cento*, CW1: 29–180.

Stokes, A. (1934) *Stones of Rimini*, CW1: 181–301.

Stokes, A. (1937a) *Colour and Form*, CW2: 7–83.

Stokes, A. (1937b) 'Mr Ben Nicholson at the Lefèvre Galleries', CW1: 315–6.

Stokes, A. (1947) *Inside Out*, CW2: 139–82.

Stokes, A. (1949) *Art and Science*, CW2: 183–212.

Stokes, A. (1951) *Smooth and Rough*, CW2: 213–56.

Stokes, A. (1955a) 'Form in Art: a psycho-analytic interpretation', in *A Game that Must Be Lost* (1973), Cheadle Hulme: Carcanet.

Stokes, A. (1955b) 'Form in Art', in Klein, M., Heimann, P. and Money-Kyrle, R. (eds) *New Directions in Psycho-Analysis* (1977), London: Karnac.

Stokes, A. (1956a) 'An Influence of Buildings on the Graphic Arts in the West', February: 1–33, Tate Gallery Archive 8816.181.

Stokes, A. (1956b) *Raphael*, CW2: 273–88.

Stokes, A. (1956c) Letter to Herbert Read, 13 November, McPherson Library HR/AS–0–33.

Stokes, A. (1958) *Greek Culture and the Ego*, CW3: 77–141.

Stokes, A. (1961a) *The Impact of Architecture*, CW3: 189–205.

Stokes, A. (1961b) *The Painting of our Time*, CW3: 207–59.

Stokes, A. (1963) *Painting and the Inner World*, CW3: 207–59.

Stokes, A. (1965) *The Invitation in Art*, CW3: 261–99.

Stokes, A. (1967) 'The Image in Form', CW3: 331–42.

Stokes, A. (1972) 'The Future and Art', in *A Game that Must Be Lost* (1973), Cheadle Hulme: Carcanet.

Stokes, A. (1981) *With All the Views*, Manchester: Carcanet.

Sudjic D. (2010) *Norman Foster: a life in architecture*, London: Weidenfeld & Nicolson.

Summerson, J. (1963) 'Heavenly Mansions: an interpretation of Gothic', in *Heavenly Mansions and other Essays on Architecture*, New York and London: Norton.

Sutherland-Edwards, H. (1859) 'Sketches and Studies in Russia: No. V, The Moscow Opera House', in *National Magazine*, 5: 98–104.

Swan, M. (1951) 'Response to architecture', in *The Spectator*, 23 March: 392.

Bibliography

Swift, J. (1886) *Gulliver's Travels*, illustrated by Gordon Browne, London: Blackie and Son.
Swift, J. (1994) *Gulliver's Travels*, London: Penguin.
Symondson, A. and Bucknall, S. (2006) *Sir Ninian Comper*, Reading: Spire and London: The Ecclesiological Society.
Tarkhanov, A. and Kavtaradze, S. (1992) *Architecture of the Stalin Era*, New York: Rizzoli.
Tavernor, R. (2007) *Smoot's Ear: the measure of humanity*, New Haven, CT and London: Yale University Press.
Taylor, P. (1982) 'A Materialist Framework for Political Geography', in *Transactions of the Institute of British Geographers*, 7.1: 15–34.
Temkin, A. (2008) 'Color Shift', in *Color Chart: reinventing color, 1950 to today*, New York: The Museum of Modern Art.
Terry, R. (1907) *Catholic Church Music*, London: Greening & Co.
Terry, R. (1931) *The Music of the Roman Rite: a manual for choirmasters in English-speaking countries*, London: Burns, Oates & Washbourne.
Thompson, E. (1995) *Colour Vision: a study in cognitive science and the philosophy of perception*, Abingdon: Routledge.
Thompson, E. (2002) *The Soundscape of Modernity: architectural acoustics and the culture of listening in America 1900–1933*, Cambridge, MA and London: MIT Press.
Till, J. (2009) *Architecture Depends*, Cambridge, MA: MIT Press.
Tovey, D. (1956) *The Forms of Music*, New York: Meridian Books.
Toynbee, A. (1972) [1972] 'Has Man's Metropolitan Environment Any Precedents?', in Bell, G. and Tyrwhitt, J. (eds) *Human Identity in the Urban Environment*, Harmondsworth: Penguin.
Treib, M. (2002) *The Architecture of Landscape, 1940–1960*, Philadelphia, PA: University of Philadelphia Press.
Troiani, I. and Sweeney, C. (2010) *House after Two Years of Living*, video, Oxford.
Turbet, R. (1995) 'An Affair of Honour: "Tudor Church Music", the ousting of Richard Terry and a trust vindicated', in *Music and Letters*, 76: 593–600.
Turnbull, D. (1993) 'The Ad Hoc Collective Work of Building Gothic Cathedrals with Templates, Strings and Geometry', in *Science, Technology and Human Values*, 18: 315–40.
Ungers, O. (1999) *Was ich schon immer sagen wollte über die Stadt, wie man sich seine eigenen Häuser baut, und was andere über mich denken*, Brunswick: Vieweg.
Ungers, O. (2002) *Oswald Mathias Ungers: works and projects, 1991–1998*, Milan: Electa.
Unrau, J. (1978) *Looking at Architecture with Ruskin*, London: Thames & Hudson.
Van Erde, K. (1971) *Wenceslaus Hollar: delineator of his time*, Charlottesville, VA: University Press of Virginia.
Various (1963) 'The Delos Symposion', *Doxiadis Associates Newsletter*, 3.7 (July).
Various/Delos 3 (1972) [1965] 'Living at High Densities', in Bell, G. and Tyrwhitt, J. (eds) *Human Identity in the Urban Environment*, Harmondsworth: Penguin.
Various/Delos 4 (1972) [1966] 'Need for More Balance in the Flow of Communications', in Bell, G. and Tyrwhitt, J. (eds) *Human Identity in the Urban Environment*, Harmondsworth: Penguin.
Various/Delos 6 (1972) [1968] 'Human Development, Densities, and Scale', in Bell, G. and Tyrwhitt, J. (eds) *Human Identity in the Urban Environment*, Harmondsworth: Penguin.
Various/Delos 7 (1972) [1969] 'The Scale of Settlements and the Quality of Life', in Bell, G. and Tyrwhitt, J. (eds) *Human Identity in the Urban Environment*, Harmondsworth: Penguin.
Venturi, R. (1983/1966) *Complexity and Contradiction in Architecture*, London: The Architectural Press.
Verbeek, P. (2005) *What Things Do: philosophical reflections on technology, agency and design*, Pennsylvania: Pennsylvania State University Press.
Vermeersch, P. and Heylighen, A. (2011) 'Blindness and Multi-Sensoriality in Architecture: the case of Carlos Mourão Pereira', in *Proceedings of the ARCC/EAAE 2010 International Conference on Architectural Research*, ARCC/EAAE, Washington, DC.

Vertue, G. (1759) *A Description of the Works of Wenceslaus Hollar*, 1st edition 1745, London: W. Bathoe.

Vesely, D. (2004) *Architecture in the Age of Divided Representation: the question of creativity in the shadow of production*, Cambridge, MA and London: MIT Press.

Vidler, A. (2009) *Histories of the Immediate Present*, Cambridge, MA: MIT Press.

Vitruvius, *De architectura*.

Vitruvius (1960) *Vitruvius: the ten books on architecture*, New York: Dover Publications.

Von Meiss, P. (1990) *Elements of Architecture: from form to place*, New York: Van Nostrand Reinhold.

Wainwright, E. (2011) 'Norman Foster, Henri Lefebvre and the Politics of Modern Architecture', unpublished doctoral thesis, Cardiff University.

Walton, P. (1972) *The Drawings of John Ruskin*, Oxford: Clarendon Press.

Wasserman, G. (1978) *Color Vision: an historical introduction*, New York and Chichester: J. Wiley & Sons.

Watson, P. (2010) *The German Genius: Europe's third Renaissance, the second scientific revolution, and the twentieth century*, London: Simon & Schuster.

Weber, M. (1958) *The Rational and Social Foundations of Music*, Carbondale, IL: Southern Illinois University Press.

Weber, R. and Vosskoeter, S. (2008) 'The Concept of Scale in Architecture: three empirical studies', in *Empirical Studies of the Arts*, 26.2: 219–46.

Weilacher, U. (1996) *Between Landscape Architecture and Land Art*, Basel, Berlin and Boston, MA: Birkhäuser.

Weisbach, J. (1844) 'Die monodimetrische und anisometrische Projectionsmethode (Perspective)', in *Polytechnische Mittheilungen*, 1: 125–36.

Weisbach, J. (1857) *Anleitung zum axonometrischen Zeichnen, nebst einem Anhange für Diejenigen, welche weder mit der Trigonometrie Noch mit der Analysis Bekannt Sind*, Freiburg: J.G. Engelhardt.

Wieser, C. (2008) 'Vom Stadtplan zum Essbesteck: Kleinteiliges und GrossMass.stäbliches', in *Werk, Bauen und Wohnen* ('Grösse und Mass.stab'), June.

Wigley, M. (2001) 'Network Fever', in *Grey Room*, 4: 82–122.

Wittgenstein, L. (1978) *Remarks on Colour*, Berkeley, CA: University of California Press.

Wittgenstein, L. (1981) *Zettel*, Oxford: Blackwell.

Wittkower, R. (1998) *Architectural Principles in the Age of Humanism*, London: Academy. First published in 1949 as vol.19 of the *Studies of the Warburg Institute*, London.

Woodman, E. (2008) *Modernity and Reinvention: the architecture of James Gowan*, London: Black Dog.

Worringer, W. (1927) *Form in Gothic*, translated by Read, H., New York: Putnam.

Wright, F.L. (1987) 'The Cardboard House' in *Modern Architecture: being the Kahn lectures for 1930*, Carbondale, IL: Southern Illinois University Press.

Wulstan, D. (1985) *Tudor Music*, London and Melbourne: J.M. Dent.

Xenakis, I. (1992) *Formalized Music: thought and mathematics in music*, Stuyvesant: Pendragon Press.

Yaneva, A. (2005) 'Scaling Up and Down: extraction trials in architectural design', in *Social Studies of Science*, 35.6: 867–94.

Youings, J. (1991) *Sixteenth-Century England*, London and New York: Penguin.

Zika, F. (2004) 'Puzzles of Color Scaling, Matching and Mixing', in Fioretos, A. (ed.) *Re: The Rainbow*, IASPIS (International Artists' Studio Program in Sweden, Stockholm).

Zika F. (2008) 'Wittgenstein's Colour Puzzles', in *Philosophical Inquiry*, 30:1–2: 191–211.

Index

Aalto, A. 203–4
absorption 91
abstract art 105, 123, 125, 150
Abu Dhabi 37, 39–41
achromatic hues 83
acoustics 88, 90–7, 141
actual-size images 119–20, 122, 125
adjusting scale 136, 140–6
Adler, G. 1–9, 182–93
aedicula 182
aedicules 9, 182–3, 185, 187–90, 192
Aegean Sea 172, 175
Aerni, G. 154
aesthetic theory 110, 112, 209
Africa 107
AHRA Critiques 6
Alberti, L.B. 4, 103, 115, 139, 184
Aldington, P. 1
Aldrin, B. 191
algorithms 23
alienation 3, 100, 172
All Saints, Crewe 183, 189
Alps 49
L'Ametlla del Valles 199
amplification 133
Amsterdam 3, 27, 75
analogical colour 84–5
Andersson, S.-I. 1
Ankara 171
anthropology 79, 85–7, 110–11, 176, 179
apartments 65–70, 202
'Apollonion' project 177
appetite 112–13
appetitive soul 113
Apple Mac 111
Arab architecture 37–40, 179
archaeology 119

archetypes 105
architectonics 159, 161, 187
architects' chairs 159–69
Architectural Association (AA) 4, 173, 183
Architectural Association (AA) School, London 90, 93
architectural scale 99–106, 137–8
architectural subjunctive 183, 185, 188–9
Arezzo 103
Aristotle 80, 111, 114–16, 143, 163–5, 188
'Ark of the World' project 108
Armstrong, N. 191
Art Deco 11–12
Arundel, Earl 24
Asia Minor 171
Asian Highway 171
Aspra Spitia 177
Assyrian 161
astrophysics 173
Athens 170–2
Atlantic 24
Auden, W.H. 180
auditoria 92
Australia 154
auto-eroticism 99
avant-garde 44, 203
axiality 56
axis systems 55–6, 62
axonometry 7, 27, 54–64
Aztecs 145

Bach, J.S. 139
Bachelard, G. 182
Bacon, F. 88
Bagenal, H. 89–97
Baghdad 171

Bakema, J. 194
Balancing Barn, Suffolk 75
baldachinos 182
Balkans 25
Ballard, J.G. 111–12
Banco Urquijo housing project 194, 197, 199–200, 202, 204
Banham, R. 38, 190
banks 197
Bann, S. 44
Barcelona 9, 194, 197, 199–200
Barceloneta housing project 194
Baroque 1
Batchelor, D. 7, 84–5
Battle Abbey 48
Bauhaus 79, 159, 196
BBC 38
beauty 177, 184
behavioural science 110
Behrens, P. 162–3
being 107
Bell, G. 175
Belov, M. 206–7
Benares 102
Benedikt, M. 3–4
Berlin 187
Berlin, B. 86
Berlin-Kay hypothesis 86
Berman, M. 174
Bernstein, L. 191
bi-scalar disorder 170
Bible 44–5, 53
biology 108–11, 173, 176
biomorphism 111
Bion, W. 105
bird's-eye view 27, 55–7
Birmingham 189
black market 144, 207
Blanc, C. 82

Index

Blefuscu 36
blindness 127
Bochner, M. 8, 118–19, 121–5
body 54, 119–27, 137, 162
    aedicules 188, 190
    chairs 165
    Delos Symposia 173, 176–7, 179
Bohemia 25
Bois, Y.-A. 123
Borges, J.L. 3
bottom-up approach 11, 17
Boudon, P. 128, 132, 134
Boullée, E.-L. 1
boxes 182–93
Boyne, C. 192
Boyne, R. 192
Brahe, T. 21
Brahms, J. 91
Braille 129, 134
brainstorming 172
Bramante, D. 1, 154
brands 39–40
Braque, G. 105
Breughel family 21
Brezhnev, L. 206, 210
brickwork 190
brightness 83
Bril, P. 21
British Library, London 106
British Museum, London 27, 30
British Pavilion 43
Broadway 37
Brodsky, A. 9, 206–17
Brouwn, S. 118–23, 125–6
Brown, D.S. 147, 159
Bruges concert hall 7
Brussels 49
Brutalism 189–91
Bryon, H. 7, 54–64
building information modelling (BIM) 129
Bulgaria 171
Bullen, J.B. 45
bureaucracy 40
Byker, Newcastle-upon-Tyne 3
Byzantium 102, 189

cabinet-making 159, 161
cabinets of curiosities 21
CAD 3–4, 129, 131, 137
calculus 108–9
Calcutta 171
calendar 145
Callot, J. 22
Calvary 185
Camberwell school hall, London 189

Cambridge 91
Cambridge Philosophical Society 55
Cambridge University 8, 55, 90–1, 94
camera obscura 49
Camus, A. 107–8, 113
Canaletto 50
Candilis-Josic-Woods project 196, 203
Canterbury Cathedral 46, 48, 136
capitalism 39
carbon dioxide emissions 65
carbon footprint 38, 40
carbon-free environments 37–8
Cartesianism 54
Caruso St John 7
Casa Contarini Fasan 50, 52
Casa d'Oro 46, 53
catapults 143
cathedrals 91–4, 96, 136, 176, 183, 207
Catholics 93, 185
CBS 170
Cerda, I. 197
ceremony 185–6
chairs 8, 159–69
Charles II 24, 29–30
Chartres Cathedral 136
chemistry 82, 87, 150
Chevreul, E. 82–3
China 65
China Hills project 65–6
Chinese 40
Chippendale, T. 159, 161
Chipperfield, D. 187
Choisy, A. 7, 54–64
chora 145–6
Christianity 113, 186
chroma 82–3
Church of England 182
churches 91–3, 96, 104, 182–6, 188–90, 210
CIAM (Congrès Internationaux d'Architecture Moderne) 170, 173, 195, 203
ciboria 182, 185–6
Cicero, M.T. 163
cinematography 4
citizenship 113, 115
City of London 29–31
city plans 27, 29–30
cityscapes 119, 212
classic architecture 183–5, 187
classical music 137, 140
clustering 70
Las Cocheras project 204
Coderch Archive 204

Coderch, J.A. 9, 194–205
coffee shops 24
cognition 112, 114
Coldstream, N. 188
collectivity 194, 204
Collingwood, W. 49
Cologne 21, 24, 190
Colomina, B. 2
colonialism 34, 38, 40, 144
colour 7, 79–87
    analogical 84–5
    basic terms 86
    charts 83–5
    circle 82–3, 85, 87
    complementary 82
    naming 85–6
    scales 79–87
    secondary 84
    systems 82–3
    tertiary 84
    theory 110
    wheel 82, 84, 87
colour-blindness 87
Colquhoun, A. 203
Columbarium Architecture 206–7, 211–16
Columbarium Habitabile 206–7, 211–16
Columbia University 174
column orders 159, 187
comma 139–40, 142, 144
communism 207, 210, 216
Communist Party 209–10, 216
Como, Lake 49
competition entries 211–16
complementary colours 82
complementary contrast law 82
complex ordinariness 147–51
computers 2, 6, 37, 41, 172–4
conceptual art 117–26
Congo 107
conic perspective 57
Connor, S. 143
Conrad, J. 100, 107–8, 112–13
Constantinople 63
Constructivism 206
consultancy 39–41, 171
context 2, 7, 9, 11–12
    cities 39
    colour scales 84
    haptics 127–8
    housing 202, 204
    small scale 24
Le Corbusier 2, 137–8, 140–1, 144–5, 159, 194, 198, 203
Correa, F. 196
Cosgrove, D. 45

234

Index

cosiness 185–6
cosmology 112–13, 115
Costa Gonçalves, M. da 6, 11–17
Costa Rica 108
'Court of Ducal Palace' 53
courtyard houses 202, 214
Covent Garden 27
Cox, D. 48
Coyne, R. 8, 136–46
Cracy, J. 48–9
craftsmanship 140, 144, 154, 161–2, 178
Crewe 183, 189
Cromwell, O. 25
Cronkite, W. 170
Crucifixion 185
crusaders 189
crystallography 55
Cubism 105
culture 79–80, 82, 84–7, 109–11
    chairs 161
    churches 188, 190
    Delos Symposia 178–9
    identity 195, 204
    police order 208
currency of equivalence 7, 39–42
Curtis, W. 2
cycle of fifths 139–40, 142
cyclical scale 3–4

da Vinci, L. 176, 185–6
Dadd, R. 7
Daem, H. 7
Daemon 115
Dallmayr, F. 7, 40–1
Danckerts, C. 27
Darwin, C. 110
Dawson, A. 147, 159
De Carlo, G. 194–6
De Certeau, M. 9
decibels 97
decorum 163
Delft 23
Delhi 171
deliquescence 206–13
Delos Symposia 170–81
democracy 114, 208, 216
demographics 172
Denmark 70, 73
density 178–9
Derrida, J. 146
Descartes, R. 54, 113
design tools 129–35
detail 11–17, 46, 48–9, 53, 131, 145, 178, 202
Detroit 171
Detskiy Mir, Moscow 212–14
developers 65

diatonic comma 140
Didden Village, Rotterdam 76
digital media 6, 84–5, 87, 109
disagreements 208
discord 139
discourse 39, 182, 198, 200
dissent 208–9, 214
distribution of sensible 207–10, 216
DnB NOR Bank project 70–1
domed spaces 63–4, 92, 102, 176
Dover 48
Dover Castle 46, 49
Dovey, K. 208
Downey, C. 127–35
Doxiadis, A. 171
Doxiadis Associates 171, 178
Doxiadis, C. 9, 170–81
draughtsmanship 48, 137
Dubos, R. 180
Duccio, A. di 102
Duchamp, M. 117
Dugdale, W. 29
Düren drawings 23
Dürer, A. 21–2
Dushkin, A. 212
Dusseldorf 123
dyes 82
dynamic design 129–31
Dzerzhinsky, F. 212
Dzerzhinsky Square, Moscow 212

Eames, C. 147, 154–9
Eames, R. 147, 154–9
East 38–9
Eastern General Hospital, Cambridge 91
eco-centres 108
eco-tech 37–8, 40
Ecole des Beaux Arts 184
ecology 172
economics 171, 175, 179, 191, 195
economy 37, 109, 209, 216
ecumenopolis 172, 179
Edwardians 11
ego 99–106
Egypt 186–7
Ehrenzweig, A. 106
Ekistic Grid 172
Ekistics 172, 174–5, 177, 179–81
Emiri family 37
Emmons, P. 3
emotion 110–16
empiricism 79, 93, 121–2
empowerment 144

engineers 55
England 5, 24–5, 28, 34
    churches 183, 188–9
    cities 39, 41
    music 90–1, 94, 97
English Civil War 25
English Heritage 4
English language 87–8, 93, 143, 182
environmental technology 37
epistemology 23, 32
errors 141, 145
Erskine, R. 3
Essen 190
Esslinger, H. 111
etching 21, 24, 31, 206
ethics 114, 160, 162–5
ethos 159–69
Eucharist 185
Euler, L. 80
Euphranor 114–15
Eurocentrism 40, 144
Europe 22, 24–5, 29, 40–1
    churches 182, 190
    detail 44
    housing 196, 203
    psychoanalysis 102
Evelyn, J. 24, 29, 31
evolution 110, 161, 173, 176
existentialism 107, 109, 190

fabrica 143
facsimiles 49
Farish, W. 7, 54–5, 57
Farnsworth, E. 154
fascism 208
Fathy, H. 178
Fayrfax, R. 93–7
Fibonacci series 137–8
firmitas 143
First World War 92, 101
Fisher, M. 2–3
five-year plans 209
Fletcher, B. 1, 207
floor plans 70
Florence 52
Fludd, R. 139
focal points 86
Fochs, C. 195
Folger Collection, Amherst 26
follies 44
Fontana-Giusti, G. 6, 21–33
Foote, J. 8, 159–69
Ford Foundation 173
form theory 58
formalism 183
fortifications 57
Forty, A. 200

Index

Forum, Rome 52
Foster + Partners 34, 37–40
Foster, H. 120
Foster, N. 7, 39–41
Fowler, H. 88, 96
Frampton, K. 190, 203
France 25, 31, 104, 184, 188
Franco, F. 196
Frank, J. 162–4
Frankfurt 21, 187
Freiburg 55
French language 88, 182
Freud, S. 8, 52, 99–100, 104, 106, 182
Friedman, A.T. 154
Frog Designs 111
frozen music 139
Fuller, B. 173–4
furniture-making 159–64, 167–8
future cities 65
Future Systems 189
future-proofing 172
futurist 112

Galileo Galilei 24
Ganges, River 102
garden structures 187
geology 48, 53
geometers 55, 141
geometry 31, 54–8, 60, 62, 115
    acoustics 90
    aedicules 189
    colour scales 83–4, 87
    conceptual 119, 121, 125
    fractal 207
    music 136, 139, 141–2, 144–5
    psychoanalysis 108–9
German Architecture Museum, Frankfurt-am-Main 187
Germania Hall 1
Germany 23, 25, 55, 57, 162
Gesamtkunstwerk 159, 162
Gestalt 79
Gibson, J. 133
Giedion, S. 203
giganticism 3, 198, 210
Giorgio, F. di 102, 138–9
Girbau, L. 196–7
glasnost 206
global city networks 9, 171, 173, 177
globalisation 174
Gobelins tapestry factory 82
Godfrey, M. 122
Godfrey, R. 27
Goethe, J.W. von 7, 81–3, 139
Golden Lane project 203
golden section 137–8, 145

Gombrich, E. 204
Google 109
Gorbachev, M. 216
Gothic architecture 46, 48, 50, 53, 136, 182–5, 188–9
Gottman, J. 172
Gowan, J. 189–90
Gran Kursaal project, San Sebastian 204
gravity 56
Great Britain 25
Great Fire of London 6, 21, 29–32
Greece 25, 170–1
Greek language 87–8
Greeks 9, 114, 161
Greenwich 25, 27, 30–1
Greenwich Observatory, London 30
Grégoire, R. 173
grid layouts 30, 37
Gropius, W. 159, 198, 203
grotesque 50
Guadet, J. 184
Gubler, J. 4
Gyre, Tokyo 67, 70

Hadid, Z. 6, 41
Hagia Sophia 63
The Hague 74
Hall, E.T. 179
Haller, L. 125
haptics 127–35
Harding, J.D. 48
harmonics 94
Harrap, D. 187
Harvard University 90, 173
Hatherley, O. 2–3
Hatton, B. 207
Haussmann, G.-E. 37
Hegel, G.W.F. 162
hegemony 144, 163–4
Heiner Friedrich Gallery, Munich 125
Hertz (Hz) 97
Heschong, L. 187
Heylighen, A. 127–35
Higgins, H. 6, 189
high-rise housing 198
historicism 161, 209
historiography 38
Hoefnagel, Jacob 22
Hoefnagel, Joris 22
Holkham 189
Hollar, W. 6, 21–33
homogenisation 179
Hooke, R. 6, 21, 29–31
Hotel de Ville, Brussels 49
Hotel del Mar, Palma 197

House of Culture and Movement, Frederiksberg 70, 73
house within 187
housing projects 3, 5, 76, 194–205, 216
hue 79–83, 85–6
Hugo, V. 44
humanism 4–6, 8–9, 54, 107, 191, 203
humidity 141
Hunt, J.D. 44

IBM 172
id 99, 104
identity 194–205
ideology 38, 114
illusionism 119–20
Imago Group 104–6
imperial system 137, 141
improvisation 141
Incorporated Society of Musicians 93
India 102
individualism 196–7
industrialisation 53, 144, 162–3, 169
industrialists 2–3
infrastructure 171
Ingold, T. 133–4
Institut du Monde Arabe, Paris 188
Institute of Contemporary Arts (ICA), London 104
interaction 88–98
interdisciplinarity 86, 97
internet 4
interstitial space 145, 204
invention 144–6
Iran 174
Iraq 178
Islamabad 171
Islington 25–7
isometry 7, 54–7
Italians 179
Italy 25, 44–5, 53, 102–3, 154, 184, 203

Jacobs, J. 178
James II 24
James, W. 110
Jameson, F. 208
Jeremiah 53
Jopling, J. 57
Josephson, H. 5
Jung, C.G. 182
jungle geometry 108–9

Kabul 171
Kandinsky, W. 81

Index

Kant, I. 80–1, 112–13, 115–16
Kastriani 175
Kay, P. 86
Kea 175
Keats, J. 52, 80
Kepler, J. 21, 24
keyboards 137
keys 140
KGB 212, 214
Khrushchev, N. 210
kinaesthetic perception 128, 179
King's College Chapel, Cambridge 91–2
Kite, S. 7, 43–53
Klein, M. 99–105
Klotz, H. 211
Knight, V. 29
Koetter, F. 194
Konrad Fischer Gallery, Dusseldorf 123
Koolhaas, R. 9
Korzybski, A. 3–4
Krauss, R. 45
Krucker, B. 147
Kube project 70
Kunstkammer 22

Lacan, J. 100, 106
Lahore 171
Lambeth 25
Lambeth Palace 27
Lancaster University 43, 45
language games 79
lapicules 192
Laplace, P.-S. 113
Latin America 171
Latin language 94, 143
Laugier, Abbé 187
Laurana, L. 102, 105–6
Lawson, B. 130
Leach, N. 208
Leatherbarrow, D. 154
Lederman, S. 128
Leibniz, G. von 115
Lely, P. 30
Leonidov, I. 206
LeWitt, S. 118
Leyden, L. van 21
libido 100
lightness 83, 85
Lilliput 34, 36–7, 39–41, 212
Lincoln's Inn Fields, London 27
linguistics 79, 85–7
lithographs 49
little boxes 182–93
liturgy 91–2, 94, 184
logic 79, 83–4, 94, 163–4, 183
logos 159–69

London 5, 7, 21–34, 39
  churches 189
  City of 28, 30–1
  detail 11, 43
  music 90
  psychoanalysis 99, 101–4, 106
  scaling 25–8
Loomis, J. 128
Loos, A. 162–4, 185
Los Angeles 147
Lourinha 127
Lubyanka, Moscow 212, 214
Lutyens, C. 189
Lutz, C. 110
Lynn, G. 108–9, 112
Lyotard, J.-F. 116

McEwen, I. 143
McLuhan, M. 173–4, 179
Madanipour, A. 174, 179
Madrid 197
Maguire, R. 182–3, 186, 189, 192
Mainz 23
major scales 137
Malevich, K. 179
Mallinson, H. 8, 107–16
management theory 40
Manchester 191
Mandelbrot, B. 189
Mann, A.H. 91–2
Mantua 184
maps 25, 29
Märkli, P. 5, 8
Markthal, Rotterdam 70, 72
Marsh, N. 88
Masdar 7, 34–42
mass housing 76, 195–6, 204
mass-effect 102–6
mathematicians 55, 189
mathematics 108–9, 144–5, 168
matryoshka 207, 212, 214, 216–17
Mead, M. 172
measurement 54–64, 81, 96–7, 117–26
  chairs 162–3, 168
  Delos Symposia 176, 178–9
  music 136–7
mechanics 55
media 1, 170, 172–3, 208–10
Mediterranean 202
Meduna, G.B. 46
megalopolis 171, 175, 177, 179–80
Meiss, P. von 5
melancholia 99
Melnikov, K. 206
Meltzer, D. 105
'Las Meninas' 22
Merian studio 23

Merleau-Ponty, M. 133
Mesoamerica 86
Mestre, X. 198–9
metamorphosis 111
metric system 5, 118, 137, 141
Meyer brothers 55–7, 59
Meyssens, J. 21
microphones 88
microscopes 24, 31, 88
Middle East 38, 175
Mies van der Rohe, L. 7, 154, 204
Mildendo 7
Milendo 34–42
military 40, 57, 62
military-industrial complex 40
mineralogy 48
Minimalism 120, 122–3, 154
modelling 55, 108–9, 129–35, 211
Modernism 2–3, 6–8, 38–9, 43
  chairs 162
  colour scales 81
  Delos Symposia 170, 181
  Movement 194, 202–3
  music 142
  Russia 216
  utilitarian 210
modulation 140, 143
modulor system 137–8, 141
moiré effect 12
Mollino, C. 165–9
MoMA 109, 117
Monument, London 30
Moore, C. 5, 187
moral philosophy 111
Moretti, L. 154
Morris, R. 117, 120
Moscow 209, 211–12, 214
Moscow Toy Company 212
Mostafavi, M. 154
Munich 117, 125
Munsell, A. 83
Munsell Colour System 83, 86
Murray, K. 182–3, 186, 189
Museum of Childhood, London 7
Museum for Disappearing Buildings 211
music 8, 88–98, 116, 136–46
musical scales 80–1, 91, 139–42
musicology 90, 92, 95–6
Muthesius, H. 3
MVRDV 3–4, 7, 65–76

narcissism 99
Narni bridge, Umbria 58
National Gallery, London 103
Naumann, C.F. 55–6
Nazis 209
neo-Classicism 11, 210

Index

neo-Conceptualism 118
neo-Plasticism 190
neo-Rationalism 187
Nesbitt, L. 214, 216
Netherlands 25
networking 173–6, 179
Neues Bauen 4
Neues Museum, Berlin 187
neurophysiology 86–7
Nevers 61
New Brutalism 189–91
New City project 109
New York 37, 210
Newcastle-upon-Tyne 3
Newcourt, R. 29
Newton, I. 30, 55, 80, 112–13, 115
Newton Memorial 1
Nicholson, B. 105
Nietzsche, F.W. 6
nihilism 162
Nishizawa, R. 3
Northcote, J. 45
Norway 70–1
Norwich Cathedral 183
Notre Dame, Paris 184
Notre-Dame-la-Grande, Poitiers 61
Nouvel, J. 41, 188
Noyez, E. 8, 117–26

oblique projection 57–8, 62
octaves 137, 139–40
Ogilvy, J. 29
oil 175
Oiza, S. de 202
Old Testament 53
Oldenburg, C. 119
Olympic Games 212
Ondák, R. 8, 117–19, 122–3, 125
ontology 107, 116
opponent-process theory 86
opposing colours 82
optics 24, 57, 129
oratory 163
organic architecture 159–60, 162, 164–5
Orientalism 38–40, 189
Orinda house, California 187
orthography 55
Oslo 70–1
Ostwald, M.J. 9, 206–17
Otterlo Conference 195, 204
Ottomans 189
overcrowding 171
overstimulation 179
overtone structures 93
Oxford 101–2, 147, 154–9
Oxford University 94

Padovan, R. 5, 142
painter's perspective 57
paints 82, 84
Pakistan 171, 178
Palatine Hill 60
palimpsests 52
Palladio, A. 139, 189
Palma 197
Palo Alto 127
Pantone colour charts 85
Paper Architecture movement 9, 206–17
parallel projection 54–9, 62
parametric architecture 6, 8, 189
Paris 30, 184, 188
Park Hill, Sheffield 3
Parkrand, Amsterdam 3
passions 113
pathetic fallacy 112
pathos 159–69
Peking 171
Pennington, R. 22
perception 7–8, 120, 127–9, 133–5, 177
Pereira, C.M. 127, 128–9, 130–5
perestroika 216
Pérez-Gómez, A. 6, 54
periodicity 93
'perpendicular' England 188, 189
Perret, A. 159
Persia 25
Personal Rapid Transit system 37
perspective 54–7, 134, 159, 161
Pevsner, N. 183–4
phenomenology 83, 86–7, 120, 182, 203
philosophy 54, 80, 101, 110–11, 113–16, 140–1, 144–5, 206
photography 119–20, 122, 124–5, 165
photovoltaic arrays 37
phronesis 143, 163–5, 168
physics 79, 87, 90–1, 113
physiology 81, 110
Piano, R. 41, 188
Picasso, P. 105–6
Picturesque 43–4, 50, 52–3
Piero della Francesca 4, 103
Pike, M. 9, 194–205
Pinakothek der Moderne, Munich 117
Pindar 171
Plate, River 171
Plato 113–15, 137, 141, 146
play 182
poetics 167, 191

poetry 112, 114–15
pointilism 7
points of view 56–7, 61
Poitiers 61
police order 208–10, 216
polite architecture 2–3
politics 206–13
pollution 178
polyphony 94
Pompidou Centre, Paris 188–9
poor 195, 204
Porter, T. 134
Portugal 127, 132
positivism 40, 54, 191
post-humanism 54
post-modernism 159
Potsdam 186
power relations 207–8
pragmatism 162
Prague 21–3
Prague Castle 21
praxis 143
pre-Raphaelites 8
primary colours 84
Princeton University 159
principalities 24–5
prisms 80
Privy Council 24
product design 111
programmatic clustering 70
progressive method 49
proportion 4, 36, 41, 108
    axonometry 62
    chairs 160
    churches 184
    haptics 128
    measurement 117, 121, 125
    music 94, 137, 139, 142–3
Protestants 186
Prout, S. 49–53
prudence 163–9
psyche 100
psychoanalysis 99–106
psychology 79, 82–3, 87, 171
    churches 182, 185
    Delos Symposia 176, 180
    identity 202
public buildings 70
publishing 4
Puritans 185
Pythagorean comma 140, 142

qualitative methods 88–98
quantitative methods 88–98

rainbows 80
Rancière, J. 9, 206–9
Rappaport, A. 210

Index

Rare Architecture 6, 11–17
Raskin, E. 1, 4
rational soul 113–15
Ravenna 102
Read, H. 104
Reaganomics 204
reality 2–3
receptor systems 179
recycling 150
reduction 133
reflection-in-action 130
Reformation 8, 92, 94–5, 185
refraction 80
refugees 171
register 53
reification 112
remaindered space 145
Rembrandt (Harmenszoon van Rijn) 22
Renaissance 8, 54, 102–4, 137–9, 184, 209
repoussoir 23
representation of space 23–4, 54–64, 130–1, 133–4
resistance 207–9, 216
resolution 131
resonance 139
reverberation 91, 93
rhetoric 114–15, 163–5, 171
Rhine 23
Richards, J.M. 180
Richards, S. 9, 170–81
Richardson, B. 121
Richmond, London 27
Rimini 102–3
Robbrecht, P. 7
Roberts, D. 52–3
Rogers, R. 188
Rogers, S. 45
Romanesque 50, 61, 103–4, 188
Romantics 8, 43, 45, 53
Rome 52, 58, 154, 185
Rorty, R. 5
Rotterdam 23, 70, 72, 76
Routledge 4
Rowe, C. 136, 194
Royal College of Music 92
Royal Exchange, London 25
Royal Exchange Theatre, Manchester 191
Royal Institute of British Architects (RIBA) 4, 88, 96
Royal Musicological Association 93
Royal Naval Hospital, Greenwich 30
Royal Pavilion, Brighton 38
Royal Society 24
Royaumont 194, 196
Rozencwajg, N. 6, 11–17

Rudofsky, B. 38
Rudolf II 21
Runciman, C. 48
Runge, O. 83
Ruskin Foundation 45
Ruskin, J. 7, 43–53, 112–13, 116
Ruskin Library 43, 45
Ruskin, M. 45
Russia 206–10, 212

Sabine, W.C. 90–1, 93, 96
Saïd, E. 38–40
St Albans Cathedral 93
St Anthony's, Essen 190
St Mark's, Venice 49
St Mary Overy, London 27
St Mary's, Oxford 101
St Paul, Bow Common 183–5, 189, 192
St Paul's Cathedral, London 30
St Radegund's Abbey, Dover 48
Saint-Savin, Gartempe 61
Saint-Trinit, Vaucluse 104
Sainte-Etienne, Nevers 61
Salonica 63
San Clemente, Rome 185
San Francisco 127
San Sebastian 204
SANAA 3
Sant' Andrea, Mantua 184
Sartre, J.-P. 110–11
Sassen, S. 171
saturation 83, 85
Sayers, J. 8, 99–106
scale 1–3, 7–8
  adjustment 136–46
  aedicules 182–3
  affinities 189–90
  architectural 99–106
  body 119–20
  classic 183–5
  colour 79–87
  cyclical 3–4
  definitions 128, 132–3
  deliquescence 206–13
  detail 11–17, 202
  differences 187
  dimensions 60, 62, 120–3, 125, 179, 187, 190–1
  dwelling 199–202
  furniture-making 159
  Gothic 183–5
  gradation 178
  haptics 127–35
  identity 194–205
  interaction 88–98
  interior 147
  intermediate 194, 204

London 25–8
massive 99–101, 106
mathematical notion 41
measurement 117
meditation 34
musical 80–1, 91, 137–42
MVRDV 65–76
negotiation 181
ontology 107, 116
pre-twentieth century 6–7
redefinition 117–26
register 53
senses 208
small 21–33, 44–5, 50, 53, 134–5, 162–3, 167, 170, 175, 177, 180, 204
subjective 57
subversion 206–7, 212, 216
switching 109
transference 160–1, 164, 168
transforming 213
twentieth century plus 8–9
urban 197–9
worm's-eye view 54–64
scaling 127–35, 160, 189–91
Scandinavia 203
Schafer, M. 139
Schelling, F. von 139
Scheppe, W. 44
Schinkel, K.F. 186
Schloss Charlottenhof, Potsdam 186
Schoenberg, A. 81
Schön, D. 130
Schumacher, P. 6
Schutz, A. 141
Schwartz, R. 190
science fiction 111, 175
Scott, G. 104
Sea Bathing Facility, Lourinha 127–8, 130
Second World War 170
secondary colours 84
Sejima, K. 3
Selfridge's, Birmingham 189
Semper, G. 161–2
Sennett, R. 140, 144
senses 81, 105, 128, 133, 177, 179, 208
sestinas 94
set texts 1
Seven Sisters, Moscow 209–10
shadows 57
Shakespeare, W. 7
Sharr, A. 7, 34–42
Shelley, P.B. 52
Sheraton, T. 159, 161
Siberia 209, 212

239

Index

signature notes 91
signature projects 41
Silodam, Amsterdam 75
site specificity 11, 42, 204
sketchbooks 46–9
Slade 106
Sloane, H. 30
Smith Group 127, 129
Smithson, A. 147, 154–9, 189, 203
Smithson, P. 147, 154–9, 189, 203
Smyth, F. 8, 88–98
Snodgrass, A. 145
social construction 111
social history 111
socialism 208–9
sociology 140, 171–2, 216
software 4
solar gain 38, 40–1
Somme, battle of 91
Songdo Landmark City 65, 67
Soto, J.R. 106
soul 113–15, 176
sound theory 139
South Koreans 65–70
Southwark Cathedral 27
Soviet Union 9, 144, 206–7, 209, 211, 216
space see representation of space
Spain 203
Spanish Civil War 196
species survival 170, 173
spectral analysis 80
spectrum 80–5, 87
Speer, A. 1
spirited soul 113
Stalin, J. 206–7, 209–10
standardisation 144
states 24
Statue of Liberty, New York 210
stereotypes 39
Stewart, S. 143
Der Stil 161
Stirling, J. 189
Stoicism 115–16
Stokes, A. 8, 99–106
Strand 27
Strasbourg 21, 23
street life 70
studiolo 22
Stüler, A. 187
Sturgis, R. 90–1
sublime indifference 107–16
Sudjic, D. 39
Summerson, J. 9, 182–3, 185–6, 188–90
Surrealism 179
Surrey 25
sustainability 42, 65, 76

Swan, M. 103
swatches 85
Swift, J. 7, 34, 37–40
symmetry 142–3
synaesthesia 81–2
synecdoche 44–5, 52
Sørenson, C.T. 1

tactile perception 128, 179
Tahiti 86
Taj Mahal 102
Tate Gallery 106
Tati, J. 159
Tavernor, R. 5
Team 10 194–6, 203–4
technology 37, 174, 178, 191
tectonics 7, 53, 58, 60–2, 64, 161, 167, 178
Tehran 171, 174
telescopes 24
Temkin, A. 84
Tempietto, Rome 1
Tempio Malatestiano, Rimini 103
Terry, R.R. 90, 92–5, 97
tertiary colours 84
Thames, River 25, 27, 31
Third World 171
Thrace 171
Tintoretto 21
Tokyo 67, 70
tolerances 141–2
tonality 91–2
top-down approach 11
topography 23, 25, 31, 49, 52, 65
topology 30, 108
Toronto 173
torus rings 109
totalitarianism 162
Toulouse Le-Mirail 196, 203
Town Hall Hotel, London 11
town planning 170–1, 198, 210
Toynbee, A. 172, 180
trade 24, 41–2
transposition 137, 140–1
Trevi fountain, Rome 52
triangulation 84
trigonometry 55
tripartite soul 113–14
Troiani, I. 8, 147–51
Trübbach/Azmoos housing project 5
Tschumi, B. 174
Tschumi, J. 4
Tudor music 97
Tunbridge Castle 46
tuning 139–44
Turkey 25
Turkish War of Independence 171
Turnbull, D. 136

Turner, J.M.W. 43, 45, 48–9, 52–3
Twentieth Century Society 4
Tyrwhitt, J. 173, 175

ugliness 111–12, 116
Ungers, O.M. 187, 190
Union of Architects of USSR 211
United Arab Emirates (UAE) 37
United Kingdom (UK) 154
United Nations (UN) 170–1, 173
United States (US) 4
Unrau, J. 46
up-views 57–8, 62–3
Upper Lawn Pavilion 154
urban design 30–2, 37
urbanisation 65, 171, 175, 177, 209, 212
Urbino 102, 105–6
Uriach house, L'Ametlla del Valles 199–200
Utkin, I. 9, 206–17

vacuum blankets 37
Van Dyck, A. 24
Van Eyck, A. 195, 200, 204–5
vanishing point 55
Vâstu Mandala 145
Vaucluse 104
Velázquez, D. 22
Velde, J. van de 22
Venice 43–6, 49–50, 53
Venice Architecture Biennale 43–4
Venturi, R. 147, 159
Verbeek, P.P. 133
Vermeersch, P.-W. 8, 127–35
vernacular architecture 38, 174, 177–8
Veronese, P. 21
vertigo 198
Vesely, D. 8
vibration 80–1
Victorians 7, 191
Vidler, A. 38
Vienna 30
vignettes 45–6, 50, 53
Villa Frankenstein 43
Viollet-le-Duc, E. 190
visual impairment 127
Vitruvian man 141, 176
Vitruvius, M. 4, 143, 163
void 206–7, 209–11
Vosskoeter, S. 128
Vries, N. de 7, 65–76

Waddington, C. 172
Wagner, R. 162–3
Ward, B. 172, 180
wars 195

waste-free design 37–8
Wastell, J. 46
water clocks 143
wave theory of light 80–1
weathering 154
Weber, M. 144
Weber, R. 128
websites 37, 139
wedges 143
Weisbach, J. 55–7
West 6–7, 38–41, 85–6, 102
    churches 182, 189
    music 137, 141
    politics 206, 209, 211
West 8 projects 1
Westminster 27
Westminster Cathedral 92–3

White, G. 110
white light 80
Whitehall Palace 27
Wieser, C. 3
Wigley, M. 173–5, 179
Wikki Stix 129
Wilson, C. St J. 106
Wirtschaftswunder 190
Wittgenstein, L. 79, 83, 85, 87
Wittkower, R. 138–9, 183–4
Wölfflin, H. 102
Wood, A. 90–1
Woodman, E. 190
workshops 131
World Health Organisation (WHO) 171
World Society for Ekistics 170

worm's-eye view 7, 54–64
Worringer, W. 183
Wren, C. 29–31
Wright, F.L. 159–60, 162, 164–5

Xenakis, I. 144

Yaneva, A. 128, 130
Ypenburg, The Hague 74

Zaha Hadid Architects 6
Zika, F. 7, 79–87
Zollverein School of Management and Design, Essen 3
zooming 4, 65
Zurich 3
Zwicky, F. 173–4